THE RETURN OF SQU/
An anthology of blogposts from the Red Brick Blog

Edited by Steve Hilditch

Foreword by Karen Buck MP

With contributions by
Karen Buck MP, Tony Clements, Alison Inman, Dermot Mckibbin, Monimbo, Steve Schifferes, and Sheila Spencer

Additional editing by Simon Hilditch

Preface

This anthology of Red Brick blogposts is dedicated to the memory of those who lost their lives in Grenfell Tower, their families, friends and the survivors, and to the many millions of people in this country who still live in unsafe, insanitary, overcrowded, unaffordable and inadequate homes or have no home at all.

From the Red Brick blog *'Beveridge 70 Years on. The Return of Squalor'* published on November 27, 2012:
In a highly competitive market the poor lose out. The return of one of Beveridge's five evils – squalor – is in evidence all around us, from the re-emergence of 'bed and breakfast', to more homeless on the streets, to rising overcrowding and sharing, to the new phenomenon of 'sheds with beds'. The housing and welfare benefit reforms, in their bewildering variety, leave millions of people facing unbridgeable gaps between income and housing costs.

From the Red Brick blog 'Radical solutions to the housing supply crisis – or just common sense?' published on February 16, 2017:
The abuse of the term 'affordable' has been taken to Orwellian levels in last week's White Paper. George Orwell might have said: "War is peace. Freedom is slavery. Ignorance is strength. Unaffordable is affordable."

Or as Orwell said on another occasion:
In a time of universal deceit telling the truth is a revolutionary act.

About the Editor

Steve Hilditch has edited Red Brick throughout 2010-2020, first with Tony Clements and then with the pseudonymous Monimbo. Steve is a former head of housing policy for Shelter and assistant director of housing for a London borough. He worked as a housing strategy consultant for 20 years, including drafting Ken Livingstone's first London housing strategy, acting as special adviser to a number of Select Committee inquiries, helping councils to implement the decent homes standard, and working on the reform of council housing finance. He was chair of Labour Housing Group and Secretary of the Westminster Objectors' Trust which brought the 'Homes for Votes' case against Dame Shirley Porter in Westminster.

Contents

Preface: the return of squalor

Foreword: Karen Buck MP

Introduction: Ten Years of Red Brick blog – the place for progressive housing debate

2010   6

    Feeling Insecure
    A long term increase in the benefit bill...
    An unfair future for social housing
    Scaremongers abound
    Housing benefit: the truth will out
    One cheer and one HuRrAh

2011   17

    Social housing investment peaks then plummets
    For one day only, I agree with Nick
    Self-financed council housing – will it do what it says on the tin?
    Changing the borrowing rules (part 26)
    Equalities laws are not 'red tape'
    John Wheatley and the Origins of Council Housing
    That vile word
    Jon Snow's 'shocking eye opener'
    What is it about our society that can make such things possible?
    Myths about migrants
    A tale of two rioters
    LibDems in denial
    Eric's troubled families
    Roxy Come Home
    'Rents will fall and no-one will be made homeless'. So what happened, IDS?
    Homeless people are 'the likes of us'
    Shooting the troubled

2012   48

    Who gets subsidised housing?
    Health and safety gone mad
    Can a new Tenant Voice rise from the ashes?
    Time to think in billions for housing

56. The magic number that should condemn Boris Johnson to a huge defeat.
Louise Casey, Jeremy Kyle and the zombie statistic
How right to buy sales push up the benefits bill
A boy called Mohamed
It's the same the whole world over….
Bed and breakfast – deja vu all over again
Affordable rent shambles continues
Dark days for the homeless
Beveridge 70 Years on. A Social State: The Return of Squalor

2013   72

Halfway house for the Coalition
You can't borrow your way out of a debt crisis. Well, yes we can.
Rents policy is a mess
Vile Products
Switching from benefits to building
Stabilising private sector rents
Rent is the new grant
The emerging consensus on private renting
John Humphrys should be sacked
The role of new settlements
The abominable yes man
A false start

2014   94

'An artificial and temporary recovery based on property inflation'
Squeezing welfare out of the system
Rolnik and the Tories: The Truth Hurts
Money should be no object for homelessness too
Half a great housing strategy – unfortunately, the wrong half
Waiting lists are becoming political devices
So what's not to like about social renting?
Time for raised voices
Regeneration or Gentrification?
'Poor doors' and a 'failed brand'
Giving away council houses
That sinking feeling
The Right to a Home – 30 years on
The homeless are not just for Christmas

2015   128

Selling the family silver

Social housing is worth its weight in gold
City Villages or ghettoes for the rich?
The super rich push out the rich push out the middle class push out the poor. Welcome to London the Global City.
Be wary of those who say they already know why Labour lost
Talking aspiration
The economic and fiscal case for social rented housing is unanswerable
The Tory message on social housing: it's for 'losers'
Jeremy Corbyn MP on Housing
A bitter pill to swallow

2016 — 154

Land ahoy!
Harold Wilson – a housing hero
Government support for the private market is more than double its spending on affordable homes
Is this how to deliver a 'One Nation' housing policy?
Troubled families: a tale of Cameron's prejudice and hubris
Still '500 miles' from home, today it is 50 years since Cathy

2017 — 166

Trump will be bad for housing too
Radical solutions to the housing supply crisis – or just common sense?
A basic right of citizenship
The mother of all monopolies
Why I care so much about housing associations
GE2017: At last someone talks seriously about housing
Tenants and the homeless must not be made to pay for the tower block fire safety crisis
Not much controversy here
Will Haringey's HDV tackle homelessness?

2018 — 189

Right to buy is not the biggest reason for the fall in social renting
So how should we set social rents in future?
Corbyn sets out Labour's housing stall
Let our Municipal Dreams flourish once more
Shifting Housing's Overton Window
Social housing green paper: not fundamental, and not much of a rethink
The Help to Buy gravy train
'Happy clappy' is not the right response
So, WHY can't you afford a home?
Home ownership is the most 'subsidised' tenure

2019   212
    A vision based on evidence
    Voluntary Right to Buy: should housing associations be 'proud to be involved'?
    Labour's 'Land Grab'
    From social mobility to social justice: how a simple policy announcement started a small war
    Labour to modernise feudal leasehold system in response to Tory inaction
    A look back at Labour's Annual Conference 2019, from a housing perspective

2020   228
    Coronavirus and housing: Government doing nothing much
    NTV – the wheel waiting to be re-invented
    Domestic abuse: #MakeaStand
    Coronavirus: the poor must not be made to pay for the crisis

Obituaries   237
    Richard Crossley OBE
    Chris Holmes CBE

Foreword

By Karen Buck MP

Things we have already learned from the Coronavirus pandemic include the fact that it both reveals and intensifies existing inequalities. The virus may not discriminate between two individuals with similar characteristics but over a whole population it is clear that the most vulnerable are hardest hit by both the health and economic consequences. And we already knew only too well that the housing crisis we have been grappling with for decades now is a graphic illustration of that inequality.

It should not be any surprise that a public health emergency is in many ways a housing emergency. It is more surprising, and profoundly disappointing, that government has turned its face away from responding to it. Taking the long view, housing conditions have improved for millions of people over the last century, of course. Public housing replaced the slums from which previous public health disasters like cholera had emerged in the 19th century, and subsequently replaced the horrors of private housing run by the likes of Rachman and Hoogstraten. The rise of home ownership fulfilled the hopes of millions more. Even as council housing contracted from the 1980s onwards, the Labour government's Decent Homes Initiative ensured that public housing, starved of investment for far too long, could benefit from much needed modernisation.

And yet. Here we are in 2020 with almost a million homes still unfit for human habitation. For those with no market power and few choices, the homes they are condemned to live in are a living hell. To our absolute shame, some of the worst conditions are those endured by homeless people, even in the Temporary Accommodation procured for them by local councils. Deregulated 'Permitted Development' schemes are in places already simply putting up the slums of tomorrow. Overcrowding is rising again, too - I am, even as I write this, making representations to my council on behalf of families of 5 and 6 who are going through the year of lockdown in 1 bed flats. And in a hideous twist, it now turns out that hundreds of thousands of new build homes are unfit for habitation in another way- with cladding and other construction defects leaving their occupiers at risk from fire, and trapped in properties they cannot either pay to make safe nor move from.

Nowhere else has there been the consistent, expert, detailed commentary on today's housing challenges that Red Brick Blog offers. I so wish it wasn't still needed.

Introduction: Ten Years of Red Brick Blog, the place for progressive housing debate

By Steve Hilditch

To mark the tenth anniversary of Red Brick housing blog, we are publishing this anthology of around 100 blogposts selected from the 800+ that have appeared on the site since October 2010. Any royalties from sales will be donated to the Labour Housing Group.

After Gordon Brown's election defeat in 2010, I sat down with Tony Clements, who had been an adviser to Labour's Housing Minister, John Healey MP, to think about ways we could highlight vitally important housing issues under the new Coalition government. Two things we didn't consider at the time were, first, that the Coalition's policies would be worse in practice than even we feared at the time; and, second, that the Tories would still be in government ten years later – we assumed, wishful thinking, that we would be preparing for a Miliband government, probably before 2015.

We hit upon the idea of starting a housing blog which would be 'the place for progressive housing debate' – our first and only strapline. It would be Labour, but not exclusively so: we wanted it to be open to a wide spectrum of opinion and a wide range of contributors, forging a critique of the Coalition but also developing the new policies that a new Labour government could put into practice.

Over its ten years Red Brick has posted over 800 pieces comprising at least 800,000 words, longer than the King James Bible and approaching the word count of the entire Harry Potter series. There were peaks and troughs in output, at the height there would be 2 or three a week, at the lows only one a month, more in the first few years than in the later years when energy faded. We went from optimism that there would be a Miliband government, to the deflating failure in 2015, to the heady days of 2017 – another defeat, but one that made the horizon seem much closer. Almost immediately, talking sensibly about housing became an impossibility after the mind numbing, unbearable awfulness of Grenfell, followed by the stultifying dominance of the Brexit issue (which was only displaced when the Covid crisis came along), Labour's sectarian implosion, and defeat again in the 2019 Brexit election. Losing to Boris Johnson was a bitter pill – as Mayor, he was on the sharp end of many a blogpost, including one entitled 'What Boris Johnson knows about housing' featuring a blank page.

About two-thirds of all the posts (those without a by-line in this selection) were done by yours truly but there have been many excellent contributors: each is named with their piece if it is included in this selection, and all are identified on the Red Brick website. Due to work, Tony stepped down as co-editor and the estimable Monimbo – a pseudonymous senior housing policy officer who has been the second most prolific contributor to the blog – joined up. In 2018 we encouraged a range of new authors and received some brilliant long form pieces which can be read in full on the website. Worthy of attention are those by true experts: a string by Dave Treanor on planning, land and tax reform; a series by Ross Fraser including one on Local Housing Companies and a long technical piece on offsite manufactured housing; pieces by Roger Jarman, including one on property tax reform, and a succession of pieces on the desperate need for leasehold reform by Dermot Mckibbin. It was also great to sign off my stint with a piece (which is included here) on tackling domestic violence by the brilliant Alison Inman, who devoted her presidency of CIH to raising the profile of the issue.

And so to 2020, with the Red Brick relaunch and my 'retirement'. There is a new relationship with Labour Housing Group, so the blog is now an LHG product, edited by a member of the EC, Chris Worrall. Chris, with support from the wonderful Sheila Spencer, Ross Houston, John Cotton and myself, has breathed new life into the old dog, with exciting new and more diverse writers and contributors, aiming to deliver about two new posts a week. It has genuinely become an open forum. We have not included posts from the revamped blog in this selection; they can be saved for a new anthology in the future.

LHG's editorial policy for managing the re-launched Red Brick emphasises its non-factional nature, wanting to encourage debate and being open to the widest possible range of 'progressive' opinion. Whatever we agree or disagree about in politics, we are united in wanting to deliver an effective housing policy for the Labour Party, one that tackles the housing crisis in all its forms whilst also building popular support.

Making the selection for this anthology sometimes felt arbitrary and excluding nearly 90% of the material was painful. But hopefully the choices stand-alone without too much context, so readers can dip in and out as they wish. I jettisoned a few personal favourites but end with the two hardest to write but most heartfelt pieces, the obituaries of Richard Crossley and Chris Holmes, who both had a big influence on my housing journey. The anthology is not intended as an organised and balanced chronicle of the Cameron, May and Johnson governments, that is a task for another day. Some posts tracked government announcements in more detail than is needed for the historical record. But hopefully the selection gives a feel for the period and the sense of outrage many of us who believe in meeting housing need have felt over the last ten years. For those who might want more, all of the pieces are archived and searchable on the new blog site at redbrickblog.co.uk

In putting the anthology together, we have done some editing to make it more easily readable, for example taking out references to events that have passed and links to other sites or documents that no longer exist or which no longer seem relevant. Sadly, because this will be available in printed form, click through links have been replaced by references where appropriate. Typos – yes there were typos – have been removed when spotted. Each piece is the product of its time – there are references to policies which even the Tories later thought better of. Some embarrassingly incorrect predictions were made which have been left in to prove that not even Red Brick is infallible.

There were times when there was a rash of posts about a single topic, so the anthology itself is a little lumpy. One such was the aftermath of the riots in 2011, when Cameron demanded jail sentences for all rioters no matter how trivial their offence and the courts and crown prosecution service meekly delivered an oppressive and illiberal demand. When it spilled over into a media clamour for the eviction of social tenants and an attempt to blame the often appalling conduct of rioters on 'sink estates', Red Brick became enraged.

Similarly, we published frequent posts on the scandal of the so-called 'Affordable Rent' product, the failure to reform the private rented sector, the undermining of the homelessness safety net, the reform of council housing finance, the infidelity of some housing associations, the 'troubled families' pretend programme, and the crisis facing leaseholders especially after Grenfell.

Housing is the theme, and we try to stick to that. It would be easy to wander off into general commentary about politics. Temptation is (usually) there to be resisted, but there are signs of frustration in various posts at the undermining of Ed Miliband (too left wing evidently) and Jeremy Corbyn (much too left wing evidently) when we desperately needed unity to get a Labour government. As something of a tribal loyalist, who defended Gordon Brown, Ed Miliband and Jeremy Corbyn for the simple reason that they were the properly elected Leaders of the Labour Party (after the treatment of Corbyn this incantation is now under threat), my most depressingly correct prediction came in 2019: 'Hatred of Blair on the one hand and hatred of Corbyn on the other. The result of this madness will be no Labour government at the next election.'

Even so, I am surprised on re-reading some posts how gentle we were with New Labour's housing record over 13 years and with 'the Eds' due to their reluctance to commit to ending austerity. No explanation is needed for Red Brick's hostility to the Tories - they turned out to be far more right wing than anyone imagined. It is more of a surprise to find no redeeming features in the performance of the LibDems in government: despite excellent party policies over the years, they failed miserably to promote progressive policies or even to act as a brake on the worst excesses of Tory housing and welfare policy.

It is so hard to judge if any blog has impact in the wider world. Lots of people say they enjoy Red Brick, and that is great. The numbers of email recipients and clicks through to the site have always been healthy. A few pieces have gone a little viral, like Jeremy Corbyn on housing during the first leadership election and, more surprisingly, my attack on John Humphrys of the BBC for a scurrilous documentary about 'welfare'. Some pieces have been picked up more widely, often on the Guardian's Housing Network when that was a thing, and sometimes on Inside Housing, occasionally by the excellent Patrick Butler on the Guardian or by Dave Hill when he wrote a regular London blog for the newspaper. Occasionally it has caught the attention of the Evening Standard or Private Eye or other journals, and linked pieces have been published on a range of other blogs like LabourList or LeftFootForward and by think tanks like Class and the Fabians.

Banging on and on about a few issues that were slow to get political and public recognition may have had an effect. Most notable was our campaign against the unaffordable 'Affordable Rent' – classic Orwellian doublespeak from Grant Shapps. We may have helped to move the argument along on a range of issues: those that come to mind include council housing finance reform, changing 'Treasury rules' governing housing investment, denouncing prejudice against tenants and media misrepresentation, calling out those housing associations who lost touch with their mission to tackle housing need, promoting the SHOUT campaign to save social housing, and the now popular activity of exposing Boris Johnson as a political fraud and trickster. Across the piece I hope we have helped to expose bad housing policies and to promote better ones.

We could also claim a little influence within the Labour Party in helping to develop a more positive story about council housing, and social rented housing more generally, tackling some of the negative stereotypes about social tenants and people on social security which, to my great discomfiture, had infected parts of the Labour Party, and raising the debate on a range of issues like borrowing for investment, the 'benefits to bricks' agenda, and the virtues of security of tenure.

So why do it? Well, top of the list for me is a near 50-year passion for the topic and an interest in homelessness provoked by watching 'Cathy Come Home' when it was shown way back in 1966, when I was an impressionable 16-year-old living in a 'Bevan house' on a good council estate in Newcastle. In our relative comfort I could not believe that people were treated like that. I've done plenty of outrage since then, and blogging is better than shouting at the TV or fulminating in the pub at the latest Tory scandal. And I get a bizarre sense of pleasure from writing a headline based on a Bob Dylan song ('Desolation Row' and 'Dear Landlord' were too obvious, 'There's a million reasons for you to be crying' and 'I'm troubled and I don't know why' were more obscure).

It has sometimes been quite hard work to keep going. Occasionally words flow, other times they just won't. Sometimes I think it would be easier just to tell everyone to read the doyen of housing blogging Jules Birch instead: his output has been phenomenal, his posts have more facts in them, and he doesn't rant so much (julesbirch.com). It's been tempting to try to comment on all housing issues as they are raised but, after all, it is a blog not a magazine and Inside Housing exists for that. Like most people, I get irritated even by good things when they appear too frequently in my inbox, so the blog mustn't impose.

I'm very grateful to the fantastic Monimbo for his support and brilliant contributions over many years, to Tony Clements for helping develop the blog idea, to LHG for a mutually supportive relationship over ten years, to Jen McClelland for her continuous support and suggestions, and to Simon Hilditch for doing many of the hard yards involved in editing disparate source material into this volume.

Above all, thanks to you for sustaining the idea, for reading, and contributing, and especially to those of you who go out campaigning on the issues. Because housing really matters.

A note from 2011

It is probably unconnected, but last week I signed up to Twitter for the first time, only to receive an email within minutes which read "you are being followed by the Conservatives". It's an alarming thought.

2010

Feeling Insecure

October 30, 2010

30 years ago, a political consensus emerged that council tenants should have the protection of security of tenure, leading to the 'Tenants Charter' in the 1980 Housing Act. All political parties supported the move – it was a Labour bill then taken up by the Tories after Thatcher won power.

The policy did not emerge from academia or from Whitehall. It was the outcome of campaigns and pressure from tenants all over the country. It was a campaign for fairness and justice, that landlords should not be able to remove tenants from their homes without going before a court and providing evidence that a term of the tenancy had been breached in such a way as to justify the tenant losing their home. It was a campaign rooted in the bad practice not only of council landlords but also housing associations who sometimes removed tenants in a punitive and capricious way with no rights of complaint or redress.

Losing your home, and probably being declared intentionally homeless as well, is a serious matter. The basic principle is that it should not be decided by the landlord acting alone, but should be based on evidence and a set of rules. That is all security of tenure and the many extensive 'grounds for possession' entails: simple consumer protection. Without security of tenure, tenants have fewer rights against eviction than I have to appeal against parking tickets.

Many people become social tenants after major disruption in their lives, especially homelessness and being dumped in temporary accommodation for months or years at a time. Many people who become tenants do so because they are vulnerable in some way, through age or disability or because they have children. A secure home provides them with the platform to rebuild their lives, to put their children in a school for more than a temporary period, for some to register with a doctor for the first time, for many to consider work for the first time. They become part of the community, neighbours, and, because they have a long-term home, feel it is worth making a local contribution. Security is the foundation of the big society. We all say we want to build more stable and mixed communities but a policy of insecure tenancies would move some people on against their will at the point where they are finally settled and likely to be contributing most.

The government has yet to explain how insecure tenure will work in practice except to say that new tenants will be reviewed after a period to see if they still qualify for a home. Insecure tenants will live in fear that their landlord will decide against them and they will be out. It is an extraordinary disincentive for people to take work or to get a better job. In my experience social tenants simply do not fit the media and government stereotype of fecklessness and scrounging: they are aspirational, but their aspirations are realistic. They are not anticipating setting up a business, becoming the next self-made millionaire, and joining the Cabinet. They aspire to getting a low paid job, enough to make ends meet, or to getting a promotion and having a bit more spare cash. They aspire to leading a better life or at least ensuring that their children do.

The government has begged the question of what will trigger eviction. Few if any social tenants will make it to the higher rate tax band so there will have to be some lower point at which a tenant is deemed to have enough to justify being kicked out. It will be a bureaucratic nightmare of means tests and reviews. To be honest, some social landlords have difficulty managing one set of tenancy conditions without taking this on as well.

Nor should we give any time of day to the argument that it is right that tenants should be moved on from 'subsidised' housing. Council housing no longer receives subsidy, it pays its own way with rent covering costs including the cost of debt. Housing associations receive grants (well, they did until the CSR) to help meet the capital cost of new homes but there is no revenue subsidy – rents cover costs and over the lifetime of a home will make a significant surplus. Even if social housing had a straightforward revenue subsidy, my response would be 'so what'. Society subsidises poor people is not a shock headline. The economy is full of subsidies and reliefs.

As a society we have failed to tackle poverty and inequality. That is why social rented housing exists and why it will continue to be essential. Over 30 years, social housing has been given the residual role of housing the poorest and most vulnerable and, by and large, it has done a hellish job well. But it has only done so by learning to respect its customers individually and as a group and by creating a partnership between landlord and tenant. We should not go back to the dark ages.

A long term increase in the benefit bill...

October 31, 2010

By Tony Clements

So what would Labour do instead? It's the standard question to us at the moment and indeed of any opposition.

It's a difficult one to answer for a lot of reasons. One of those reasons is that whatever you do, you have to graft it on to what the other lot have done during their time in power.

One of the things Labour is likely to face coming into office again in the future is a considerably higher housing benefit bill. Yes, really – despite the caps and restrictions that will do real damage to mixed communities, the CSR paved the way for a rising bill in the long-term. Here's why:

George Osborne announced two weeks ago that capital funding for 'social' or affordable housing would be cut. He says by 50%, in truth it's more like 75%, but that's a different issue. So how will the Tories justify their claims that they will build more affordable homes? By increasing 'social' rents to 80% of market rents and then allowing housing associations to borrow against these new higher revenue streams to build more homes. OK, well that *could* stack up. But how will people on the waiting lists be able to afford near market rents? They are often often workers on very low incomes, carers, disabled, workless etc? Well Nick Clegg has the answer: "People on low pay on those new rents will be compensated in full through housing benefit."

So, in a nutshell, it's a shift in the cost of subsidising housing from up-front capital to build homes to putting more people on higher levels of benefit, so they can afford near-market rents.

They've moved the bill from the Department of Communities and Local Government to the Department of Work and Pensions – nifty footwork from Eric Pickles.

That's great for cutting big capital budgets now in order for the Chancellor to say he's wiped out the deficit before the next election: it's rubbish for the taxpayer in the future who has to shoulder the long-term costs.

It's like a great big housing PFI: avoid the capital investment up-front, pay more in the long-term.

p.s. I think there's good reason to think that the benefits system won't cover these costs 'in full' as Nick Clegg says, but that's for another post.

An unfair future for social housing

November 22, 2010

It's too ambitious a task to analyse Grant Shapps' social housing consultation paper[1] in one post. I hope people will read it and make their comments forcefully to the government. But there are a few points I think are worth stressing.

1. Localism is a great dodge. It allows you to slide away from all difficult questions by saying you are just enabling the landlords and it will be down to councils and housing associations to decide for themselves how much the new powers are used. The paper has no predictions of how many of each type of new tenancy might be created in future and it avoids any substantive discussion of how 'well off' a tenant needs to become before they are evicted at the end of a short tenancy. So it's a postcode lottery, what happens to you and your home depends entirely on an accident of geography and chance. Given that the stated justification for the policy is to give more opportunities to the 1.8m on waiting lists, it is astonishing that there is no estimate, however rough, of how many people might benefit from the policy over a period.

2. The proposed change to the homelessness duty guts the legislation as we have known it for 33 years. Local authorities will be able to discharge their duty to a homeless household by finding a private letting for the applicant, who can no longer refuse it, even though landlords will still have to offer 'reasonable preference' to vulnerable homeless households under their allocation policy. The paper complains that "those owed the duty can effectively insist on being provided with temporary accommodation until offered social housing" as if being in TA is some luxurious option. In fact, TA makes it almost impossible for people to work, frequent moves mean families do not settle and children are seriously disadvantaged. The average stay in TA is one year outside London and 3 years in London. No-one would suffer that if the private rented option was a reasonable one for them. People suffer it because social housing offers the only hope of a decent and secure home at an affordable rent to enable families to rebuild their lives in a settled home.

3. Some extraordinary claims are made – for example that the reforms will help overcrowded families. How exactly? There are no proposals to tackle underoccupation amongst existing tenants and zero existing large homes will be

released to help the 260,000 overcrowded social tenants. Even more astonishing is the claim that the proposals will promote 'strong and cohesive communities' when the opposite is the almost certain outcome of a more rapid turnover of tenants with new tenants not being able to put down roots and become net contributors to their neighbourhoods.

4. The new 'affordable rent' tenure, or 'flexible tenure' as they now seem to prefer, is aimed to provide homes for the same people who might be offered social rent now. But it is open to the landlord to decide the rent, the length of tenancy and, within a broad framework, the terms. The paper at least is honest when it says this is "a significant first step towards those greater freedoms for social landlords." How will people on waiting lists, homeless people or any other prospective tenant know what kind of tenancy they will receive, for how long and at what rent? Chaos awaits.

5. The paper has one traditional charlatan's trick – if you can't change the reality, change the way it is counted. One reason for the growth in waiting lists since 2002 was labour's decision that they should be open to anyone to apply. As a result, waiting lists have become a more accurate count of not only the need for social rented housing but also the demand – and it is huge. Social housing is a popular option with many people and they want more of it. But in future councils will be able to dictate who qualifies to join the waiting lists, leaving it open to local political manipulation as was the case prior to 2002. And no doubt the government will claim that waiting lists have been slashed since they came into power.

6. And my two favourite hobby horses. First the claim that social housing is subsidised when everyone at CLG knows that council housing is running a surplus, including the cost of debt, which is likely to grow over the next few years. Even calling houisng association homes subsidised because they have capital grant is questionable – they make a large surplus in the long term. And secondly, the use of the term 'lifetime tenancy' as if it was a legal or technical term, is extremely irritating. This phrase was invented by those opposed to security of tenure to try to make it sound ridiculous. Security of tenure simply means that the tenancy is not time limited and the landlord has to have grounds for possession and to get a court order to repossess. Simple consumer protection.

[1] 'Local decisions: a fairer future for social housing', published by the Department for Communities and Local Government in November 2010

Scaremongers abound

November 28, 2010

By Tony Clements

During the election the Tories were very keen on painting Labour as a negative party, who wanted to whip up unfounded fears about the Tories' secret and malicious plans. On cancer tests, cuts, and Sure Start, among others, the cry of scaremongering went up from Dave, George and co.

It's an effective political technique that undermines the credibility of criticism by arguing that it is extreme and that those making it are desperate, with only the power of fear to play on.

Such a skirmish took place on the housing front. People who pay attention to housing will remember a story from Inside Housing in April; rattled by Labour claims that the Tories would hike social housing rents and abolish security of tenure, Mr Cameron came out to bat himself to rebut such claims. He said these claims were part of a 'scare campaign', Labour's allegations were 'simply untrue' and that the Conservatives believe in the 'security [social housing] provides'.

Within months of their election they are set to abolish security of tenure and allow social housing rents to rise to 80% of market rents.

Regardless of if you think these measures are good or bad, they broke their promises and were perhaps even telling porkies at the time.

Anyway, it's an unattractive habit of political people to rake over lost election claims, seeking retrospective justification. But does this episode tell us anything about our government now and in the future?

Didn't Clegg and others jump to say Labour were scaremongering over housing benefit cuts compelling people to move out of their communities? Remind me, what was Eric Pickles' response to the (Tory-controlled) Local Government Association's assessment of the impact of cuts on council services? He accused them of scaremongering.

Just a thought: Rather than scaremongering being the last resort of desperate parties, aren't accusations of scaremongering becoming the first resort of our government when they've been caught bang to rights?

Housing benefit: the truth will out

December 6, 2010

In a recent post I made the observation that government impact assessments, and especially equality impact assessments, tended to reveal more about a policy than all the other official documents put together, and that looking at any policy from the point of view of those most likely to be worst affected tends to expose the downside or weak links in the argument.

The point is well supported by the DWP impact assessments on the housing benefit changes, or more correctly the Local Housing Allowance changes, published last week.

At constant prices, and taking account of the recent minor concessions in the proposals, the LHA savings will start in 2012/13 and build up to £1040m in 2014/15, slightly offset by piddling amounts for increased discretionary payments and an (extremely welcome) allowance for an extra room for a carer. In 2014/15:

- removing the £15 bonus for people achieving a rent below the LHA rate (the shopping around incentive) will save £550m

- setting Local Housing Allowance at the 30th percentile of local rents will save £425m, and

- capping LHA rates will save £65m.

The first point to note is the relatively small saving from the 'cap', given that virtually all government comment on the LHA issue has focused on excessive benefit payments to people in high rent areas, especially in central London. 17,400 households are affected – often very severely - by the caps. The much higher saving from the '30th percentile' change will have far more impact. It will affect more than three-quarters of a million households in all parts of the country.

Nearly everyone will lose: over 900,000 households, a stunning figure. The national average loss is £12 per week, from an average benefit of £126, but the hardest-hit group, households needing a five bedroom property, will lose an average of £57 per week as the five bed rate is withdrawn entirely. All the regions/nations are hit, with London top with an average loss of £22 per week. The biggest groups numerically are those in the one- and two-bedroom categories, who will face average losses of £11 and £15 respectively. The lack of grip on the reality of what it is like to live on a very low income is illustrated by the argument that "only four per cent of cases will have a shortfall of over £20 a week" – well, that's all right then.

DWP refuse to make an assessment of the number of households that will have to move. They say they can't predict behaviour, and customers have options – for example, "some may start work or increase working hours", others "may be able to renegotiate their rent with their landlord and others may have resources such as savings they can fall back on". To be fair, they do note that the Greater London Authority's estimate that over 9,000 households may need to move in London as a consequence of the caps, and that 6,800 of those will be families; and Shelter's estimate that between 68,000 and 134,000 households may have to move nationally.

"David Cameron insisted today no one will be made homeless by limiting 'extravagant' housing benefits"
– Daily Mail

Contrary to the assertions of leading members of the coalition, including David Cameron, the impact assessment notes "a risk of households falling into rent arrears leading to eviction and an increase in the numbers of households that present themselves as homeless" and that "any resulting population movement could have wider impacts. People who move may need to rearrange their children's schooling, healthcare arrangements or, where relevant, social services support; they may also need assistance with finding accommodation."

Other specific groups affected by the changes include:

Disabled people, especially those who may have to move across a council boundary, because care and support packages do not move with the person and settled arrangements will be disrupted as the new authority carries out a new assessment. This "could lead to gaps and delays in new arrangements being put in place and consequential distress for the individual".

Large families, who often have poor employment prospects and a much increased risk of poverty: for them, the "cap could affect their risk of overcrowding and the associated health and educational effects".

Ethnic minority groups, who tend to have a higher proportion of large families, will be likely to be affected disproportionately. Further research may be commissioned in this field as there are "limitations in current data".

The key quote from the impact assessment:

"the impact assessment recognises that there are a number of risks as follows:
- increases in the number of households with rent arrears, eviction and households presenting themselves as homeless;
- disruption to children's education and reduced attainment;
- disruption to support services for people with disabilities and other households with care and support needs;
- increase in the number of households living in overcrowded conditions; and
- a decrease in the number of and quality of private rented sector properties available to Housing Benefit tenants."

The truth will out.

One cheer and one HuRrAh

December 19, 2010

In trying to look beyond this government's irksome habit of claiming credit for things agreed before the Election, at least it can be said that the snail's pace move towards the abolition of the housing revenue account national subsidy system continues in vaguely the right direction.

Having announced already that he planned to stick with most of John Healey's proposals, announced it again as part of the November consultation on the reform of social housing, and announced it yet again as part of the Localism Bill package, Grant Shapps has now announced a 'route map' towards reform - in advance of a more detailed announcement next month! The route map makes it clear that more detail will emerge over the next year before implementation in 2012, no doubt offering Mr Shapps further opportunities to announce his great, but inherited, reform. Who said spin was dead?

Brought up on a council estate in Kenton, Newcastle, I have always had an emotional belief in council housing, and have often been outraged at the stigma attached to the tenure, the appalling media misrepresentations, and the snobbery. Although what Thatcher did to council housing was unforgiveable, I was hugely disappointed that it turned out to be not very New Labour either. But the rationale for council housing is not just emotive. Based on a system of rent pooling, so that surpluses from older homes cross-subsidise the cost of new ones, it was also a robust financial model. It could have provided hundreds of thousands if not millions of extra homes if it had been managed properly over the past 30 years.

The Tories' failure to invest in managing and maintaining the council stock left Labour with a huge problem in 1997, including a backlog of disrepair estimated at around £19billion and an incoherent rent policy. Labour made some well-meaning attempts at reform, such as the introduction of rent restructuring, the Major Repairs Allowance and the Decent Homes Programme, but funding for the latter carried the clear political price tag that direct management of the stock by councils was unacceptable to the government.

As some councils in the national HRA subsidy system had large historic debts and others had none, the system was unbalanced and rent pooling became unmanageable. It also became increasingly unpopular with tenants and councils in those areas where a third or even a half of local rents were taken for distribution elsewhere. Despite producing growing surpluses nationally, all of the participants were unhappy with the outcome, even those that gained from redistribution. As an annual system, there was no certainty about income and it was impossible for councils to plan long term and improve efficiency. Tenants simply could not engage with the key decisions that affected their homes and communities because they were only understood by a tiny number of civil servants and professionals. In its latter years, the Labour government became less hostile to the idea that council housing should have a long term future, and understood that a more local system suited the times. It embarked on the hugely complex exercise of unravelling the system.

The Localism Bill contains powers to implement the local system proposed by Labour. In future, councils will keep their rental income and use it locally to manage and maintain their own homes and service their debt. To get to the point where all councils have sufficient income to meet these costs, there will be a one-off payment between central government and each council, which will reallocate existing housing debt between councils in a final settlement based on 30-year business plans for each landlord. This is possible because the national system is in surplus – i.e. tenants are paying more in rent than council housing costs to run.

The Communities and Local Government department's task is complicated: they have to incorporate the implications of the new government's shifting policies, for example on rents, as well as making important assumptions about inflation and the 'discount rate' (currently assumed to be 6.5%) used to determine the 'net present value' of each council's housing business.

I have two main concerns. First, John Healey planned to allow councils to keep their right to buy capital receipts, whereas the Tories will retain the current system that returns 75% of net receipts to the Treasury. There will also be a cap on councils' overall housing borrowing. Hope that HRA reform would trigger a resurgence in council housebuilding has been dashed. The overall receipt to the Treasury from all the various calculations is currently projected to be around

£6.5b, but tenants may come to view this as being paid for out of a large rent increase next year of over 7%.

Secondly, Labour would have localised the HRA within the clear framework of the regulatory regime. There would have been an external check, through the Tenant Services Authority, and a place for tenants to go if, for example, their council set up backdoor arrangements that took funds out of the HRA to benefit the general fund. It is still not clear how regulation will operate without the TSA, and this will make tenants in some areas nervous about what their landlords will get up to.

At least we can look forward to further announcements.

2011

Social housing investment peaks then plummets

January 11, 2011

An early glimpse into the new edition of the UK Housing Review, to be published at the start of February, reveals that investment in social housing has reached its highest level for 20 years but is due to plummet again when the cuts take effect in April 2011.

The review describes how overall gross social housing investment in Great Britain rose again in 2009/10, to the highest level in real terms for almost 20 years – up by over 80% since the previous decade. The strongest annualised growth was seen in Scotland. Taking account of all private finance investment, the Review concludes that

"the last two years have seen overall investment in social housing at its highest sustained level (in real terms) for three decades.

"Going right back to the 1970s, in only in one earlier year – 1989/90 – was expenditure higher. This resulted from a coincidence of exceptional factors – peaking right to buy receipts in the late 1980s housing market boom, together with landlord action to pre-empt government spending restrictions that were announced before they took effect."

For the Chartered Institute of Housing, which trailed the Review this week, Director of Policy and Practice Richard Capie said: "The last two years have seen record investment in social housing across Britain, both from central government and importantly through private finance. This allowed the provision of more homes, essential community regeneration and important improvements in existing homes. We have now entered a very different era, with 50% cuts in cash terms to housing budgets in England and around 19% in Scotland. We are in the midst of a housing crisis with fewer than half the homes we need being built. This latest research shows the sheer scale of the dramatic cuts we are now seeing in new housing. These are a body blow to first time buyers, low income households and the construction sector."

Figures on cuts to housing investment for 2011-14 for England are taken from the National Affordable Housing Programme which was £8.4bn in 2008-11 and will be £4.5bn in the three years from 2011/12. Accounting for the inclusion of mortgage rescue and the recovery of empty homes this represents a cash terms cut of 50%. In Scotland the draft budget prefigures a cut in housing and regeneration spending from £488m to £393m, a cash cut of 19%. The Scottish Federation of Housing Associations estimates that allowance for spending brought forward in 2010/11 means that the real reduction in 2011/12 will be over 30%.

The starkness of the figures adds strength to points made recently by Tony about how the anti-recession stimulus is running out with potentially dire consequences for the construction sector of the economy. *The UK Housing Review is edited by Professors Steve Wilcox and Hal Pawson.*

For one day only, I agree with Nick

January 19, 2011

It became a catchphrase during the Election TV debates and I haven't found a lot to agree with Nick Clegg about since the coalition took over. But, just as Red Brick agreed with Grant Shapps when he made sensible remarks about the need for a period of stable and not inflationary house prices, now it is time to agree with Nick in his comments about the extension of the Freedom of Information legislation.

Labour had plans to extend FoI to cover some additional agencies (such as University admissions services and the Association of Chief Police Officers) which the current government is also going to pursue, but Clegg spoke about going much further and my ears pricked up when 'housing associations' got a mention. Since FoI came in, we have had the strange position where the regulators (Housing Corporation then Tenant Services Authority) were covered by FoI but the organisations they regulated were not.

Clegg said that "free citizens must be able to hold big institutions and powerful individuals to account... There are a whole range of organisations who benefit from public money and whose activities have a profound impact on the public good... citizens must first know what goes on in these institutions."

It is Clegg's suggestion that private bodies performing "functions of a public nature" should be covered by FoI. That catches housing associations – although careful definition will be required to avoid any suggestion that the change might trigger the re-classification of housing associations as public bodies (thereby running the risk that their loans – around £40bn - might transfer to the public sector balance sheet). The FoI Campaign has argued for years that private providers of health and social care and other public services should be subject to the Act, which contains safeguards around information that might be commercially sensitive. As Clegg says, there should be a simple rule that organisations that benefit from public money should be subject to public scrutiny.

I suspect that housing associations are probably no better and no worse than most bodies that are subject to the FoI already. But non-disclosure and a lack of public scrutiny can make organisations too cosy in their internal procedures, and then it is easy to fall into bad habits. Public scrutiny (especially through Inside Housing's annual survey and league table) has made a difference to housing associations that had a penchant for paying over the odds for their senior staff. But I think they are often unnecessarily secretive, for example many do not publish routine information like non-confidential Board papers. Tenants often complain that they cannot get hold of financial and other information that council tenants get routinely from their landlords. And you hear the occasional story about Chief Executives' expenses, posh dinners and trips abroad, all of which should see the light of day.

I argued unsuccessfully to the TSA that the principles of FoI should be part of the new regulatory code, thereby avoiding the need for an extension of the legislation. That didn't happen, and now regulation itself will be severely restricted (Clegg got that one wrong), so the only way forward is to extend the Act. The principle has to be right, the risks can be avoided, and I don't accept the line that it will involve 'too much work'. If it also helps change the culture of some HAs, it might have the added benefit of making the government's plans for tenant scrutiny more effective.

Self-financed council housing – will it do what it says on the tin?

February 5, 2011

By Monimbo

I hesitate to say that the government has published its final proposals for the self-financing of council housing[1], since they've made so many announcements about it they are rivalling the quantity issued by the previous government. And strangely enough, despite this the broad shape of the package is pretty much the same as that put forward by John Healey when he offered his 'prospectus' last year. One key difference, of course, is that a prospectus implies choice, whereas the current package will – after a bit of negotiation around the edges – be imposed by statute from April 2012, on all 171 councils that still have housing stock.

On the face of it, the figures involved look alarming, and no doubt some on the left will use them to oppose self-financing outright, as they did when Labour put it forward. The headline figure is that councils will take on around £19bn of new debt, to enable them (in effect) to buy their way out of the system. While the LGA originally demanded that all 'historic' debt be written off, this was always an unlikely call on public funds, even more so with Mr Osborne in charge at the Treasury. More recently, among local authorities there has been gradual and – almost – universal acceptance of the principle that extra debt would have to be taken on as the price for escaping from the so-called 'subsidy' system. (The word 'subsidy' increasingly means, of course, that tenants subsidise the Exchequer, not the other way round.) And the other side of the coin is that a minority of councils will have part of their debt paid off.

Inevitably, the Treasury had its fingers in this pie well before the general election. The cap on each council's borrowing, which restricts them to the levels to be included in the settlement itself, was already envisaged in Labour's prospectus. Not only that, but it was always likely that the Treasury would ensure that it kept the surpluses the government would have earned from council housing in the future, however much these are correctly argued to amount to 'daylight robbery' from tenants.

In terms of the arithmetic, the spreadsheet experts have so far concluded that the current deal is similar to, and perhaps even a bit better than, the one in John Healey's prospectus. However, whatever the overall deal, what will matter to authorities is how their individual figures work out. Given that there is a fair amount of local detail in the latest paper, this is where the focus of interest on the figures is likely to shift.

There is already a danger, of course, that hard-pressed councils whose revenue support grant has been cut are looking at their housing revenue accounts to see if they can help make up the shortfall. Labour was alive to this, and included updated guidance about maintaining the 'ring fence' around the HRA in its prospectus. In the current document, the guidance has been dropped and there is only a brief reminder that the ring fence needs to be kept. It seems to me that it's always been down to tenants to be vigilant on this issue. Their vigilance needs to be even greater when, after April next year, the only income to the HRA will be their rents. The first call on rents will be to pay the debt charges, then maintain the stock, then run the landlord service. Councils and tenants can't afford to let *any* of their rental income be siphoned off to make good cuts elsewhere.

There remain several points of contention about the caveats in the overall deal the government has put on the table, and all of these are a result of those greedy Treasury fingers looking for the meat in the pie. The new one to emerge as part of Mr Shapps' package is that councils will have to continue paying three-quarters of right to buy receipts back to government. Labour can hardly rail against this iniquity, since they introduced it, but credit was due to John Healey that through his package it would have been brought to an end. The Treasury have locked their fingers round this tasty morsel, and must now somehow twist the settlement so that it reflects 30 years of future stock losses through right to buy. This introduces a high and unnecessary degree of uncertainty, since predictions of right to buy sales are invariably wrong.

The Treasury also wants the facility to reopen the settlement if circumstances change. One of these might of course be a wayward forecast of the effects of the right to buy, but the very prominence of this caveat is making councils think that 'self-financing' might be maintained only as long as it suits the Treasury. This is not what the deal is supposed to be about.

However, it's the debt cap that really grates with councils, in part because of the context of overall spending cuts. If it was a bad idea under Labour, it's a far worse one when grants from central government and other sources of finance apart from borrowing are likely to be very scarce, to put it mildly.

The debt cap, the continued repayment of receipts and the constant threat that the settlement might be reopened are all eroding councils' supposed autonomy. Interestingly, as was revealed by the Local Government Chronicle last month, councils have an unlikely ally in the deputy prime minister, who is said to have asked for councils' borrowing powers to be reconsidered in a letter to Eric Pickles about the imminent local government finance review.

Of course, if the Treasury were to listen, at last, to the case for taking council borrowing out of the main national accounts, they could use self-financing to get council debt off the government's books completely. Council housing is anyway now classified as outside government by the Office for National Statistics. Because most of its income comes from charges (rents). Where councils have ALMOs, these are considered separate public corporations (like, say, the BBC). Taken together with likely changes to the accountancy rules about housing revenue accounts and the separating out of housing debt, this could be the moment for the Treasury to take a step towards giving council housing – like housing associations – *real* autonomy. However, none of us will be holding our breath.

[1] *'Implementing self-financing for council housing'*, published by the Department for Communities and Local Government in February 2011.

Changing the borrowing rules (part 26)

March 18, 2011

A rare opportunity to welcome an initiative by a bundle of ten councils of all political persuasions – Tory, LibDem, Lab and NOC – arose this week. The issue is an old one on which a dedicated band of experts have campaigned for 20 years or more. And the question is whether George Osborne is any more likely to listen than any of his predecessors as Chancellor. My feeling is not because the tradition of orthodoxy runs deep at HM treasury.

Changing the borrowing rules has been a celebrated cause, where everyone except the people who matter most, in Whitehall, favours change. In essence, in the UK borrowing to invest in council houses has been included in the main measure of public sector borrowing, and therefore subject to strict control. Other countries especially in the Eurozone, do things differently, and we could count council housing and other public corporate activities as separate trading activities where borrowing is determined by the business plan of the organisation involved and its revenue streams – and governed by the prudential code - rather than being controlled by an artificial national count of all debt that only the Brits use.

Detailed work led by the CIH in the 1990s (their report was entitled 'Challenging the Conventions') led to high hopes that the new Labour Government would change the rules. Some adjustments were made, mainly with the prudential borrowing regime, which helped, but the breakthrough never arrived. The research for the CIH report was undertaken by the (then) leading Coopers and Lybrand accountancy company, now part of PWC. They then did follow-up research with financial institutions, revealing in a second report called 'Consensus for Change' that the City was wholly relaxed about the proposed revision to borrowing measures and that it might lead to over £1 billion of extra investment being available for council housing.

This new initiative, supported by councils from all over the country as well as all political persuasions, takes the campaign into yet another decade. They assert that the change would not affect UK credit ratings, would ease unemployment in construction, and would help deliver the Government's aspiration to build more homes during this spending review period. Their current estimate is also that an additional £1bn could be raised for investment in new housing.

HM Treasury being what it is, silence will probably be the response. I don't think they have ever issued a serious rebuttal of the arguments. Time will tell, but some of us have already grown old and grey waiting for this sensible reform.

Equalities laws are not 'red tape'

April 20, 2011

One of the more offensive acts of this government has been to put the Equalities Act 2010 up as a topic for debate on its 'Red Tape Challenge' website.

Housing organisations have been at the forefront of promoting good policy in equalities and diversity for many years - the latest evidence being CIH's publication this month of its guide to delivering housing services to lesbian, gay, bisexual and transgender customers - and should be ready to make the case for the retention of the Act in its entirety, together with its supporting regulations.

The 2010 Equalities Act pulled together the previous diverse strands of discrimination and equalities law into a coherent whole and added new duties and responsibilities. It harmonised the legislation to provide a single approach wherever possible.

Extensions included the new duty on public bodies to consider socio-economic disadvantage when making strategic decisions, wider definitions of discrimination, harassment and victimisation, stronger duties to help eliminate conduct which the Act prohibits, to advance equality of opportunity and foster good relations between people who share a relevant protected characteristic and people who do not, the use of positive action, amendments to family property law to remove discriminatory provisions and additional statutory property rights for civil partners.

What has caused so much offence is that all the other topics posted on the Red Tape Challenge website seem to involve changes to regulations whereas the equalities topic invites comment on the entire Act, which is of course primary legislation only recently passed by Parliament.

That is not to say that the other topics are unimportant – the website reads like a list of all the things where more not less regulation is probably needed (eg Major Hazard Industries, Biodiversity, Pensions).

It is worth a look at the comments contributed to the Red Tape website on equalities. It is pleasing to note the relative lack of hateful comments (compared to many website discussions on this topic) and the many positive and supportive comments.

So what is the government up to? The equalities website says that the government's approach is as follows: "We do not want public bodies to have to show people these things: how they worked out whether their rules and services were fair; what they looked at when they checked that their rules and services were fair; who they involved when they were working out their equality goals; how they were going to check whether they had met their goals. We will not make public bodies tell us how they will work out how they are going to check that they are meeting their goals. This is because it will not help public bodies make equality better."

Accusations of 'red tape' and 'box ticking' are often little more than a back door attack on the purpose of the regulations themselves. I suspect this is exactly what is happening on equalities. The whole housing sector should be watchful.

John Wheatley and the Origins of Council Housing

May 6, 2011

By Steve Schifferes

Council housing has a rich history. It transformed the housing conditions of millions of people. It owed its origins to a small number of visionary pioneers. In a special post, Steve Schifferes recalls the life of a pivotal figure, John Wheatley.

John Wheatley, a leader of the "Red Clydeside" group of Labour MPs in the 1920s, was a key figure in the development of housing policy in the UK, and the architect of the 1924 Housing Act which built nearly 500,000 homes in the interwar years and put council housing on a firm financial and political basis for the next 50 years.

At a time when the very concept of council housing is under unprecedented attack, it is useful to look again at Wheatley's legacy.

Wheatley's concern about housing stemmed from his own impoverished background as the son of an Irish miner in the Lanarkshire coalfields. Wheatley himself went down the pits at age 12, and lived in a one-room terraced house with his eight brothers and sisters, parents, and lodgers. The children all slept together in a bed that was rolled out at night. There was only a communal toilet and water had to be hauled from a common tap. Wheatley later described the degrading conditions of such housing in his pamphlet 'Mines, Miners, and Misery', where he blamed the mine owners for dehumanising their workforce.

Wheatley managed to escape from the pits through self-education and eventually managed to become a successful businessman, setting up a printing firm which printed religious calendars and local papers. His financial success allowed him the freedom to carry out his political activities without interference, and he was able to subsidize the printing of leaflets and the organisation of meetings.

Wheatley had not started out as socialist but as an Irish Nationalist, and was a leading member of the United Irish League in Glasgow before he joined the Independent Labour Party in 1906. Wheatley was also a devout Catholic, and his first act was to set up a Catholic Socialist Society, to convince the Irish Catholic community that there was no incompability between religion and socialism. He ran foul of the Catholic establishment in the City, and in 1912 an angry mob converged on his houses to burn him in effigy for his heretical beliefs – an event he watched with equanimity from his front porch.

Wheatley soon became active in local politics, serving as a councillor for Shettleston, and when it was amalgamated with Glasgow, as leader of the Labour group on the City Council. Glasgow had the worst housing of any major UK city, with the majority of its population living in unheathly one or two room tenement blocks with little sanitation. Death rates for the poorer wards were very much higher than in the affluent West End. And housebuilding had virtually ceased as the "housing famine" increased, putting pressure on accommodation and rents.

From the outset, Wheatley argued that only the government could supply the answer to the housing problem by building reasonably priced housing for workers. He sought to capitalise on the successful activities of the Glasgow City council to help subsidise the cost of building such housing, proposing that the surplus from the municipal tramways be used to build "Eight pound (per year) cottages for Glasgow citizens."

What transformed the housing issue in Glasgow was the First World War. As a major munitions centre, Glasgow's population expanded rapidly with an influx of workers to the shipyards and armaments factories. The result was a squeeze on housing, especially affecting existing tenants whose husbands were in the armed forces. The ILP under Wheatley – despite its anti war stance – began agitating over the evictions of servicemen's wives, calling the landlords the "huns at home." By October 1915 they had built a mass movement, led by women, of rent strikers who prevented evictions and marched on the sherriff's court. When the workers at the Parkhead Forge (led by a Wheatley ally, David Kirkwood) threatened to go on strike to support the rent strikers, the government conceded and introduced rent control throughout the UK for the duration of the war.

Wheatley himself was always clear that rent control was a temporary measure due to the failure of the private rented sector, and the real answer was the provision of state-subsidised housing. In 1922 he was elected to Parliament, and in 1924 he had a chance to put his ideas into practice when he was appointed Minister of Health in the first Labour government.

There had already been two failed attempts to involve the national government in the provision of housing after the war – the Addison Act in 1919, which aimed at providing "Homes Fit for Heroes" but fell victim to the Geddes Axe and was cut by the Coalition Government as too expensive. In 1923 Neville Chamberlain introduced a housing act designed to subsidise private sector provision, but little housing was built.

Wheatley built the foundations of his housing policy carefully, first working to gain an agreement between builders and the building trades on the expansion of the apprentice system to ensure there was the workforce to expand housing production. He also sought agreement with building materials suppliers to limit any price increases, and carefully consulted the local authorities. Under Wheatley's plans, local authorities would receive long term 40 year subsidies to build council housing under municipal control with a guarantee against any losses. Wheatley aimed to eliminate the housing shortage in ten years, with house building rising from 135,000 per year to 450,000 houses per year in the final year of his plan. Wheatley aimed at a high standard of housing suitable for skilled workers and available to all, "homes not hutches" as he called it.

Wheatley fell out with the Labour leadership under Ramsay MacDonald over his attitude to the 1926 General Strike, and due to his left wing views was not reappointed in the 1929 Labour government – and remained a fierce critic of its orthodox economic policy in the face of the growing world economic crisis. He died in 1930, just before the Labour government fell and the pound was devalued.

MacDonald joined a new National government dominated by the Conservatives. That government abolished the Wheatley Act as too expensive and returned to a policy of slum clearance with its emphasis on the rehousing of "slum dwellers" in houses and flats of lower quality. This led to a number of rent strikes by existing tenants, who objected to having their rents increased in order to subsidize the rents of the new tenants, who at that time could not afford council housing.

Wheatley's legacy lived on, however, through the post World War II expansion of council house building – and council housing became the basis for Labour's rise to power in the major urban centres.

Steve Schifferes is Professor of financial journalism at City University. Formerly a producer at London Weekend Television and a BBC journalist, he also worked at Shelter, the National Campaign for the Homeless.

That vile word

June 1, 2011

I was once in a meeting of a housing association which was discussing buying land and developing homes in Stevenage. "I've been there" chirruped the Chief Executive, "it really is chavland". I have been in plenty of other meetings where senior housing folk have talked about their clients in disparaging terms. I can recall one Housing Director in the north responding to a presentation on the Decent Homes programme by saying "There's nothing wrong with our houses, it's the people that need fixing". Fortunately, most people who work in the profession are more enlightened and have a more balanced view and a better choice of words.

As a fan (mildly obsessive) of EastEnders I get outraged by every storyline that involves any character visiting a council estate. They are always the same. High blocks, lifts not working, rubbish strewn everywhere, hoodies gathered menacingly outside, drug dealers hovering, noisy music blaring, people shouting, and in the middle of it some poor character suffering terrible deprivations, and desperate to get back to the square where decent folk live (now there's the joke).

I used to start talks by asking people if they knew where the Jasmin Allen estate was. Invariably they knew it was a bad bad place where police only went in big groups because it was run by gangs and the residents appeared to throw rocks at them on every visit. Everyone thinks they've heard of it and the penny eventually drops that it was in The Bill and was fictional. I believe the filming was done on an estate in south London famous for being visited by Tony Blair on his first day as Prime Minister.

I was got going on this topic by a recent Polly Toynbee piece on 'the vile word' chav. How right she is that the use of the word chav is just one part of a sustained effort to 'foster the loathing of a feral underclass' thereby diverting public resentment about economic and social failure from the rich to the poor.

Polly quotes Baroness Hussein-Ece – a LibDem Equality and Human Rights Commissioner no less – who tweeted: "Help. Trapped in a queue in chav land. Woman behind me explaining latest EastEnders plot to mate while eating largest bun I've ever seen." And then of course this week we have Iain Duncan Smith, hand wringing in public, and in private getting his department to place stories in the media – and picked up endlessly by the BBC – about the 'top ten' most ridiculous stories told by some benefit scroungers.

For this government (LibDems should look suitably ashamed, I expect it from the Tories) and their supporters this is all part of the softening up exercise for the cuts. Everyone's on the fiddle, no-one wants to work, they're breeding like rabbits, they get subsidised housing and don't even pay the rent, so we should take their benefits away from them. Even decent politicians run in fear from the stereotype and feel it is necessary to back some variant of 'welfare reform'.

The outcome is that it is so much easier to make cuts that really hurt people. We have blogged about some of these before. The latest news this week, from the heads of Britain's main charities dealing with mental health, concerns the 'devastating effects' welfare reform (i.e. cuts) is having on the mental health of hundreds of thousands of people.

The long title of Owen Jones' book 'Chavs' being published this week is 'the demonization of the working class'. That's what is really going on and council tenants get the worst of the stigma. Some politicians and housing professionals need to read it and begin choosing their policies and words more carefully.

Jon Snow's 'shocking eye opener'

June 30, 2011

I doubt very much if he will recall it, but I met Jon Snow in 1973 when I organised a conference on homelessness in London's West End on behalf of Voluntary Action Westminster and he was the main guest speaker. Jon worked at New Horizon Youth Centre but he was already a stunningly charismatic and committed man.

I understand he has kept in touch with New Horizon ever since. I have only come across him once since, when he devoted almost the entire Channel 4 News to a brilliant analysis of the Westminster Auditor's guilty verdict on Dame Shirley Porter's gerrymandering.

On the basis of these two little episodes I have taken it as read that he had a feel for housing issues as they affect people at the very sharp end. He himself says that what he saw of poverty and homelessness in the West End in the 1970s has informed his life ever since.

Jon has now revisited the bad end of the housing market for a Dispatches programme which airs next Monday. He calls it 'a shocking eye opener'.

On his blog, Jon says:

"This month I have spent hours in flats and houses in which you would not leave a dog for an hour. I have smelt the dank fungi that leaches its way across the walls of a two-bedroom flat in Rochdale and wandered between rows of garden sheds to the West of London in which rafts of men live two, three, and four, to a shed. At night you hear the voices in the dark, see the chinks of light through the boards, hear the clank of cooking pots as they prepare supper at the end of a working day.

"It perplexes me that society can be so consumed with the state of education and health provision in Britain, and yet turn so active a blind eye to the true state of where people actually live."

At a time when it seems to be increasingly acceptable to blame the poor for their poverty and the homeless for their homelessness, and politicians line up to talk about housing benefit as if everyone was getting tens of thousands of pounds to live in luxury, the programme will show what life is really like at the bottom of the housing market in the worst of the private rented sector.

It is, says Jon, 'a shocking and upsetting watch'. And as the government rips the homelessness safety net to shreds and cuts housing benefit to the bone, let's hope it makes them feel just a little embarrassed.

The shocking thing is that it isn't shocking to anyone who has worked in the lower end of the sector over the last 30 years. When I worked there in the 1980s, I can recall a house being discovered by environmental health officers in Haringey which had 50 people living there in shifts. The growing housing shortage is clearly making things worse, and it is inevitable that the housing benefit cuts will make the scramble for the cheapest and worst homes even more intense.

Anecdotal evidence tells me that there are fewer environmental health officers and housing advisers working in the sector than there were then, and the Chartered Institute of Environmental Health's journal EHP regularly reports cuts in posts and services. Back then, in boroughs like Haringey and many others, programmes like Housing Action Areas meant that the poorest areas were identified and additional powers taken for small areas of particular housing stress. Local teams of housing advisers (who understood tenants' rights) and environment health officers (who understood property law and enforcement) worked together to go systematically from house to house dealing with bad conditions. Although landlords sometimes responded by ending a tenancy, it was the council and not the tenant that was responsible for action being taken, making it clear to the landlord that getting rid of the tenant was no way out, thereby making tenants feel less vulnerable. Picking up a small number of homeless people as a result of a large programme of intervention was seen as a price worth paying. The method was carrot and stick – grants were available to help with the works, but we would not shy away from compulsory purchase when it was necessary.

Things seem to have got worse over the years despite many changes in the legislation and the introduction of the health and safety rating system. The service and enforcement of notices seems to be as complex and bureaucratic as ever. The sector has grown but resources, especially the number of housing environmental health officers on the ground, seem less, and it is less common to have local teams who get to know the landlords and develop relationships with them. The system seems to have reverted to responding to tenant complaints rather than planned programmes of inspections focusing on the riskiest properties.

A system that puts tenants at risk – of eviction, and occasionally of harassment – if they complain will never work effectively. It is interesting that the CAB's advice on getting repairs done starts with the warning: "Trying to get a repair done may put a tenant at risk. People with limited security may face eviction if they take action against their landlord." This is the central conundrum in dealing with bad conditions in the private rented sector.

Labour's proposed reforms following the Rugg Review were a start but are now abandoned, and the current government's laissez faire attitude is seriously deficient. Anyone watching Grant Shapps' interview with Jon Snow would spot the complacency and, frankly, lack of concern. There is nothing wrong with emphasising that most landlords are good, and that most tenants are satisfied, but this is no excuse for failing to have a strategy to tackle the bad landlords and the bad properties.

Private renting is the last great unmodernised industry, run by amateurs and too often driven by the dream of the quick buck. The landlords' organisations seem far more responsible and less defensive than they used to be: they also support action against rogue landlords and support the professionalisation of the industry.

There seems to me to be a great opportunity – rising demand, good returns, a flat property market – for radical reform that will benefit tenants and landlords together. Taxation of private renting needs reform to encourage investment in repairs and improvements. I would argue for a stronger measure of security of tenure and the abandonment of the worst aspects of the local housing allowance changes as well. But the way forward for private renting must be based on proper regulation against a clear code and standards, a professional service, clear contracts between service provider and consumer, and swift intervention that is driven by council inspection and not tenant complaints. Just like any other industry that has a major impact on people's lives.

What is it about our society that can make such things possible?

August 9, 2011

There are some similarities between what has happened in Tottenham over the past few days and the riot of 1985. Both were triggered by a death during a police operation and a family demanding answers about what happened, followed by a march on Tottenham Police station and people feeling ignored and disrespected. Then, crowds gathered on Broadwater Farm estate which became the venue for the subsequent riot. The riot had nothing to do with the estate, it was about policing, and the location could equally have been Tottenham High Road then as now. But the pressure cooker exploded and the appalling, and I believe still unsolved, mob murder of PC Blakelock cemented the notoriety of the estate.

Talking our way through hundreds of riot police, three of us opened the Broadwater Farm Neighbourhood Office at 7am the following morning, dealing with many terrified people. Teams of council staff arrived spontaneously and began the clean-up. Shops and cars had been burned out but there was remarkably little damage to the residential parts of the estate – extraordinarily, the glaziers were hardly needed – although the impact on residents' morale was palpable.

Local politicians and neighbourhood staff were outstanding in the aftermath, and especially Bernie Grant, who showed enormous courage in the face of a despicable media campaign of vilification. He devoted many years of his life afterwards to making the Farm, and the wider Tottenham area, good places to live and strong communities. He eventually got the relationship between the community and the police onto a new footing.

Everything that has been said about the criminality of the current riots, the appalling firesetting and looting, is fair comment. A large number of people, many very young, have done very bad things and they should be arrested for them as soon as they are identified. It hurts, but we have to understand that many of the rioters have done this to their own communities; it is not good enough to say it was all done by people from somewhere else.

It will take a long time for communities to recover, but there were signs all over the news today of councils responding magnificently and communities pulling together and supporting each other. I have been struck by the many interviews with community activists and leaders who are stunningly articulate about what is happening in their areas, why things have been going wrong, and what needs to be done. They give the lie to the many derogatory things that are said about working class areas. In many cases they are already the Big Society but without the resources and wherewithal to withstand the tsunami of post-recession policies that have caused hope and aspiration to evaporate.

A twin track approach is needed. Obviously, the police response has to be better and the community deserves to be better protected. Cuts to police numbers should be withdrawn. There will be many operational lessons to be learned, especially when so many communities come under attack at the same time. What is so different from 1985 is the speed with which the rioting spread through so many different areas across London and further. The Blackberry phenomenon needs to be understood for the future, the police seemed clueless in the face of it.

But those that can **only** condemn and talk of clampdowns and state retribution are making a big mistake. Even Mrs Thatcher sent out Michael Heseltine to find out what was happening in Liverpool after the Toxteth riots. Boris Johnson hasn't got a clue. His one-dimensional response, repeated by David Cameron, about 'sheer criminality' is just not good enough, and Ken Livingstone is much more sure-footed and grounded in reality when big issues like this arise.

If it has no other dimension than criminality, if it has nothing to do with economic and social conditions, and policing, why has it happened now? Is it completely unrelated to the closure of youth centres, the removal of EMA, rising youth unemployment, and rising numbers of young people being stopped and searched on the streets, which they see as harassment and disrespect? If poor communities are constantly accused (even by some Labour politicians) of fecklessness, worthlessness (to the point of being told they shouldn't have children if they can't afford them) and scrounging, and a feeling of hopelessness is added by the unfair and unequal impact of the recession, is it a surprise that the outcome is a destructive form of alienation that eventually expresses itself in violence?

If bankers ruin the global economy then earn millions in new bonuses, if politicians and policemen are perceived to be on the make (even if most aren't), if a media empire indulges in criminality as a matter of routine, if we only measure worth in material possessions, we should be traumatised but not astonished when youth also display heartless avarice and grab what they can. Maybe Laurie Penny is right when she wrote in her blog last night that "people riot because it makes them feel powerful, if only for a night".

For the future, we should take our lead from the dignified comments of the furniture store owner, distraught at the loss of his building, which had served the local community for 150 years, who was right to condemn but also had the perspicacity to ask why, what is it about our society that can make such things possible?

Myths about migrants

August 25, 2011

On Red Brick we've taken an interest in trying to test out and bust a few of the myths in housing.

One area where there are more myths than most is in migration policy and the access that 'foreigners' have to social housing. It's interesting that social housing is often portrayed in the media as being the lowest of the low, except when it is occupied by immigrants, in which case it is a wonderful national asset that should only go to 'British people'.

Migration Watch gets a lot of sympathetic coverage in some parts of the media and their latest use and abuse of statistics comes in a 'study' on social housing and migration in England, in which they claim that the social housing requirements of new immigrants will cost the taxpayer £1 billion a year for the next 25 years. They say that *"45 additional social homes would have to be built every day, or nearly 1400 a month, over that period to meet the extra demand"* and *"The impact of immigration on the availability of social housing for British people has been airbrushed out for too long. Either the government must cut immigration very substantially as they have promised or they must invest very large sums in the construction of extra social housing".*

At least I can agree with the last 13 words of that quote.

John Perry, who blogs at the Migrant Rights Network, has analysed Migration Watch's claims and the Migration Observatory has published a detailed briefing on the real facts about migrants and housing.

Perry demonstrates that there is no automatic link between the number of new households that are projected to be formed by migrants and the provision of social housing. On current government spending plans migrants would have to take virtually all of the funding available and new homes provided for the claim to be true.

Yet few if any new migrants will actually get these homes. The percentage of new social lettings going to foreign nationals is 7%, most of whom have lived here for many years in order to qualify. The Migration Observatory points out that 75% of new immigrants go into the private rented sector, and that is probably where the serious issues around migration and housing lie.

The veracity of Migration Watch's analysis can be summed up by the graph they include which shows the 'cumulative stock of migrants' and 'households on waiting lists' on the same chart, as if they were correlated in some way. You might as well correlate Newcastle United's league position and the frequency of cyclones in south east Asia.

With his Chartered Institute of Housing hat on, John Perry has also written a helpful guide on the role of housing providers in relation to UK migration and how to handle national policies and trends, published by the Joseph Rowntree Foundation.

The paper comments that *"Migration policy often focuses on the number of new migrants entering the UK, but little is done to support neighbourhoods where migrants already live. Central government is withdrawing from these issues at a local level, placing more importance than ever before on regional and local leadership."*

It then highlights the ways in which housing providers have already taken steps towards better neighbourhood cohesion and integration and suggests ways in which they could do more because they are well placed to do so. It also explores the perceived and actual competition between migrants and host communities for housing.

Migration is a complex and emotive topic where exaggeration is rife and 'facts' are often exploited by the media to promote a particular political agenda. The housing world generally and many individual providers have a terrific record in promoting community coherence, work that is needed more than ever after the events of the last few weeks. There is an appetite in the sector to do even more and the CIH/JRF guide and the MO briefing are invaluable and highly recommended tools.

A tale of two rioters

September 1, 2011

Picture the scene. Two 15-year-olds caught up in the riots. Both enter a building and steal something, no violence involved but it's clearly burglary. Both are caught by CCTV, arrested, charged, and brought before the Courts. Both are sentenced to six months in jail. The justice system has worked.

But there is one difference between the two children. One lives with his parents in a small terraced house that they bought 25 years ago and have brought their three children up in. No-one in the family has been in trouble before. The other lives with his parents in a small terraced house that they got from the council 25 years ago and have brought their three children up in. No-one in the family has been in trouble before.

What does justice have to say about this? Both have been dealt with, punished seriously for their crime. Both will have the blight of a criminal conviction and prison sentence hanging over them for years to come. But it's fair treatment.

The first boy, when released, will return to his family in their family home and try to take up his life. There is some security and stability as he rebuilds. It's hard but possible.

The second boy, when released, finds that his family has been evicted by the council from the family home because of his crime. They were declared intentionally homeless, so they won't be rehoused. They have taken two private rented rooms in a shared house at a cost of nearly twice the council rent they were paying. Dad thinks he can't afford to keep working. The youngest child is bedwetting, a result of the trauma of eviction say the medics. Mum is suffering from depression and is struggling to keep her job. They are not able to take the oldest boy in. He drifts off to stay on someone's sofa. There is no security and stability from which to build. It's very hard and it feels almost impossible.

What does justice have to say about this? None of this is fanciful; anyone involved in housing knows that this story reflects the reality.

There is no doubt that the mood is about retribution. Polls show that more people want tenants evicted than don't. But neighbours who are home owners or private tenants probably don't want anyone convicted of a serious crime living next to them either. And the determination of some councils to evict, and the government's determination to make it easier for them, will not apply more generally to your common or garden murderer or rapist or burglar.

It may allow politicians to sound tough. It may be what people want. But it isn't justice. It's double punishment, it's guilt by association, it's discrimination on the grounds of tenure, pure and simple.

Labour, nationally and locally, should have nothing to do with it.

LibDems in denial

September 23, 2011

They say politics is a rough old trade, but any hope that there might be a frank debate on housing during the Party Conference season were dashed immediately at the LibDem conference in Birmingham. The line was just to deny that their policies have any downside at all.

LibDem President Simon Hughes MP knows that attack is often the best form of defence. He set the tone at the start of the week by giving the impression that the worst thing happening in housing at the moment is that Frank Dobson MP is a council tenant, or as Inside Housing quoted Hughes as saying, he lives in 'a bloody Camden Council flat'.

Then we had Andrew Stunell MP's subterfuge: trying to pretend that 'affordable rent' homes are social housing, stretching credulity to the limit. He also made much of the Coalition's efforts to bring empty homes back into use without mentioning Eric Pickles restrictions on the use of Empty Dwelling Management Orders to protect property owners' 'fundamental rights'.

Finally we had Pensions Minister Steve Webb MP. Surely a man with such expertise in the field of tax and benefits would have something intelligent to say about the housing benefit reforms. None of it. His line was that while Labour accused him of adopting a policy akin to the slaughter of the first born, the truth was that cash spending on housing benefit at the end of the Parliament would be the same as at the start, around £22bn. So all is well, he is just 'reigning in the remorseless growth in spending'. No mention of rent inflation, or of policies, like affordable rent, that are driving up housing benefit costs, or of the increasing caseload of private tenants having to share the available cash, or of the policy of pushing homeless families into the more expensive private rented sector. And certainly no mention of Boris Johnson's description of the policy as 'Kosovo-style cleansing'.

Never can a LibDem audience have been so supine. It looked to me like they think that the only hope of political survival is to keep their heads down and claim that they are having influence. In housing they have nothing to show for their efforts because they have gone along with the Tory agenda in its entirety – the end of social rent, moving towards market rents, reducing tenants' rights, laissez-faire in the private rented sector.

It will be interesting to see how the Labour Conference pans out. We are told that there will be honesty about the record in office, which should start with an admission that far too few homes were built. But this has to lead to new policies that will produce many more homes – market homes and genuinely affordable homes. There will need to be a radically new approach to capital investment, so I will be paying as much attention to Ed Balls as I will to Caroline Flint.

Eric's troubled families

October 22, 2011

By Monimbo

The latest Pickles obsession is troubled families: 120,000 of them costing the state (or is it the overall economy? That's a bit vague) at least £8 billion per year.

This sounds like a lot of money, and while the usually diligent Fact Check has looked into it, I'm not convinced that they have demonstrated that it's anywhere near accurate. A small part of the cost is attributable to services that all low-income families receive, while most of the cost is based on a global figure of £2.5bn which relates to a smaller group of 46,000 families considered by the Department of Education. These 46,000 families are the ones where, in addition to their other problems, the children are in trouble with the law. The £2.5bn is the cost of the 'reactive spend' these families require, such as children going into care, hoax emergency calls, vandalism and a range of other things which look very difficult indeed to measure in terms of incidence let alone cost.

What is a 'troubled family'? Apparently it is one where 'no parent in the family is in work; the family lives in poor quality or overcrowded housing; no parent has any qualifications; the mother has mental health problems; at least one parent has a long-standing limiting illness, disability or infirmity; the family has low income (below 60% of the median); or the family cannot afford a number of food and clothing items'.

The strange thing is that this says nothing about the 'problems' the family causes. The Guardian said that one Salford family required 250 interventions in one year, including 58 police call-outs and five arrests; five 999 visits to A&E, two injunctions and a council tax arrears summons. This sounds horrendous, but there must be many families that fit the Cabinet Office definition that aren't causing this sort of mayhem.

Well, I'm sure it's right that some families do cost a lot of money because of their anti-social behaviour and crime, but the Pickles approach suggests a fixed, potentially manageable social malaise which can be 'solved', which is the kind of problem beloved by civil servants and ministers but which often hides a range of more complex and challenging issues where the remedies require co-operation between different agencies.

What's striking about the presentations on the scheme on the Department of Education website is not only how many agencies might be involved, but how – service after service – these are ones being affected by cuts in local authority and other budgets. When times are harsh, it's precisely the 'extra' services like Sure Start and the additional help which failing pupils get in schools that are likely to be affected.

So, as in other areas of government, Eric will give back with one hand what he first took away with the other one.

Almost at the time of the announcement, indeed, there was a report of how 73% of a sample of 22 family intervention projects have seen their budgets cut and have had to reduce the services they provide to over 1,100 families. It is a fair bet that many of these feature in the 120,000 national 'total', and of course family intervention, promoted by Labour, has been shown to work in many cases.

Another characteristic of Eric's announcements is to blame problems on the failure of local authorities to realise that the issue (in this case, troubled families) is complex and requires multiple interventions. It is almost as if behind each family is a set of blinkered council departments who have no idea that the family is demanding the attention of different agencies and are incapable of picking up the phone to discuss the issues with colleagues. In Eric's ideal world, local authorities would have staff who are as bright as he is and would see the virtues of joint working, or at least know how to phone the police. In reality, I know most housing officers would say that they do try to co-ordinate action but when budgets are being cut so drastically it is extremely difficult.

The Daily Mail, of course, loved this story and signed up to the government's simplistic approach. It said that ministers want one dedicated official to turn up at people's homes to get them out of bed for work, make sure their children go to school or ensure alcoholics or drug addicts go to rehab.

Do not despair! That apostle of joined-up approaches, Louise Casey, will bang heads together and make them see sense. She has been appointed as the Tsar that will sort everything out, set tight targets and ensure they are complied with. Now Louise is a sensible person who has a track record of tackling these issues, so her appointment is certainly not a bad one but she – more than anyone – must realise the complexities of the issues involved and the even greater difficulty of tackling them in a time of deep spending cuts.

She must also know that local agencies often *do* collaborate to find solutions, otherwise family intervention centres wouldn't exist. She is also aware of the pressures on many agencies not to solve the problems but to pass them on, by excluding children from schools or evicting difficult families from social housing (something on which Eric's colleague, Grant Shapps, favours tougher action, of course). But this only sends them into the private sector where they'll get less help.

As a point of reference, Tony Blair in a speech in 2007 said that 2-3% of families had deep and persistent problems, so perhaps Pickles could have made a passing acknowledgement of the previous government's success in reducing the numbers so radically. Of course, in 2007 the government had no more idea of the real magnitude of the problem than it does now, but I do wonder whether the scale has been brought down to a more manageable 120,000 for political reasons.

Times are harsh and public money is scarce. If a smaller number of families are causing mayhem (even being blamed for the riots), at previously uncalculated and enormous cost, then perhaps Eric (aided by Louise) has more chance of riding to the rescue and sorting them out. When he has, no doubt we will be given the evidence of how much money has been saved when the families are eventually put on the path of rectitude. I'm sure we'll read about it in the Daily Mail.

Roxy Come Home

November 11, 2011

Albert Square is the only place in London where the housing market appears to be stable and there is a plentiful supply of homes for anyone separating from a partner or being kicked out of their last place. Phil Mitchell and Ian Beale appear able to buy homes in the Square at will, normally with the relevant amount of cash.

The show normally prides itself on its 'gritty realism' and its research into controversial topics, trying to get the facts right, and frequently advertises help lines when distressing stories are being broadcast - for example, around the cot death of Ronnie Mitchell's son James or Whitney Dean being forced into prostitution.

However, they never seem to concern themselves with housing. Last week no help lines were advertised when Janine illegally evicted Roxy with no sign of a legal procedure, just walking in and removing her stuff. In previous weeks, the landlady attempted forcible entry and clearly harassed poor Roxy and her small child. Parents might also be perturbed at the rather cavalier way a children's officer took Roxy's daughter off her and gave her into the care of Jack Branning under what was said to be a Temporary Residence Order. Shades of Cathy Come Home.

When we talk about rogue landlords, we would do well to keep Janine Butcher in our mind. Not that Roxy deserves much sympathy, having done similar things to previous tenants of her own before she squandered her inheritance from her Dad, the beautifully evil Archie Mitchell. (It's also a mystery as to why Janine refers to Roxy as a Chav when her Dad was a successful rich criminal who lived in a very large house on the south coast before moving in with Peggy, but I've gone off at a tangent.)

Another recent storyline, involving young squatters, seemed well out of touch with reality as the property seemed to be transformed magically into a care home of some sort, by an amazing stroke of luck the squatters got to live there (I admit I may have missed an episode and misunderstood something here, or I may have happened upon the E20 spin-off, but the same principles apply).

Unfortunately, Walford Council is never much help. They do not appear to have a housing advice or tenancy relations service, and it looks like the CAB has never made it to Walford either. The council only ever appears in a bad light, run either by corrupt or otherwise unhelpful and stupidly bureaucratic officials with the single policy of doing whatever annoys the residents of the square. I do have a distant memory of one storyline when (I think) Michelle Fowler went off to work in the housing allocations department of the council, where there were strange goings-on. It didn't end well.

So, here's a plea to EastEnders producers and the BBC. When there is an illegal eviction, please remember that this is an experience many people in this country have every day. And just as you do for other difficult storylines, putting Helpline information on the screen at the end of the show is the minimum you could do.

It would be even better if a charming Housing Officer came along to prevent the eviction, accompanied by a Police Officer willing to make an arrest.

'Rents will fall and no-one will be made homeless'. So what happened, IDS?

November 16, 2011

By Karen Buck MP

Government Ministers have consistently argued that the changes in local housing allowance would lead to reduced rents in the private rented sector and would not lead to more homelessness. Labour MP for Westminster North Karen Buck spoke at the launch of the NHF's Home Truths report this morning, and writes exclusively for Red Brick below.

A year ago, Iain Duncan Smith said in the House of Commons debate on Housing Benefit:

"The purpose of these (HB) changes is to give a real impetus to getting the rents down to make affordable housing more available in some areas... Through the emergency Budget and spending review, we proposed a set of housing benefit reforms designed to bring back under control a system that has been out of control. I accept that the responsibility of Government is always to get the balance right as we protect, incentivise, and ensure fairness in the system. Critically, for housing, that means getting the rents down..... There should be no need, with the discretionary allowance, for people to be made homeless. That is just the nonsense with which Labour Members want to scare everybody."

One year on, we now know that the mean rent increase in London was around 12%.

We are facing an unprecedented crisis of supply and affordability. This has not all occurred since May 2010 - and some of the present problems have roots in the decision to switch subsidy from 'bricks and mortar' to personal subsidy three decades ago. Still, recent developments have intensified the problem acutely.

Over the last year, homelessness has risen sharply, reversing a fairly steady medium term decline. The recent pattern by which homelessness/temporary accommodation has been diverted via the prevention and relief of homelessness strategy is faltering, because families are reluctant to abandon future security as the PRS becomes increasingly unaffordable. (Meanwhile, there are over 100,000 households to whom local councils accepted homelessness duties but then diverted them into the private sector who will be at risk of re-presenting as rents rise and benefits fall.)

The central issue remains one of the supply of affordable homes, especially for rent, but whilst we are seeing the final wave of new supply coming through as a result of the Labour government's investment, the future looks less hopeful because of the Orwellian 'affordable rent' model and housing benefit cuts.

'Affordable rents' as the means of filling the grant gap mean not just places like Westminster become unaffordable - an 'affordable rent' set at 65% of market rents would require a household income of £65k to cover the cost without benefit - but so do poorer places like Haringey and Newham. In Haringey, a rent set at 80% of local market rents would require a household income of £31k for a 1 bed flat, and in Newham a 2 bed flat would require a household income of £27k. This at a time when the median income for social housing tenants is £12k.

The Household Benefit Cap and Housing Benefit cuts, meanwhile, are estimated in a recent report by London Councils to leave 133,000 households unable to pay their current rents.

Even if this proves to be an over-estimate, staggering numbers of households face a dramatic shortfall in their income and are at risk of upheaval and homelessness as private rents continue to soar. Boroughs with lower housing costs can anticipate a sharp increase in numbers of incomers, many with high service and support needs.

It is worth noting that unemployment, the freeze in real wages and rising housing costs have already contributed to a rise in the number of private sector Housing Benefit claimants, especially in the suburbs- the London Borough of Redbridge, which includes part of the constituency of the Secretary of State for Work and Pensions, saw a 65% increase in Local Housing Allowance claims in a little over a year, the largest increase in the country. Some of the areas facing the biggest cost pressures are not the Knightsbridge's and Mayfair's of popular myth, but places like Hillingdon and Croydon, whilst Newham will be amongst the places worst hit by the overall Benefit Cap.

Supply may be the solution over the medium and longer term, but in the very short term we need DCLG and DWP to sort out their differences and develop an integrated approach to housing need and homelessness before they escalate.

Homeless people are 'the likes of us'

November 25, 2011

Michael Collins is styled as a biographer of the working class, with his best known work being 'The Likes of Us' published in 2004. The book's rosy view of working class culture in history and how it was destroyed by social change was controversial, with black writer Mike Philips saying *'the book... appeals to the most destructive form of nostalgia'*.

Recently Collins has meandered through the history of council housing. I mainly enjoyed his TV film history 'The Great Estate: The Rise and Fall of the Council House' earlier in the year, but took issue with his analysis of what had gone wrong over the last 40 years and in particular the blame he attaches to the 1977 Housing (Homeless Persons) Act, an argument he returned to this week in a piece for the Independent. The core of our difference is that I think the homeless are 'us' too.

Comparing a distorted view of how awful council housing is now with an exaggerated view of how great it used to be only benefits those who wish to undermine its future. The golden era was just as mythical as the right wing press's modern view that it is a failed sector populated by 'Shameless' characters, everyone skiving, dependent on benefits and getting their home by conning the State that they were homeless.

I don't look back on my childhood in Newcastle, on the Montagu Estate in Kenton, as some great heyday when everything was right in the world. Still in the desperation of the post-War housing shortage, it was without doubt a pretty good deal: a brand new Bevan house, with partial central heating, front and back garden, close to both the Town Moor and the countryside stretching towards the tin hut called the airport. Virtually all the men were in work, most had skilled trades or were clerks, so I suspect there had been social selection going on. It could still be a tough place, with gangs and fights and flick-knives, and we didn't venture onto neighbouring estates. Periods when men fell out of work, as most did from time to time, were hard. There were no shops, just travelling vans, and no community facilities apart from the neighbourhood school. The front door was the colour the council said it would be, no-one had security of tenure and anyone not paying their rent got kicked out. So, my nostalgic memories are reserved for Len White or Stan Anderson playing at St James's Park (now forgodsake the Sports Direct Arena) and a youthful visit to the Club A Gogo to see Eric Burden and the Animals.

So where specifically do I think Collins gets it wrong? Let's start with his tirade against the homeless persons' act. *"It was Labour who demolished a fair letting system. In 1977, the homeless were made a priority and a system of "need" was introduced that was open to abuse. Unsurprisingly, a lot of "homeless" people appeared, to the annoyance of locals who had waited patiently for years on the housing lists.'*

This revision of history, that allocating council housing according to housing need is the root of the sector's perceived problems, has been gaining currency, influencing 'Blue Labour' and the Labour's front bench. The reality is that the impact of the homelessness legislation on allocations after 1978 was slow. The Act encouraged a high degree of gatekeeping (and still does), and there was a high refusal rate for applications, rigorous application of the 'intentionality' rule, and many people suffered the purgatory of a period spent in bed and breakfast or single mother's hostels. It was a process no-one would choose to go through if they had any real alternative. Local connection was vigorously applied and people with a connection to another place were sent back. Virtually all homeless applicants were local and on the waiting list. Crucially, the homeless only became a significant proportion of total allocations when supply collapsed in the 1980s as homes were sold and not replaced. Most homeless people would have been rehoused off the waiting list before becoming homeless in the 1970s when supply was much better.

I also disagree with Collins when he says *'The Government should clarify who the houses are for. In the past it was clear who was entitled.'* My view is that it was only in late 1960s and early 1970s, following 'Cathy Come Home' and the rise of Shelter, that council allocations policies came under greater scrutiny. Before that there was a variety of local practices, but rarely were they transparent. Applicants were subject to subjective assessments of their housekeeping standards by home visitors, and the practice was often discriminatory as the poorest were kept out. In many areas, individual house allocations were made by councillors, a practice that would be condemned today.

Collins lauds 'sons and daughters' schemes which *'ensured extended families remained on the same estates, in the expectation that further generations would remain locally'*. But it is worth remembering that in many places black people were excluded either by schemes that favoured existing families or by direct discrimination. The National Front used the phrase 'sons and daughters' to mean 'no blacks'. It was right that these practices were challenged vigorously by the Community Relations Commission and others.

There's plenty wrong with council housing, now as in the past. But it is better run and managed than it ever has been. Tenants have gained security of tenure and reasonable rents in a profit-making and improving sector. Five million households have expressed their demand to live in it. Council housing is a success story, just as it was in the past, and could have a great future. Its role in providing decent housing to millions of ordinary people deserves proper recognition and proper assessment – with a lot less spin.

Shooting the troubled

December 18, 2011

Cameron and Pickles finally flipped this week. Only they could tell the world, without a shred of humour, that they were going to tackle 'troubled families' by appointing 'trouble shooters'. Of course, this might appeal to some of their backbenchers when they have finished with their Nazi-dress stag parties[1].

When interviewed, Pickles seemed not to have a clue what he was talking about and couldn't even describe what the 'trouble shooters' would do. Frankly, he didn't seem up to the task set by Cameron a year ago when he said he wanted to 'turn round every troubled family in the country' by the end of the current parliament.

There is of course a serious point here, and no-one would complain about developing the good work done in Labour's family intervention projects. But many of the services that are most relevant to these families are precisely those that are being cut as the Government's deficit reduction plan bites.

Serious doubts have emerged about the figure of '120,000 most troubled families' who 'cost the state £8 billion a year'.

Who are these families? Well, according to much of the media, they are the 'Shameless' families who live on benefits, refuse to work, don't send their children to school, adopt ASB as the family sport, etc etc, the typical everyday Daily Mail stereotype of the feckless working class. John Redwood MP calls them 'the worst problem families' who use up 'a small army of state employees'. Even the better news organisations said these were 'dysfunctional' 'problem' families. Sky News used examples of domestic violence, repeat offenders, people who have been in care, and children excluded from school.

Really, who are these families? Over at Fullfact they have tried to track down the figures, stretching back to research done for the Social Exclusion Unit many years ago. The '120,000 families' figure turns out to be a reworking of the SEU's estimate of the number of households who scored on five out of seven indicators or disadvantages. But none of the indicators concerned ASB or criminality or school exclusions or benefit fraud convictions, and it would be possible to be one of the 120,000 without being on out-of-work benefits at all. The SEU indicators are not measures of bad behaviour but of poverty, overcrowding, disability, mental ill-health and low income as well as worklessness. It's not even clear whether we are talking exclusively about families with children at all and whether, for example, older people are included.

Cameron said the Government has estimated how many troubled families are in each area but this sounds like a very dodgy bit of arithmetic, taking an old figure based on different criteria and dividing by the number of local authority areas. It is very different from having a list of households to work with and councils will struggle to operationalise the new policy even if they wanted to and even if they could afford to.

I'm happy to support more money being spent on co-ordinating services to low income households, although it is the height of cynicism for the Government to expect local government to put in 60% of the cost. There are a lot of agencies involved offering a bewildering array of services with different eligibility criteria, so better co-ordination and more targeted service delivery seems like a good thing to do. I suspect however that if the 'trouble shooter' starts by assessing the services received by the household then looking at what they need and what they are entitled to the cost will go up rather than down.

The 'Shameless' stereotype is now so strong that the automatic assumption in all debates is that it is a true depiction of the workless poor – see the newspapers but also watch/listen to the supposedly intelligent programmes like Any Questions and Question Time which are stuffed full of right-wing demagogues peddling these myths.

Family intervention was indeed aimed at the tiny number of families who really could not cope with raising a family and needed intensive (and non-judgemental) support. But this is not what Cameron and Pickles are up to. They are on a propaganda mission, to convince the public (with the mighty media machine behind them) that the real issues are fecklessness and inadequacy and not poverty and unemployment. In short, blame the poor and not the bankers, and certainly not the Tories.

And slightly off-piste: was anyone else rather shocked to hear Boris Johnson on the Marr show this morning say that he expected one nation to drop out of the

Euro, but then comment that the upside would be that ouzo would be lot cheaper. Hilarious or not, isn't he meant to be leading our capital city with a little integrity and dignity? I wonder what the many Greeks living in London think of his little joke?

[1]*Tory MP Aidan Burley was exposed for attending a stag party at a French ski resort where his friends chanted Nazi slogans and wore SS uniforms. He subsequently apologized for "any offence that was caused".*

2012

Who gets subsidised housing?

January 8, 2012

By Monimbo

New proposals by Frank Field and David Davis to boost the right buy have raised the ever-topical issue of whether social housing is 'subsidised' and, by implication, the wider question of whether other sectors are, and if so by how much. This is an issue regularly addressed by the annual UK Housing Review, and armed with a sneak preview of this year's edition, edited by Steve Wilcox and Hal Pawson, I've been checking it out.

Let's start with the sector that's really cushioned by the government. Yes, that's right, it's you owner-occupiers, especially if you have paid off your mortgage. How so? Well the benefits to mortgage payers were wiped out when tax relief ended in 2000, but all owners enjoy capital gains tax relief now worth £5bn (net). Those with no or only small mortgages also benefit from not being taxed on the value of their home (as used to be the case through Schedule A). This is worth an astonishing £11bn. Add back in the taxes that owners *do* pay, and the net subsidy is a romping £12bn. Even if you dismiss the tax on the imputed value of a home as an academic notion which shouldn't enter the balance sheet, then the outcome is that owners pay no net taxes at all. But, as Steve Wilcox points out, the existence of these tax advantages means that house prices are far higher than they might otherwise be, benefitting existing owners and adding to the hurdles faced by first-time buyers.

Private landlords don't enjoy the same tax advantages as homeowners but they benefit from a less restrictive regulatory regime, which means they can access interest-only mortgages. Furthermore, the recent growth in numbers of landlords who own only one or two houses is undoubtedly fuelled by homeowners who can afford a deposit to buy another house to rent out. Taken together, Wilcox argues that the effects of the tax and regulatory regimes benefit existing owner-occupiers most, then landlords, with first-time buyers (especially those who can't afford a deposit) at the bottom of the pile.

Let's turn to subsidy for renting. All tenants, of course, are eligible for housing benefit. The average HB payment for private tenants, at £114 per week in England, compares with £82 for housing association tenants and £73 for council tenants. Obviously, this is largely a function of higher rents. But those who claim that social housing is 'subsidised' because it charges lower than market rents often fail to point out the costs that then fall on government through the HB budget.

How much is the economic subsidy due to lower social rents actually worth? Well, quite a lot, given that social rents run at about 60% of market levels: some £7bn annually. But, again as Steve Wilcox points out, the gap will close (slowly) as the government's 'affordable' rents kick in. And this will in turn have a knock-on effect on HB costs.

It could however be argued that the 'economic subsidy' for social housing is as artificial as the implicit tax reliefs for homeowners, given that no (sensible) government would raise social rents to full market levels. But, oddly enough, those who go on about this subsidy to social housing don't tend to draw attention to the similar one for owner-occupiers.

But surely social housing gets direct subsidy? We are all aware of the social housing grant for new homes and historic subsidy for council housing, but much of this has been paid off, given that average council debt is now only £17k per house. And council housing has now been making a 'profit' since 2008, recognised by the handsome payment to the Treasury implied by the debt settlement that will take place when council housing gives up all future subsidy on April 1 this year. Council housing in Scotland has meanwhile been running without direct subsidy for years, and Scottish councils have been building lots of houses recently, partly from their rental income. As will increasingly happen in England, Scottish council tenants are *themselves* cross-subsiding new tenants.

And finally, we shouldn't forget to add into the reckoning the *direct* subsidies to homeowners. They get renovation grants, support for mortgage interest (for owners who lose their jobs), right to buy discounts and shared ownership schemes, together worth a princely £1.7bn in 2010.

This all means that the only straightforward answer to the question 'who gets subsidised housing?' is that everyone does, from the Queen downwards. Singling out council and housing association tenants as 'subsidised' may be politically convenient to the likes of Field and Davis, but it doesn't square with the facts. As I've said before, let's argue for the introduction of self-financing in England on April 1 as the date on which everyone should stop calling council housing 'subsidised'.

Health and safety gone mad

January 25, 2012

Like benefit recipients and council tenants, Health and Safety gets a very bad press. But the call from the London Fire Brigade to the Mayor to respond to the growing problem of 'back garden developments' or 'beds in sheds' as part of his revised housing strategy brings home the reality.

Their evidence should be compulsory reading for all those who knock health and safety regulations or believe that it is wrong to interfere in the market. And it's not just London – examples similar to theirs can be found in many cities and towns in the country.

The Brigade is issuing an increasing number of prohibition notices to prevent properties being used as housing. Rita Dexter of LFB has identified a range of *'potentially lethal fire traps'* such as converted sheds, industrial units and garages being used as accommodation, with residents relying on highly risky methods of heating lighting and cooking. *'They are also being exploited by unscrupulous landlords who are happy to take their money without any regard for their safety,'* she said.

Examples quoted include a death in a fire in a garage, a group of commercial buildings where 150 people were living, and an office block with 17 rooms with over 50 people living in them with no fire safety features at all.

The need to tackle dangerous housing was the central feature of the LFB's response to the Mayor's Housing Strategy and their lobbying of Government for stronger building regulations. They identified a series of major risks, including the need for better compliance by housing authorities with their Housing Act duties, especially in relation to tall residential buildings and buildings with timber frames, fire setting in empty residential buildings, beds in sheds, and both overcrowding and under-occupation.

On **under-occupation**, they cite the problem of an increasing number of mainly elderly people retreating into living in one room and switching from traditional to *'intrinsically more unsafe'* forms of heating. On **overcrowding**, they called for the housing strategy to *'say more about the consequences of overcrowding'* because of the risk from overuse of electric appliances and blocked escape routes.

On the day when the ludicrous former Archbishop Lord Carey said the major moral dilemma facing the country was the deficit and tackling 'welfare dependency', one glance at the real evidence from the fire authorities of people who are so poor they have to put themselves at risk of serious harm makes you wonder what planet people like him inhabit.

Can a new Tenant Voice rise from the ashes?

February 23, 2012

One of the best projects I've been involved with over the past few years was chairing the group that led to the creation of the **National Tenant Voice**. The NTV was the third leg of Labour's regulatory system for social housing – the smallest and cheapest part – together with the Tenant Services Authority and the Homes and Communities Agency.

The aim was to create a new type of organisation which would bring tenants' and residents' views to the table in Whitehall, facilitate scrutiny of landlords' performance at all levels and help promote tenant and resident self-organisation around the country. The views it represented would be based on research and wide consultation with tenants and residents, including those not represented through existing tenants' and residents' associations.

It was a complex project because the NTV had to be complementary to the existing structure of national tenant organisations, which fully supported its development, and because it was to become a non-departmental public body, and the rules surrounding NDPBs are ferociously complicated (it makes you wonder how there are so many of them).

The NTV operated through a National Tenant Council of 50 members – a very impressive body of people active all around the country – and had just got going and appointed a Chief Executive – Richard Crossley, who had done most of the work to set it up – when the Election happened. Grant Shapps thought that spending £1m on tenant representation was a waste of money and it was axed almost immediately. He did however provide some funding for a review of where the tenants' movement might go next and the report of the review has now been published and attracted a big spread in Inside Housing magazine.

The 'New Dawn' review, also co-ordinated by Richard Crossley, rightly concludes that the abolition of the NTV has been a major blow to the tenants' movement and to the aspiration that tenants, with proper resources behind them, might be enabled to have a real influence over national policies and sit at the table on a more equal footing with the well-resourced landlord and professional organisations as well as the Government. It looks at options for new structures to evolve but concludes that these will take some time.

The issue of resources remains at the heart of the debate about the future of the tenants' movement. With virtually no funding, organised tenants locally make a huge difference to the quality of life on estates and do a huge amount to make landlords accountable. Many of the criticisms of tenant organisation stem from the fact that they operate on a shoestring and usually have few funds to organise events and consultations.

The report concludes, and I agree, that:

There is recognition in the sector that the sector itself should make funding available for tenants to have a voice at national level. In the consultation we carried out, a payment of an amount per tenancy to support influence at national level was supported by an overwhelming majority of those consulted. Just 1p per tenancy per week would give a budget more than the original budget of the NTV. This will need to be explored further.

Councils and housing associations pay large amounts for membership of their national organisations which, correctly, have a major influence on the development of policy or at least make sure the views of the organisations are known. Tenants are often aggrieved that these subscriptions are effectively paid for out of their rents but any request for funding for tenants locally or regionally or nationally is treated as if it is some outrageous demand and is normally only ever available with strings attached. Tenants are often furious, for example, at having to apply for funding to attend meetings and conferences that the landlord attends as a matter of routine.

The time has come for tenants to be able to fund their own representation out of their own rents and for landlords to co-operate willingly in this.

The abolition of Labour's infrastructure for social housing regulation is being replaced by a national committee that will be focused on money and much less interested in performance and services provided to tenants. The gap is supposed to be made up by a greater emphasis on local tenant scrutiny. But without funding this will fail and without an effective and properly funded national tenant voice, Government will not get to hear about it until it is too late.

The New Dawn report is dedicated to Terry Edis, the Chair of NFTMO and an inspirational tenants' leader, who died recently.

Time to think in billions for housing

March 5, 2012

It is now widely accepted that the last Labour Government did not give enough priority to building new affordable homes. It made the planning system more proactive and it had a good record in some areas of housing investment, especially in tackling the enormous inherited backlog of repairs and improvements to the social housing stock. And its classical Keynesian response to the recession put large extra amounts of investment into new homes from 2008 onwards. Unfortunately, that investment – homes started under Labour but completed under the Tories – has obscured the disastrous collapse of the genuinely affordable housing programme since May 2010.

Looking forward, unless we think big, the lack of supply and the resultant high value of housing will be problems that blight the country for a generation. And it is increasingly clear that the broad policy framework, no matter how well conceived, will not deliver the needed homes unless the financial model is right. And that means not only making sure that each scheme is viable but also delivering sufficient investment in total with the right amount of subsidy to make a sufficient proportion of the homes affordable.

There are two big ideas around that could make the kind of difference – billions – that is needed.

First, to bring about a grand shift in the balance of investment by pension funds. All we pensioners have done badly out of a model that depended too much on the appreciation of stocks and shares – when they stopped appreciating, pensioners lost out. There is potentially a synergetic relationship between pension funds – which need good returns over the long term – and housing investment – which produces relatively weak short term but excellent long-term returns. Most development for rented homes makes a loss in the first few years and a rising profit after that – because borrowing costs are reasonably constant over the lifetime of the home but rental income keeps rising year after year. If, and there have been some exemplars, many more deals could be struck whereby the investing pension fund received a lower return at the start, which then rose over time, thereby matching the income stream, affordable housing could be produced with a much lower need for initial subsidy.

The second idea which is bubbling under is *quantitative easing through housing investment*. The Bank of England has printed hundreds of billions of pounds through its QE programme. Essentially this means that money is created electronically and used to buy back gilts from banks, pension funds and insurance companies, strengthening their balance sheets and boosting their capacity to create new investments. The hope is that these institutions, with artificially boosted balance sheets, will in turn put more real resources into the economy by lending to businesses. The problem is that this is a chain with weak links and it is based more on the hope than a requirement that it will boost lending.

A more purposeful alternative would be to use QE – technically the Bank of England Asset Purchase Facility Fund (APF) – to create funds which come directly into housing by buying housing bonds. The purchase of corporate bonds, as opposed to the purchase of gilts, has been a very small part of QE so far. Some amendment might be needed to the APF's rules, but in theory at least APF could buy local authority housing bonds (although there is a problem with falling foul of the public borrowing rules, see below) or bonds issued by housing associations or their intermediaries (which would count as private sector activity). Such bonds are highly rated by the credit rating agencies.

Even if the Bank of England is not willing to use APF to buy housing bonds, these two ideas could be brought together in a more circuitous route: the Bank buys gilts from pension funds, the pension funds use their extra capacity to buy housing bonds, preferably on a more sustainable long term financing model.

The issue about local authority bonds and public borrowing has been raised on Red Brick before. Although over the years people campaigning against the 'Treasury Rules' have seen some helpful shifts in policy – the creation of the prudential borrowing regime for example – the Treasury has remained obsessed by total public sector borrowing *including* government-owned trading corporations (which in turn includes housing). In many other countries borrowing by government-owned corporations is not included in the main measure of public borrowing because they are deemed, like private corporations, to be able to finance their own borrowing from their own business plans. Instead other countries measure 'general government' borrowing. The fact that these definitions are Treasury-made and not inviolable is shown by the fact that the nationalised banks are already treated differently from other government-owned bodies.

Professor Steve Wilcox's chapter in the new UK Housing Review includes an excellent round-up of the arguments against this Treasury orthodoxy. He argues: *'Adopting those international fiscal measures would enable public corporations to play a far more active role in promoting economic growth.... there are obvious examples in terms of housing policy where switching to international fiscal measures would open the door to a far more active role for local government.'* Indeed the strength of this argument is reinforced by the growing evidence that housing investment pays for itself through increased tax income and reduced benefit expenditure – borrowing should be regarded differently if the Treasury gets its money back.

These are complex issues that have huge implications for housing, where policy is more dependent than in any other area, with the possible exception of transport, on borrowing for long term investment – investment that, because of rising rents, is highly profitable in the long term.

My knowledge is probably extended to the limit by writing this post, but there are others who understand this world of high finance and could develop detailed proposals. But it needs political will to do so: political will that unfortunately was absent during the Labour government years. The opportunity of going into the next Election with a genuine offer of many more homes, and a worked-out plan to deliver them, is a prize which is at least worthy of detailed examination.

56. The magic number that should condemn Boris Johnson to a huge defeat.

April 12, 2012

If policies alone decided Elections, Ken Livingstone would be romping home as the next London Mayor.

Instead he faces a photo finish with Tory Boris Johnson. *'Look at Boris, isn't he a laugh'* is no way to run one of the world's five greatest cities. But his celebrity status only tells half the story: Johnson is a cunning and ambitious right wing Tory who is running an unremittingly negative campaign with such hugely powerful media support that even people on own Ken's side start to believe some of the things that are said.

Ken has always had an extraordinary ability to define the policy needs of the moment. On fares, he saw that the need in the 1980s was to use spare capacity and get people back on the tube again; by 2000 the need was for massive investment in new services; and now in 2012 the need is to put money back into the pockets of struggling Londoners.

Similarly, in housing. In his first Mayoralty, 2000-2008, Ken was not given significant housing powers until near the end, when he became responsible for housing strategy and was given considerable influence over the Homes and Communities Agency investment budget. But he realised from the start that housing was one of the great issues facing Londoners and set about using his general planning powers and the strength of his Leadership to create a pro-development and pro-affordable housing culture in London. Even the Olympic bid was turned into a housing development proposal. Recalcitrant developers and boroughs were pushed and pulled into place.

It didn't always work, and the affordable housing numbers built up painfully slowly, but build up they did. By 2008 Ken had his planning and housing strategy in place and he had won the biggest affordable investment programme in London's history from Gordon Brown.

Boris Johnson has been dining out on Ken's 2008-11 housing programme ever since he was elected, taking credit for completing homes for which he had no responsibility. All the while he has been working to undermine the principles on which Ken's programme was was based. Lags and lead-in times in housing are such that 2011-12 was the first year when housing development could be said to be the result of Johnson's and Grant Shapps' policies rather than Ken's and Gordon Brown's. And the result in the first six months of the year (the last available figures) was that **the number of affordable housing starts in a city of millions was 56**.

Ken's Manifesto, published yesterday, contains housing policies that are again fit for the times. He will do everything in his power to get development, and affordable development in particular, moving again. He will do everything in his power to defend social tenants from an unprcedented attack. But his practical focus is on the reality of housing in London's rapidly expanding private rented sector. Unable to afford to buy and unable to access social housing, millions of Londoners are now dependent on private renting and are angry at the poor value for money they receive, with many paying out over half their income on somewhere to live.

The practicality of the Manifesto is demonstrated by the proposal to set up a London-wide not-for-profit lettings agency. Livingstone's boldness in terms of policy is shown by the fact that he is the first politician in many years that has dared to raise for debate the issue of rent control - and to undertake to campaign for a London Living Rent, mirroring the hugely successful campaign for a London Living Wage.

The last word goes to the Guardian's London blogger Dave Hill:

Ken Livingstone's programme for London is obliterating Boris Johnson's in so many ways it's almost embarrassing. I preferred Ken to Boris in 2008 too, but not by a massive margin. His vast policy superiority this time may turn out to be at its greatest in the area of housing.

London's housing problems are not the sort that are best left to the market, which is the natural default position of the total Tory that Boris is. Housing policy is another compelling reason for Londoners to give one of their two mayoral votes to candidate Livingstone and neither to candidate Johnson.

Louise Casey, Jeremy Kyle and the zombie statistic

July 20, 2012

With her background at Shelter, Louise Casey understands the power that a strong case history can have in humanising and illustrating a complex policy issue. But her report on interviews with 16 families, in her current role as Head of the Government's 'Troubled Families' project (or Troubled Families Tsar if you prefer), published this week, leaves a bad taste in the mouth.

The problem lies not so much in the project itself, which builds on the previous and successful work on family intervention, but in the spin and the dirty politics that lie behind it. A potentially useful programme is being dressed up for media consumption to make a point.

We have commented before that Ministers seem absolutely determined to portray these 'troubled families' in a particular way, to caricature them as depraved not deprived. That way they hope the public will conclude that all we have to do is address the personal behaviour of a tiny minority, heaping the blame on the so-called dependency culture rather than poverty and failing services.

The original estimate of the size of the problem, which led to the adoption of the oft-repeated '120,000 families' figure, was based on 2004 data which took a much wider view of indicators of multiple deprivation, including poor housing, no qualifications, mental health problems, disability, and inadequate income to cover basics. The criteria for the selection of families are now much more targeted at involvement in crime, risk of going into care, school truancy, and domestic violence, factors that have very little to do with the original 120,000. This has been expertly exposed by Jonathan Portes and by Fullfact. As the New Statesman says, 'This zombie statistic refuses to die'.

The excellent Fullfact have challenged the way CLG spins the 16 as being somehow representative of the 120,000, which they aren't, and then spins the 120,000 as being somehow representative of a whole underclass, which is misconceived.

It looks like the project itself is being steered away from families experiencing multiple deprivation (which might require public resources to resolve) towards the Prime Minister's idea of neighbours from hell (and he has experience given what we have discovered about his neighbours in Chipping Norton), and towards Eric Pickles' notion of people we should understand less and condemn more. Gone are the criteria relating to poor housing and disability and low income. And nowhere is there reference to the fact that existing Family Intervention Projects have been subject to cuts so there are fewer services not more.

Casey's report on the selection of 16 families is undoubtedly grim. The stories of violence and abuse are shameful and disturbing. As always, there are a few families that fit the *Shameless* stereotype and you do wonder what young people are being taught about contraception. But ultimately the report reads like a script from the loathsome *Jeremy Kyle Show*: pointing at the Chavs and moralising about their sub-human behaviour. Despite being mainly in the families' own words, it feels like it has been put together by a redundant News of the World journalist.

I couldn't get past case study 7 and jumped to the end. Here we find an assessment of the evidence that is largely balanced and occasionally insightful. But most journalists didn't get that far and so more lurid headlines are generated. *'Criminal culture at the heart of feckless families: Shocking report lifts lid on incest, abuse and spiral of alcohol abuse'* said the Daily Mail. No wonder that Zoe Williams in the Guardian concluded: *'I believe the ulterior motive is the demonisation of the poor'*.

The problem with the whole underclass theory is that many of the behaviours that are identified are classless. Undoubtedly they have a much harsher impact, and are a lot harder to resolve, when the family is also badly housed, poorly educated, and very poor – but that is the bit the Government doesn't want to recognise. Having a child with ADHD, or a parent with mental ill-health, as many of the 16 families have, would devastate most middle class families with good incomes. Alcohol and drugs can have a huge impact on even the wealthiest families, witness the Rausings; but children from wealthy homes don't normally end up in the disastrous care system. Sexual abuse and violence have been perpetrated by the most religious as well as the most godless. And as for incest...

The problems faced by the 16, or the 120,000, and indeed many more families, are rooted in poverty and bad housing whatever their individual pathology or personal failures. The latter will not be treated without also treating the former.

How right to buy sales push up the benefits bill

August 4, 2012

By Monimbo

How much of the recent growth in private renting is being fuelled unintentionally by right to buy sales? And what impact is this having on the housing benefit budget? This question was posed last month by Paul Dimoldenberg, based on the evidence he turned up of almost 40% of properties sold under the right to buy in Westminster having ended up in the hands of private landlords. As he pointed out, this means that money is being spent not only on funding big discounts for the original purchasers but then year-in-year-out on the local housing allowance payments to the many low-income tenants now housed in them, who otherwise could have been in council lettings.

While converting a property to a private let is particularly attractive in Westminster, new work by Nigel Springings and Duncan Smith[1] shows that such sales are now taking place all over Britain. Unfortunately there is little systematic data on private rented properties, and no national figures which would show how big the role of RTB actually is. But Springings and Smith have reviewed a range of studies which show that while Westminster may be at one end of the spectrum, there are plenty of other places where RTB properties have moved sectors (again). For example, in one Birmingham estate 43% of RTB properties had ended up as private lettings, although 20% was the Birmingham average. Overall they say that there is evidence to suggest that up to 30% of properties eventually convert into private lettings.

Of course, not all of these are then let to benefit recipients, and again the evidence is only partial. But they point to a couple of local Scottish studies which found that around half of private sector benefit recipients were in ex-RTB properties. Their own study looks in detail at Renfrewshire, where just over 16,000 council houses have been sold under RTB. What they unearthed is that, of the local housing allowance (LHA) claims being made in the area, 43% come from ex-RTB properties, involving just over 9% of the ex-RTB stock. These houses and flats are, on average, let at rents about £40 per week higher than the council charges for adjoining properties it still owns. In a low-rent area like Renfrewshire, this means that the hidden cost of RTB in higher benefit payments is still some £3.2 million annually.

Having looked in detail at one Scottish authority, the authors apply the methods (making suitably realistic assumptions) to Camden – obviously, an area with much higher demand and far higher rents. Their fairly conservative estimate is that right to buy in Camden – where sales as a proportion of stock are much lower than in Renfrewshire – has resulted in a hidden annual subsidy of £18 million in LHA payments.

The authors quite understandably aren't able to resist making an assessment of the cost of this hidden subsidy across the UK. Obviously they have to make some heroic (but still realistic) assumptions, and they conclude that the extra cost of LHA for tenants in RTB properties compared to the same tenants in council houses is a staggering £2 billion per year. Apart from anything else this is roughly the amount by which the total housing benefit bill has gone up in the last twelve months, and as he also said this increase is being driven by the growth of the private rented sector. What studies like those by Springings and Smith are starting to show is that much of this is also driven by old right to buy sales.

A logical response might be to slow down the promotion of right to buy while someone assesses its long-term costs in more detail. This is of course exactly what the government is *not* doing, having recently increased discounts. Hardly a week now goes by without fresh government efforts to persuade people to buy their council houses.

There's a further irony here. Grant Shapps is fond of talking about 'subsidised' council housing in the context of his anxieties about Bob Crowe and other better-off council tenants. As he must know but doesn't say, he can only be referring to the historic subsidy for council housing, since currently it doesn't get any actual subsidy. This is based on the purely theoretical idea that councils should 'really' charge full market rents, and that lower social rents are therefore a subsidy. Now we see how people's ignorance of housing finance can be further exploited: not only does he fail to talk about the similar subsidy involved in selling right to buy properties at hefty discounts (of up to £75,000 each), but he'll no doubt keep equally silent about the annual £2 billion subsidy for the right to buy in extra housing benefit payments.

[1] *Unintended consequences: Local Housing Allowance meets the Right to Buy*, in People, Place & Policy: Volume 6, Issue 2.

A boy called Mohamed

August 6, 2012

The contrast between the euphoria of the Olympics and the riots that were in full swing exactly one year ago could not be greater. It's hard to believe this is the same London and the same Britain.

For me the moment of the Games so far was the extraordinary reception for Mo Farah, in the race and on the podium. Real name Mohamed, an immigrant from Somalia, a Muslim, a Hounslow state school boy, he suddenly became a great British hero. After the ludicrous criticism of the opening Ceremony by an ignorant Tory MP and some Tory media, the huge support for every competitor, whatever their origin, has reinvented multiculturalism. You can be a British Somali immigrant, of mixed race from Sheffield, a girl from Stratford, a boy from Kilburn or from the playing fields of Eton, nobody cares and, when it comes to sport, everyone is equal in the public estimation.

My normal answer to the question 'what do you think about multiculturalism?' is that I think it would be a good idea to give it a try. Despite all the talk, it was pursued half-heartedly and blown off course by the gale of fear called Islamophobia. The key idea of multiculturalism was very simple: that you can be British and black, British and Irish, British and Somalian, that you can be British and support India at cricket, that you can mix cultures and respect all, and that British society should be open and flexible enough to celebrate all of the diversity this brings. It was an integrationist philosophy, but it challenged the notion that Britishness is a narrow vision of an all-white English village with a cricket square and a pretty church. The nadir was reached when Cameron misrepresented multiculturalism as 'segregation' and claimed that it was responsible for forced marriages and fostered extremist ideology, directly contributing to home-grown Islamic terrorism.

Most of the retrospectives on the riots have been sensible, focusing on the alienation of young people of all races and creeds, their frustration with the police and poor prospects, and the triggers that led to criminal behaviour. We have not had repeats of the initial attempt to scapegoat black people and council estates. Owen Jones' series for the Independent and an Inside Housing piece on the role of communities and local agencies were particularly good.

Even the normally repugnant Andrew Gilligan in the Telegraph offered a serious commentary: *'what's surprising is how little change there has been. With the country in Games rapture, and the only flames in London now of the Olympic variety, the incredible events of last August seem, like the victims, to have fallen out of public consciousness. Their impact on policy, and politics, has been minimal. ..... Youth unemployment is 12 per cent higher this summer than it was at the time of the riots. But the austerity drive is hitting much more deeply now. The procedure for investigating police killings seems as sclerotic and ineffective as ever. More than a year after the shooting by police of Mark Duggan – whose death sparked the Tottenham riot – his family are still no clearer how it happened.'*

Meanwhile Communities Secretary Eric Pickles seems to only rejoice in the size of the sentences handed out to those arrested, still talking vacuously about mindless criminality and rehearsing the corrupted statistic that the Government is 'going into the homes of 120,000 of the nation's most troubled families to address root causes.' He has nothing to offer to the debate.

Austerity for the poor. The stripping out of services and facilities for the young. Stigmatisation of people who can't get jobs or require state benefits. Growing poverty and inequality. The Olympics serve to illustrate what ordinary people born into poor circumstances can achieve given the right support and opportunities. A year on from the riots, nothing has been learned and nothing has changed.

It's the same the whole world over....

September 19, 2012

In the early 1970s I went to Berlin for a European conference of community activists. At the time I was doing community work in north Paddington, working mainly with tenants living in private rented accommodation subject to the pressures of gentrification, and with council tenants on poorly-managed Westminster and GLC estates.

Berlin was an extraordinary contrast, the close juxtaposition of a capitalist city and a communist city, separated only by a wall. In West Berlin, we saw much high quality housing but also large areas of appalling slums where local community activists worked with working class tenants and squatters to argue for improvements. One day we went from the American sector through Checkpoint Charlie, across no-man's land under the scrutiny of machine gun towers, and into the East. Wandering about randomly we found rows and rows of concrete apartment blocks, workers' housing that met a certain standard but could only be described as drab and uniform. The contrast between East and West led to several long nights of debate about the inadequacies of both political and economic systems, with the only broad conclusion being that neither served the interests of the workers or the poor very well.

I've had this habit, perhaps even a compulsion, since to look out for workers housing wherever I visit. In beautiful cities that everyone raves about, like Barcelona or Vancouver, it didn't take long to find some private slums and some public high-rise concrete blocks. They were there even in Reykjavik, although not so high rise (and beautifully warm) but concrete and distinctive with an invisible architect's board saying 'social housing for the poor'. New workers housing in China was much more attractive than most but it was the sheer scale of provision that was so astonishing. Despite the volume of building, Shanghai also had large areas of slums – hugely overcrowded with communal taps in the courtyards – which seemed to be largely reserved for immigrant workers from other provinces.

I suspect there aren't many people who have wandered round the projects on Lower East Side in New York and asked random residents how the refuse disposal system works – I was intrigued by buildings that looked rather like British social housing but with an extra 20 stories on top.

I was set on this train of thought by a tweet from Tom Watson MP, drawing attention to an article in the New York Times, called The Land that Time and Money Forgot, discussing how New York's housing projects are now the last of their kind in the country and that they may also be heading for extinction. The author, Mark Jacobson, says *"Across the U.S., public housing, condemned as a tax-draining vector of institutionalized mayhem and poverty, whipping-boy symbol of supposedly foolhardy urban policy, has largely disappeared. Chicago knocked down Cabrini-Green, St. Louis imploded Pruitt-Igoe, New Orleans flattened Lafitte after Katrina. Only in New York does public housing remain on a large scale, remnants of the days when the developments were considered a bulwark of social liberalism, a way to move up."*

Reading through Jacobson's fascinating social history of the projects, there are threads that seem common to most countries mentioned so far. Societies that suffer from rampant disease that affects all classes have to make sure that the poor live in sanitary conditions. Then liberal reformers usher in an era of idealism aiming to provide decent housing for all. Then the social problems emerge and there is a crisis of belief. Then the neo-liberal era where people living on prime real estate fear for their homes as developers move in to provide luxury homes.

Two lessons strike me from the above. First, very different systems all produce two solutions for the poor: private slums or under-resourced social housing, which may not be always be very good but meets minimum standards and is affordable and offers some security. And, secondly, there are always long queues of people wanting to get in to the latter because the former is so much worse.

Bed and breakfast – déjà vu all over again

October 5, 2012

TV is an incredibly powerful medium and last night's Newsnight investigation into the use of bed and breakfast accommodation for homeless families got the point across more effectively than a hundred reports.

Tim Whewell has an understated style and gave clear explanations both of the policies that have led to a new explosion in the use of B&Bs and of the laws that are being broken by councils. The families that featured were articulate and were given an opportunity to explain their circumstances and the issues they faced.

Essentially, a number of councils, mainly in London, have faced a surge in homelessness and they have a duty to secure accommodation at least whilst enquiries are undertaken. Having kept the use of B&B under firm control for many years now, the lack of available accommodation at an acceptable price – the Government were warned! – has once again led to families being kept in B&B longer than the statutory maximum of 6 weeks and at huge cost to local taxpayers. Conditions, as we saw in the programme, which featured Croydon, are often scandalous; we saw examples of dangerous overcrowding, with families virtually living on a bed in a room with no circulation space, wholly inadequate bathing, toileting and cooking facilities, fire hazards and infestation. Owners are making money hand over fist.

The numbers have risen alarmingly over the last two years and the programme revealed a significant amount of denial and buck passing. Jon Rouse, ironically the former chief executive of the Housing Corporation and now of Croydon Council, tried to pretend all was well and under control when the evidence of the film was the complete opposite. How he can claim the properties were regularly inspected is beyond me and was clearly beyond the evidence gathered by the independent environmental health officer used in the investigation.

Buck passing was clearly central to the briefing given to new Lib Dem Minister for defending the indefensible, Don Foster – who was almost as embarrassing on his first Newsnight interview as his boss Nick Boles when he appeared last month after the reshuffle to talk about planning. Foster was fresh from the Lib Dem Conference where a new policy was agreed which completely contradicts everything he will now be doing in Government. But his main line of defence – we give these councils money to manage homelessness, so it's their fault not ours – reminded me of the great Michael Green, sorry Grant Shapps, when he was Housing Minister. At least Shapps didn't hide like his replacement, Mark Prisk, who should have fronted this rather than leaving it the rather lost and hopeless Foster. Shapps also tried to blame the councils, last year writing cheekily to the worst offenders expressing his shock at the use of B&B, but it is a localist con. The fault for lack of supply and the increasingly harsh attitude to the homeless lies firmly with central Government.

Whewell's report gave me a strong sense of *déjà vu*. It was so reminiscent of the 1980s when a range of councils reached a sudden tipping point and couldn't keep up with the numbers of families becoming homeless. Low emergency use of B&Bs turned into frequent use and then before anyone knew where they were it was out of control. Hundreds, thousands of people in hotels across the whole country. It took years to get it back under effective management, at huge cost to the people involved. We are now looking over the same precipice.

The most depressing echoes of the 1980s were the conditions the families were living in, the rooms, the hallways, the bathrooms, the kitchens, and their desperation. Not even Nick Knowles could take that on. No doubt next week we will get flowery language from Cameron Gove and Pickles about their commitment to children getting a good start in life. But the true impact of their policies can be found in the hotels of Croydon.

Affordable rent shambles continues

October 25, 2012

Over the past few months I have been pursuing Freedom of Information requests concerning the Government's 'Affordable Rent' programme. We have expressed concern about this programme ever since it was scribbled on the back of a fag packet in a hurried response to George Osborne cutting the housing investment budget by more than 60%.

The basic idea was to slash the amount of subsidy per rented home by requiring providers to borrow a larger share of the cost privately, recouping this through a huge increase in rent. There were many in-principle objections to the policy: it would use up housing associations' capacity to borrow and significantly increase their risks; it would be unaffordable for most people coming in to social housing (despite the Government claiming disingenuously that it would meet the same needs); it would make more people – in and out of work – dependent on housing benefit and increase the benefit bill, which would have to 'take the strain'; and it was allied to the Government's policy of reducing security of tenure for new social tenants.

The policy did however expose a fault-line in the social housing world. The cynical branding of the scheme as 'Affordable Rent' caused endless confusion and still does. Some providers and some councils were hostile to the new scheme, mainly due to high rents, but others embraced it enthusiastically, notably those that were already dropping social rented housing and moving towards market-based rents. Even those that were hostile were seduced by the argument that this was 'the only game in town' – it was better to build 'Affordable Rent' because the alternative would be to build nothing. Some exceptional councils like Islington found ways of keeping a social rented programme going. The policy also had widely different impact in the regions – rents at up to 80% of market levels is a disaster in the south but were lower than some existing social rents in parts of the north. So a nationally consistent response was hard to achieve.

Two factors characterised the policy from the start: incompetence and delay. Virtually a whole year of output was lost as providers struggled to understand the new rules and prepare complex financial plans and risk assessments. As a result, 'affordable' housing starts tumbled towards zero and the programme became hugely back-loaded into the final year, substantially increasing the risk. Even now most of the schemes are 'indicative' not real planned homes on real sites. The programme had unclear objectives: Who was it for? What size mix was required? (for example Boris Johnson in London has consistently said he wants more family homes). To what extent should providers cross-subsidise from small homes to family homes to keep those rents down? Who was making the decisions - the provider, the government and HCA, or the local council? Was social rent excluded entirely? What would happen in existing schemes subject to s 106 deals?

Endless negotiations and threatened stand-offs followed, to the extent that only this week the HCA announced that the final contract has at last been signed. Information about the programme has been scarce and questions were met with the reply that the information was commercially confidential. The CORE statistics on new lettings revealed some information about the small sample of properties that had come through the system, but we need to know what it is planned for the whole programme. When Ministers started bragging about how many 'affordable homes' would be produced, and Boris Johnson boasted that rents would be 'only' 65% of market rates in London, the door opened for FoI requests seeking information about the basis on which these claims were made.

Communities and Local Government responded properly with the information that they had, which wasn't much. But it did reveal that across England 82,000 existing social rented homes would be 'converted' from social rents to 'affordable rents' to help pay for the programme. That is a significant share of re-lets – homes that were provided under previous schemes to be let at genuinely affordable social rents that have been hijacked for this purpose. CLG also revealed the national average rent and the regional distribution. However, their information was based on the initial bids of providers and not the signed contracts which followed negotiations, and it became clear that CLG had little idea of how the programme was developing. The FoI response did however reveal more information about 'Affordable Rent' than CLG revealed to the Public Accounts Committee when it prepared its recent report into the programme.

The Mayor of London was altogether more slippery about responding to the FoI requests. Sometimes the more someone talks about transparency the less they practice it. The GLA argued that it was too expensive to collect the information until I pointed out that the Mayor had already made statements on issues like output and rents, so he had clearly been briefed. They argued that the information was commercially sensitive but I made clear I was after monitoring data not details of contracts. Finally they released anonymous information about provider contracts, the average rents they would charge and the relationship between these rents and market rates.

But then it became clear that the information was wrong. When Inside Housing magazine tracked down the provider with the highest average rents they claimed the information was wildly incorrect. Of course, both Red Brick and Inside Housing are entitled to rely on information provided by statutory agencies and the error belonged totally to the Mayor, who has now been forced to re-issue the information with an apology.

I am relieved to discover the highest average rent for a provider is not over £440 per week as the original information said. But this experience reiterates the point that the amount of public information available about the programme, and especially the biggest segment of it in London, is inadequate, as the Public Accounts Committee found. The HCA has published more information, on providers, funding and numbers of homes, but not rents and not expected completion dates. The GLA has published much less about London. Even though it is much smaller than previous programmes, 'Affordable Rent' is the main Government effort; it is still a large amount of public money and we are entitled to scrutinise what is being provided with it and whether it meets proper housing objectives.

Omnishambles, did I hear you say?

Dark days for the homeless

October 29, 2012

In the heady days before and after the passage of the 2002 Homelessness Act I worked with Shelter on its plans to make the most of the new legislation. Although there were several important changes to general entitlements, the point that most excited Shelter and its then Director Chris Holmes was the introduction of duties on local authorities to review homelessness in their areas and to formulate statutory homelessness strategies.

Holmes wanted Shelter to transform itself from being an external critic of local government to becoming an active partner in a joint enterprise to end the scourge of homelessness. Although only partially successful, a lot of groundbreaking work was done across the whole country.

In the decade since, the optimism about being able to tackle homelessness at its roots has dissipated, to be replaced by a much harsher blaming culture and, now, under the Coalition, the dismantling of the homelessness safety net.

In the years immediately after the Act, councils, encouraged by a highly active team at CLG, introduced a range of new strategies and policies so that the management of the homelessness function improved significantly. Councils were, however, under huge and increasing pressure due to the shortage of social housing. Over time it became hard to distinguish between well intentioned policies, such as homelessness prevention and providing housing options services, and increasingly tough gatekeeping exercises where the main purpose was to reduce and divert demand. In particular, the Government's top target of reducing the number of homeless households in temporary accommodation by 50%, on the surface an aggressive and progressive policy, drove many authorities down the gatekeeping path to the point where rules were stretched to the limit and sometimes broken. Because the key indicators – numbers in TA, homelessness acceptances – were moving in the right direction little attention was paid to what was going on. And, despite the growing barriers, those people accepted as unintentionally homeless and in priority need knew that at the end of a very long hard road a social rented home with a genuinely affordable rent and security of tenure would provide a platform for them to rebuild their lives.

As the years progressed, homeless people became parcelled up in the campaign by elements of the media and politicians like Ian Duncan Smith to stigmatise and demonise all 'welfare' recipients. Some Labour politicians signed up to the new blame culture and some gave in too easily to the pressure it brought, but the Coalition has turned it into an art form. Homelessness is primarily an outcome of our generation-long failure to build affordable homes, but people on housing waiting lists are encouraged to blame the homeless for taking all the homes. Why should 'they' get all the homes when 'we' hard working families cannot? The image of the teenage single mother getting pregnant to get a council flat has become an icon alongside the shirker lying in bed all day living the life of Riley on the state and the lower orders breeding like rabbits just to get more benefits. The name of the game is blame the victim and divide and rule. The truth is that homeless households are little different from the general population represented on local housing waiting lists.

I think it is fair to say the homelessness safety net is being dismantled. The next step is that, from November, defined homeless households who would normally have had the right to be offered a council or housing association home will have to accept private rented accommodation if it is offered by the council (under certain terms). As we become a backward country in social policy terms, the analysis that it is reasonable for homeless households – by definition families with children or people who are vulnerable in some way – to be 'discharged' into the high cost and low security private rented sector has attracted surprisingly little comment from the social housing movement. Even within the sector homeless people are blamed for everything from causing their own homelessness to exploiting the system to being responsible for concentrations of deprivation and anti-social behaviour on estates.

The myths and stereotypes are winning the argument and to turn it round we need to show rather more old-fashioned solidarity.

Beveridge 70 Years on. A Social State: The Return of Squalor[1]

November 27, 2012

Seventy years ago the Beveridge Report announced the pursuit of a new settlement, one that would dramatically change the structure of Britain for the better. With this in mind, what can Beveridge's analysis of society teach us about the Giant Evils of today and how can we use this to chart an alternative course for a welfare state – or Social State – fit for 2015?

The large majority of people are adequately or well-housed. That's why housing is the dog that never barks when Elections come around. But for more than a generation – since Thatcher ended council housebuilding – we have failed to build enough new homes of all types to keep up with rising demand. And chickens are coming home to roost.

The core failure to build is the root cause of our now familiar problems. House prices are far too high due to scarcity and easy credit. Rents have followed suit. Social housing is frighteningly scarce. Escalating housing benefit is the inevitable outcome of the growing dependence on expensive private renting rather than cheaper social renting. To its credit, Labour tackled the enormous investment backlog in existing social homes, but failed to build enough new affordable homes until Gordon Brown's Keynesian fling following the banking collapse.

Three decades of failure were followed by a huge lurch backwards as Eric Pickles and Iain Duncan Smith pursued their prejudices. Housing investment was cut by over 60%. Virtually no new social rented homes are being built, only the Orwellian 'affordable rent' – homes at up to 80% of market rents. Demand from both ends – people excluded from home ownership and a rising tide of homeless and displaced people – has become focused on private renting, and rents have rocketed. Even William Beveridge couldn't solve the problem of rent and we have not tackled it properly in the 70 years since.

In a highly competitive market the poor lose out. The return of one of Beveridge's five evils – squalor – is in evidence all around us, from the re-emergence of 'bed and breakfast', to more homeless on the streets, to rising overcrowding and sharing, to the new phenomenon of 'sheds with beds'. The housing and welfare benefit reforms, in their bewildering variety, leave millions of people facing unbridgeable gaps between income and housing costs. Benefit recipients are deliberately demonised. Yet the rapid growth in new housing benefit claims is coming from people in work who can no longer meet their housing costs.

The new Government in 2015 will inherit a housing emergency. But the crisis can be tackled if there is the will. So what needs to be done?

First, we need a big increase in the building of social rented homes. Construction caused the second dip in the recession and might cause the third. Housing schemes sit on the shelf and could be activated rapidly. Housebuilding is labour intensive, creates strong multipliers through the supply industries, does not suck in imports, and reduced unemployment means that the Treasury gets most of the investment back. Building social rented homes (which eventually pay for themselves) means the housing benefit bill would start to fall as families living in expensive private rented homes or hugely expensive temporary accommodation move to much cheaper social rented homes. After the successful reform of council housing finance, many Councils have considerable capacity to finance and build new homes. A more radical reform of the public borrowing rules could unlock a wave of investment that has been stymied for many years by Treasury orthodoxy.

Secondly, we must restore a pro-active planning system that aims to meet community needs. Tory theory that higher developers' profits would encourage more housebuilding is misconceived. It just leads to higher profit. Land values should be controlled through land value taxation and more public ownership. The creeping segregation we are seeing under the Tories should end; we should fulfil Aneurin Bevan's vision of 'the living tapestry' of the mixed community.

Thirdly, the Banks must be made to work for new home owners. Even if first time buyers can afford repayments, they cannot raise the huge deposits that are required. There are ways of easing this but it is unacceptable for the Banks to be so unresponsive when they have had such extraordinary support from the taxpayer.

Fourthly, we must regulate letting agents and private renting, starting with the most squalid homes. Standards must be raised and bad practice tackled. Longer tenancies should become the norm and rent caps should replace benefit caps.

Finally, we must restore the homelessness and benefits safety nets. Housing benefit caps are likely to stay but must reflect conditions in the real housing market and not leave people having to choose between food and rent. The Coalition has effectively ended the homelessness safety net. Forcing families to move hundreds of miles from London – the majority of London boroughs are now doing this; it is not just a 'rich central London' issue – is a disgrace because of the human cost involved and especially the impact on children.

[1] *This article by Steve Hilditch was published by the think tank Class (the Centre for Labour and Social Studies) to help launch their project* **A Social State 2015: what can Beveridge teach us about the giant evils of today?** *The project looked at a range of welfare state concerns from education to welfare, employment to housing and health and universalism.*

2013

Halfway house for the Coalition

January 7, 2013

We should rejoice that today marks the point at which the Coalition is half over. From now on there will be fewer days of suffering ahead of us than there are behind us. As Cameron and Clegg do another relaunch, it is salutary for a housing blog to look back at the Coalition Agreement and see how what they have done compares to what they promised.

This is easier said than done, because the Agreement had little to say about housing and nothing to say about many of the more controversial policies they have pursued in power. And that is the root of my central criticism of the LibDems – if the Agreement is what they signed up to, with no obligation to support other policies not contained therein, why did they subsequently embrace enthusiastically so many Tory policies that were not in the Agreement and diametrically the opposite of what was in their own Manifesto? Were they weak or stupid? It must be one of those. More than in most areas, housing policy has been developed according to a private agenda within the Conservative Party and the LibDems have chosen to go along with it when they could have taken a much more oppositional stance without breaching the Coalition Agreement.

Some of the policies included in the Coalition Agreement have been pursued, such as: scrapping regional spatial strategies; reform of the housing revenue account; bringing empty homes into use; increasing the right to buy. And there are others where progress is more debatable: continuous improvement of energy efficiency; creating new community trusts to provide homes for local people; 'maintain the green belt' (remind Planning Minister Nick Boles about that one).

What is astonishing is the lack of mention of a long list of policies the Coalition has since pursued: the ending of new homes for social rent; the creation of the 'affordable rent' tenure at up to 80% of market rents; the 60% cut in public housing investment; flexible tenure; the bedroom tax; reducing the homelessness safety net; cancelling Labour's plans to regulate the private rented sector – to name but a few. It is also worth mentioning that the Agreement does not even mention the phrases 'housing benefit' and 'local housing allowance' and the word 'cap'. Nowhere is there any reference to the overall benefit cap.

There is no doubt that the LibDems would have been well within their Coalition rights to oppose or to refuse to support these policies but were too feeble to do so. Indeed, LibDem Minister after Minister – in CLG and DWP – stood up to defend them and to support policies that are wholly contradictory to historic LibDem policies or even the new and excellent LIbDem housing policy adopted at their last conference.

The reason for being so disappointed with the LibDems is that it was well known before the Election that a private housing agenda was being developed by the Tories with the help of leading figures in the housing world. In particular, the infamous Localis pamphlet set out clearly the direction the Tories would take towards market rents and the denial of rights to social tenants. The LibDems should have known what was coming and had a clearer strategy for resisting it.

There is a general belief that the Coalition will be brought to an end before the General Election so that the Conservative and LibDem parties can develop distinctive policies during the campaign. No doubt at that point the LibDems will revert to their previous and current policies, which on paper are excellent and attractive. But the real measure will be 'what did you do in Government?' The Coalition has been disastrous for housing policy and the LibDems have been fully complicit. Whatever the paper policies, they should not be trusted again.

You can't borrow your way out of a debt crisis. Well, yes we can.

January 27, 2013

Nick Clegg has been on the media a lot in the last few days saying, amongst other things, that the Government should not have cut capital expenditure so fast in the early days of the Coalition. This is a welcome statement although not accompanied by an apology for getting it so disastrously wrong – in housing, the cut was 60% and it has caused immense damage.

On the Marr Show today, he said the Government was committed to finding *'innovative'* ways of raising funds for capital investment but ruled out a return to the *'bad old days'* of traditional Government borrowing. But, he added, *'if people have ideas about how we can provide further capital investment into our infrastructure, without breaking the bank, of course we are open to that.'* Red Brick is glad to help.

It seems everyone is talking about getting capital investment through 'innovative' methods of financing these days – although it flags up in my mind the experience of 'funny money' loans in the 1980s (interest rate swaps and sale and leaseback of council buildings come to mind) and the expensive disaster of the Private Finance Initiative in the last two decades. The pressure is on because the

Chancellor's economic strategy is so obviously failing and growth is nowhere to be seen, so they are casting around desperately for new ways of financing capital that are somehow consistent with 'Plan A'.

The best questions are often the most straightforward ones. Recently we have asked *'why do we stick to borrowing rules that clearly discriminate against public corporate investment?'* and *'why do we not do more housing investment when the 'multiplier' effect is so strong that the Government gets its money back?'* Today's question is **'what is wrong with borrowing anyway?'**

A blog last year by leading economist Jonathan Portes, Director of the NIESR, provides most of the answer – there is nothing much wrong with borrowing even when there is a large deficit.

Portes sets out his basic argument like this: *'with long-term government borrowing as cheap as in living memory, with unemployed workers and plenty of spare capacity and with the UK suffering from both creaking infrastructure and a chronic lack of housing supply, now is the time for government to borrow and invest. This is not just basic macroeconomics, it is common sense.'*

His logic has a number of steps:

- First, the economy has shown no growth since Autumn 2010 and may not regain its 2008 position until 2014. In the UK it is now a far longer period of depressed output than the Great Depression.
- Secondly, public sector net investment has been cut in half over the last 3 years and will be cut further over the next 2. Falling construction output has become a central factor in the lack of growth and a key reason for the double and possibly the triple dip.
- Thirdly, the cost of borrowing is historically low and below the rate of inflation. It costs basically nothing.
- Fourthly, the Government could fund a £30 billion (2% of GDP) investment programme through the traditional method of issuing gilts for a cost of about £150 million a year. Or as Portes says, it could be funded through the ill-fated pasty tax or closing a few loopholes in the tax regime.

We need to get out more and take these arguments to the public.

Rents policy is a mess

March 11, 2013

By Monimbo

Three years of ad hoc changes to social sector rents have left them in chaos. What do we do now to restore a sensible rents policy?

A new report from CIH and London & Quadrant, We Need to Talk About Rents, is an attempt to begin a much-needed debate. Much-needed because rents are not only crucial to the sector's affordability, but also because they drive investment and are a key element in defining the purpose of social housing.

Why is policy a mess? Although the rents policy which Grant Shapps inherited from Labour had in its time been controversial, at least it embodied affordability and consistency, and was known and accepted by lenders. Shapps didn't so much dismantle the policy as ignore it, sticking on new bits without any regard to the overall outcome.

Furthermore, while the remnants of the policy still embrace the crucial link to average regional incomes, most of Shapps' initiatives have pulled in the opposite direction, eroding affordability and – surprise, surprise – helping push up the housing benefit bill. So as pointed out in the latest UK Housing Review, not only will we eventually have 67,000 new houses let at rents that are far much less affordable, but we have so far sacrificed lower rents on over 70,000 properties that have been switched to 'Affordable Rent' to support the borrowing needed to build the others. The ratio of homes removed from the social rent portfolio to pay for AR homes is likely to be 3:2, i.e. three are lost from social rent for every two gained for AR. This confirms the result of a Freedom of Information request done by Red Brick last year.

As everyone suspected would happen, and as the Review also points out, the limited experience of the new AR lettings at higher rents shows that they are nevertheless going to the same target group as social lettings, i.e. 79% of lettings are to tenants partly or wholly dependent on HB in both cases: there is no sign of more AR lettings going to better-off tenants. In other words, housing benefit will again 'take the strain' and tenants trapped in benefit dependency will face higher barriers to escape it. Duncan-Smith must have been looking the other way when this policy change was slipped through.

As the CIH and L&Q discussion paper points out, even more important than the immediate practical effects are the longer-term consequences. One of course concerns the sustainability of an investment model which reduces the average grant input to only 14% of the cost of a new dwelling (from a previous average of 39%), relying for the rest to be loaded onto rents or to come from asset sales or free land.

But arguably even more important is the role that rents policy plays in any vision for what the aims of social housing are. Here, Shapps and now Prisk have vacillated between aiming the sector at higher earners through AR rents, penalising higher earners through the still-threatened pay-to-stay policy, pushing more benefit dependent families into the sector through LHA changes, pushing them back again through the bedroom tax, and encouraging local authorities to give the impression they can reward long-term, working residents through their allocations policies – even though in practice landlords are struggling with the chaos caused by the combination of rising homelessness and the tenant transfers now needed because of the bedroom tax.

The only comfort to be drawn is that it is not only in England that policy is in confusion. The report makes clear that policy changes in Australia, Canada, France and Sweden have also had unintended consequences. In Canada for example, a programme very like our Affordable Homes Programme and with almost the same name now caters for new, better-off tenants previously excluded from Canada's small social sector, but adds nothing to the much-needed supply of lettings at 'rents geared to incomes', leaving providers unable to cope with demand.

The report doesn't reach conclusions, as it's a call for debate, but it does ask if rents could support a redistributive element so that richer tenants help keep rents down for poorer ones. Something similar has just been proposed in a report by Demos for Family Mosaic and Home Group. While this may be a desirable objective, it seems unlikely that it can squared with rents being relied on as a source of investment, unless grant rates can be restored to something much more generous than 14%.

The lesson for Labour's housing policy is that it can't put rents policy into the 'too difficult' box, it is too important for that. The risks of ignoring the issue are evident from the way the Tories' half-baked policies have pulled in conflicting directions. A debate is needed about social rents and the wider issue that lies behind them of what the sector is for. The Tories have ducked it; Labour shouldn't.

Vile Products

April 3, 2013

After Frederick West was convicted of despicable murders, no-one wrote a headline saying he was the 'Vile Product of Home Ownership'.

After Harold Shipman was convicted of mass murders, no-one wrote a headline saying he was the 'Vile Product of Full Time Employment'.

It is disgusting therefore that the Daily Mail produced the headline 'Vile Product of Welfare UK' after the conviction of the child killer Mick Philpott.

This was not the hyperbole of a headline writer who has drunk too much coffee and got carried away. Exploiting extreme cases is a key tactic in the Mail's mission to demonise the poor. And they are not alone: as Owen Jones in particular has argued many times, it is a theme of many papers and is picked up slavishly by the radio and TV. That's why people like Philpott are so attractive to the media, and why he was invited on shows like the despicable Jeremy Kyle Show and starred in a documentary by Ann Widdecombe: to illustrate to the world how monstrous and degenerate welfare recipients are.

This is deliberate politics. The best way to defend benefit cuts is to attack benefit recipients, and Philpott offered a perfect opportunity. Holding a sick bucket just in case, I read the Mail columnist AN Wilson's piece. He says: '[Philpott] *is a perfect parable for our age. His story shows the pervasiveness of evil born of welfare dependency*'; '*the trial.... lifted the lid on the bleak and often grotesque world of the welfare benefit scroungers*'; '*those six children, burnt to a cinder for nothing, were, in a way, the children of those benevolent human beings who, all those years ago, created our state benefits system*'; and, '*Whole blocks of flats, whole tenement buildings are filled with drug-taking benefit fraudsters, scroungers and people on the make.*'

In this way the case is made. The Duncan Smith narrative that our problems as a society arise from 'welfare dependency' is justified by example. Focus shifts from the swingeing and punitive cuts that he is implementing. After all, he is only trying to save benefit recipients from becoming Mick Philpotts. Unemployment is not a systemic failure; look, these people chose to be unemployed to get the benefits. And typical council tenant: having more children just to get a bigger house.

When former Children's Minister Sarah Teather was sacked, she blew the whistle on what was happening inside Government. As Toby Helm wrote in the Guardian: '*She accuses parts of government and the press of a deliberate campaign to 'demonise' those on benefits.... With vivid outrage she describes the language and caricatures that have been peddled. 'I think deliberately to stoke up envy and division between people in order to gain popularity at the expense of children's lives is immoral. It has no good intent."*

The Mail and the Government are in this together, and it is shameful.

Switching from benefits to building

April 28, 2013

The welfare reform debate inside the Labour Party appears to have reached a crossroads... again. There are three basic positions vying for attention: those that think some cuts and reform are justified because of the deficit; those that think welfare reform is popular with the public therefore Labour should go along with it in order to win; and those that think the current scale of cuts are not justified economically and that, even if they were, they should not be targeted on the poorest.

I am in the third camp, but it does not mean that I am not in favour of major reform. And I am strongly in favour of Labour winning elections. But the debate needs to go a lot deeper than the 'how to deal with the deficit' and 'strivers versus scroungers' arguments that Labour constantly gets pushed in to.

The welfare debate cannot be removed from the wider context of society. Income inequality has been rising since around 1980, according to figures produced by the Resolution Foundation's Commission on Living Standards. In 1977, of every £100 value generated by the economy, £16 went to the bottom half of workers in wages. By 2010 this had declined to £12, down 26%. Annie Quick in the New Statesman this week comments that the bottom fifth would be £2,000 a year better off – their incomes would have been 18% higher – if the income distribution had stayed the same.

The decisive shift towards greater inequality came in the 1980s under Thatcher; the trend continued under Labour and there can be no doubt it has accelerated again under Cameron. The prevalence of sub-minimum-wage jobs (where there is a scandalous lack of enforcement), devices like zero hours contracts, self-employment and labour casualisation, and pay cuts, mean that there has been a substantial squeeze on wages at the lower end of the scale. This squeeze on wages is now in turn being used to drive the case for cutting benefits; the Tory line that people should not get more out of work than in work (they don't but that's a different point) has gained a lot of traction. The Tories have engineered the position where the in-work poor and the out-of-work poor are racing each other towards penury.

In housing, there is a strong case for reform of the housing benefit system but it is nowhere near the argument that Iain Duncan Smith puts. We should start by repudiating the Tory narrative that HB is 'out of control'. The size of the HB bill is the direct and predictable consequence of rising unemployment and policy decisions taken over many years – the failure to build in response to the collapse in affordability of home ownership; the minimal building of benefit-light homes for social rent; the sale of council houses which become privately rented at twice the rent or more; the policy of pushing more poor people into private renting generally; demographic change. The most rapid increase in HB claims has been from people who are in work: it must annoy the Tories to realise that the more they complain about HB the more working people realise that they can claim it – and the higher the bill goes.

That we have ended up in a bad place is undoubtedly true – 95% of the money going into housing goes to help people pay the rent rather than building homes – but we are here as a consequence of deliberate policy. Governments have wanted to marketise housing, increase rents and, in the words of former Tory Housing Minister Sir George Young, 'let housing benefit take the strain'.

This week's statement by Labour's shadow work and pensions secretary Liam Byrne that the way to get the housing benefit bill down is to build more affordable homes is therefore very welcome. This is a genuinely radical shift in thinking and emphasis and leads to potential reforms that deserve strong support. Byrne told the Evening Standard that the initial step must be to get people into work through the jobs guarantee and *'to show how savings can be made on housing benefit by increasing the amount of homes there are for people to go to.'* He said: *'Billions are spent with private landlords yet we ask nothing in return. We are spending £24 billion on housing but hardly building any houses. No wonder rents are soaring. We simply cannot go on like this.'*

Labour should put its energy into thinking through practical policies that achieve a switch from benefits to building. A coherent switching policy would work in tandem with principled opposition to the appalling bedroom tax and the clearance of poor people from more affluent areas. The Tories are offering punishment of the poor, Labour could offer a genuine alternative – cutting benefits by putting people back to work and building homes that people can live in with much smaller benefit support.

We should not pretend it is easy. In 2012 the IPPR report Together at Home recommended a radical shift in public spending away from benefits and back towards bricks and mortar. Finding the precise mechanisms for achieving this has its difficulties because the investment has to be made before the savings in benefit can be realised. In my view, IPPR went down the wrong path by suggesting that this could be achieved by what they called 'progressive localism', rolling all housing budgets together and then localising them, leaving it to local discretion what the balance between benefits and investment should be in any particular area. As with council tax benefit, this would lead to an entirely unhelpful postcode lottery and potentially bizarre conflicting policies within the same housing market areas.

The answer lies in matching our housing aims closely to our aims to achieve growth in the economy. The collapse in construction activity was central to the second dip of the recession and almost caused the third. The sector continues to decline despite all the talk and Government meddling with planning and the rest. Labour has to be even bolder in its commitment to affordable housebuilding. A modest increase in investment subsidies, say back to 2008 levels, could generate a large council housebuilding programme and help housing associations to build many more genuinely affordable homes at social rents. The multiplier effects would give the economy a major boost in the right way: creating lots of jobs without generating inflation and without sucking in imports. By rehousing people in receipt of housing benefit (in work or not) currently living in expensive private rented homes (and in particular temporary accommodation), the benefit bill would start to come down.

Housing investment could be the way out of Labour's welfare reform dilemma. We could achieve cuts in the cost of benefits. We could have an attractive policy based on getting people off the dole into real jobs. And we could shift decisively away from policies that punish people for being poor.

Stabilising private sector rents

June 12, 2013

The private rented sector continues to move up the political agenda.

This week the London Assembly's Housing and Regeneration Committee published a considered and sensible report about the sector called *Rent Reform: Making the Private Rented Sector Fit for Purpose*. The report contrasts the problems of the sector in Britain to the successes in many other continental countries where regulation and affordable rent levels are the norm.

Some of the facts listed by the Committee are fascinating. The private rented sector in London has grown by 75% in 10 years, is now bigger than the social rented sector and in 12 years' time on current trends will catch up with home ownership. Private landlords receive over £13 billion in rents from over 800,000 London tenants. Median rents grew 9% in 2012, rising to £1,196 per month, which can be compared to gross monthly incomes under the minimum wage of £990 and £1,368 for the Living Wage. In two-thirds of London boroughs the cost of private renting is more than half average wages. For working and non-working tenants, the cost of Local Housing Allowance grew 36% between 2009/10 an 2011/12 to more than £1.9 billion.

The profile of private renters has also changed dramatically, reflecting the groups who have been squeezed out of social renting and priced out of home ownership: low income households and 'generation rent'.

The Committee makes a wide range of recommendations although it is the analysis of rent levels that is probably the most interesting. Learning from the experience of other countries and our own history, they do not recommend rent control as we have previously known it but a new 'rent stabilisation' approach which is a feature of many mature European private rental markets. Linked to longer tenancies, especially for families, this approach looks to make rents more predictable throughout a tenancy. The report also speculates about the possibility of linking rent increases to an inflation index.

Lettings agencies come in for criticism, as well they should. Their interests are different from those of both landlords and tenants because they benefit most from frequent turnover and increases in rent between tenancies. Tenants lose out due to rent inflation and landlords lose out because they experience more void periods. The Committee goes along with reputable agents who have been calling for regulation and also supports the Livingstone plan to establish not-for-profit agencies.

It is rare to find any consistency of opinion between Boris Johnson and his London Assembly Tories and the Government, but they are united in their view that nothing much should be done about the private rented sector in London. In a dissenting note, the Tories on the Committee argue against any form of 'artificial control' of rents, arguing that it is only increased supply that will bring rents under control. This basically means doing nothing at all while we wait for demand and supply to come into some form of balance. And it begs the question as to why an increase in supply of 75% in 10 years has failed to bring rents under control.

There is so much steam in the rental market at present, with buy-to-letters outbidding first time home buyers and rents racing well ahead of incomes and prices, that some form of intervention is essential. Employers have started complaining about the impact that housing costs are having on their businesses and their ability to recruit staff. The Committee quotes evidence that the supply available to people on Local Housing Allowance is being heavily squeezed, with for example only 5% of lettings in Barnet falling within the LHA cap. David Cameron and Iain Duncan Smith's promise that rents would fall due to the benefit changes looks embarrassingly wrong; instead many more low-income people are being forced out of the capital altogether.

With the Tories committed to the free market and Labour resistant to anything that looks like 'old-style' rent control, the rent stabilisation model looks like the best option available, but more work is needed on the detail.

Rent is the new grant

July 6, 2013

At the CIH Conference last week, Housing Minister Mark Prisk said that the new funding settlement for housing would involve *'something for something'*. To get a small slice of the increasingly tiny Government subsidy for new rented homes, providers will have to make a bigger contribution from 'their' own resources.

Government has been in confusion as to whether there would be a second round of 'affordable rent' (that's the one with rents at up to 80% of market levels) ever since the first round was announced. Back in 2011, then LibDem Minister Andrew Stunell said that 'affordable rent' would be a *'one-off that will not be repeated'* and that a new model would be needed after 2015. At the same time, the then Tory Minister Grant Shapps/Michael Green said there would indeed be another round, and that the Government would be looking for increased cross-subsidy from other activities to fund new homes. Not for the first time, Stunell was wrong. Although some providers, mainly those that lost sight of their social purpose years ago, were delighted to be moving away from social rent, most warned that the 'affordable rent' model should not be repeated because of the pressure it puts on their borrowings and viability, pushing their capacity to the limit.

Oblivious to these warnings, the Government has gone even further down the road of removing grants, requiring providers to borrow even more on average to build each home in the new programme. Prisk said the cost of this additional borrowing should be met from 'efficiencies', 'conversions' and 'disposals'.

Mr Prisk seems not to be aware that there is a difference between 'efficiencies' and rent increases and property sales. *'With all this money and this commitment, there will be expectations about efficiencies,'* he said, *'In considering bids for grants, we will expect providers to bring forward ambitious plans for maximising their own financial contribution .... We expect providers to take a rigorous approach when looking at every relet and asking how they can use them to build more homes for more families. I expect the result to be a significant change in the number of homes that are either converted to be let at affordable rent or are sold when they become vacant.'*

So there we have it. More homes are to be provided by 'converting' more property from social rent at 40-50% of market to 'affordable rent' at 70-80% and by flogging off more existing stock. And to get grants, providers will have to demonstrate that they are doing as they are told.

Prisk said that under the current programme *'a modest level of relets have been converted to Affordable Rent'*. The only official estimate I have seen is that it might be up to 82,000 homes stolen from the social rented stock: how many more does he envisage to pay for the new programme? A civil servant had to move quickly to explain what Prisk meant, but it's not much of an assurance: *'Landlords will not be expected to convert all re-lets to affordable rents in the new funding programme,'* he stressed.

Very helpful. *'Not all'*. But it is odds-on that we are heading for a position where a majority of social rent re-lets are 'converted'. In essence, **the replacement for the grants is huge rent increases**.

The Government has always claimed that the 'affordable rent' product would be let to the same people as social rent. The only likely outcome of that policy, when combined with a high rent regime, is that more new tenants would be on benefit and for higher amounts. A recent study confirmed that new tenants occupying 'affordable rent' homes were even poorer than those already occupying 'social rented' homes, the opposite of the social housing allocations policy that the Government is trying to pursue. Once again housing benefit is taking the strain.

The 'affordable homes' programme, which includes 'affordable rent', has a budget of around £957m a year for three years from 2015/16, about £1 for every £20 the Government spends on housing benefit. Given their obsession with cutting HB, there is a clear contradiction within Government policy. We need to intensify the argument for a major switch to capital rather than personal subsidies in the coming months.

The emerging consensus on private renting

July 18, 2013

What goes up may come down. Only 10 years ago, the growth of home ownership was believed to be inexorable: people would talk of it reaching 90% of households. But without much advance warning, it peaked in 2003 and has fallen from 71% of households then to 65% now (figures for England).

Virtually all net housing growth in the last 10 years has been in private renting. Although the *number* of home owners has remained fairly constant, in the mid 14 millions of households, and the *number* of social renters has also been fairly constant at around 3.8m, the number of private renters has grown from 2.2 million to 3.8 million households (in percentage terms from 10.8% in 2003 to 17.4% in 2011-12). Now people talk about the growth in private renting being inexorable...

This truly astonishing turnaround in the housing market – which pre-dated and was not caused by the global financial crisis, even if the credit crunch reinforced the trends – has raised a whole new set of dilemmas for policy-makers. Some issues remain the same – the crap end of the market is still crap, and still nothing much gets done about it. But new issues have emerged, and I would highlight four:

- Many of the households coming into the sector are families with children who have been excluded from social renting or from home ownership, but the arrangements in the sector have not changed to reflect the different needs of such families.

- Many new landlords are in a position where the non-payment of rent by their tenant means the non-payment of a mortgage for them – despite high rents and a long-term capital gain they are not necessarily coining it in week by week. Although buying to rent is often described as being 'the new pension fund', we still know very little about the new landlords, and in particular whether they are in it for the long term or just until some other investment with a better return comes along.

- Many new landlords are also amateurs at the job and are more likely to be dependent on a lettings agent or manager. Lettings agents in particular are not the friend of the landlord or the tenant – they want turnover because finding new tenants brings in the cash and the possibility of a rent hike, whereas landlords' business plans are easily wrecked by an unplanned void period. Tenants face an ever-increasing set of fees and charges to access a home.

- One of the effects of the clamp-down on local housing allowances has been to push people out of the more expensive areas into the 'cheaper' areas (everything is relative). This has had little or no effect on rents in the expensive areas, where demand is strong, but it is having the effect of pushing rents up in the cheaper areas because there are now more people competing for the same number of 'affordable' vacancies.

The upshot of all this is that some new thinking has been needed about the sector. The old remedies – leaving it all to the unrestrained free market, as favoured by the right, and stringent rent control advocated on the left – will not do the job and carry too much risk. There is no silver bullet and a package of new policies are needed. A lot of good policy work has been done (but only outside Government, I am sorry to say) by a range of organisations and think tanks, including landlords' organisations and responsible agents, and something resembling a consensus is beginning to emerge with the broad aim of stabilising and modernising the sector. This approach is about moderating rent increases, encouraging far longer tenancies, registering landlords, heavily regulating lettings agencies, and reinforcing the role of local authorities in improving standards and stamping out rogues.

Today's report from the CLG Committee of the House of Commons on the private rented sector is firmly in this new mainstream. Its analysis seems spot on and its key recommendations – around better regulation, the key role of local authorities, ending sharp practice, better court procedures when things go wrong, and changing the culture of the sector so it becomes more family-friendly – allied to the Committee's continuous exhortation for more house building in all tenures – reflect the emerging view about the best way forward.

Whilst the Government has its head in the sand – the last people to recognise that an unfettered free market doesn't work for landlords or tenants – Labour has done a lot of work in this area and the Shadow Housing Minister, Jack Dromey, is to be commended for taking time over the detail, consulting widely with all parties, and publishing intelligent policy papers about what should be done.

To get housing right over the next decade, we have to take action in all tenures: we have to enable more people to become home owners, we have to provide far more social rented housing at genuinely affordable rents, but we also have to find a new stable settlement for private renting which is fair to tenants and landlords: homes at good standards on fair terms.

John Humphrys should be sacked

July 31, 2013

A niche housing blog like Red Brick doesn't expect any story to go viral – that's reserved for royalty, pop stars and funny animals doing tricks. But in October 2011 our attack on a programme on welfare researched and presented by Radio 4's John Humphrys became our biggest ever hit.

The Red Brick piece – *'John Humphrys, hubris, and welfare dependency'* – criticised the basic premise of his hour-long BBC documentary that: *'a dependency culture has emerged.... A sense of entitlement. A sense that the State owes us a living. A sense that not only is it possible to get something for nothing but that we have a right to do so.'* The programme was a year in the making, we were told, and involved a (no doubt) all-expenses paid trip to the USA.

We pointed out that Humphrys apparently got paid nearly £400,000 a year to be rude to people on the radio in the mornings, which didn't seem to make him particularly qualified to comment on the incomes or behaviour of the extremely poor.

But our ire was stirred most by the fact that he trailed his programme in a feature article in the Daily Mail built around a large picture of the fictional Gallagher family and the headline 'Our Shameless Society'. He knew exactly what he was doing. He knew what the Mail stands for, he knew what message the 'shameless' imagery would convey, and he knew which audience he was pandering to.

Now, nearly two years later, in a rare victory against the forces of darkness, a complaint made by the Child Poverty Action Group (CPAG) about the programme has been upheld by the BBC Trust, which concluded that the programme breached its rules on impartiality and accuracy.

CPAG Director Alison Garnham commented: "*This programme, like too many media stories, failed the public by swallowing wholesale the evidence-free myth of a 'dependency culture' in which unemployment and rising benefit spending is the fault of the unemployed."*

The Trust however rejected part of the complaint that Humphrys had presented a personal view in contravention of guidelines for senior current affairs presenters on controversial issues, stating that the sentiments he expressed were: "*...judgements based on his personal experience rather than opinions which could be interpreted as a personal view."*

This is arrant nonsense and a whitewash. The programme started with a highly personal recollection by Humphrys of his own background in Splott in Wales and his poor upbringing; it followed him around as he personally visited various (I would suggest carefully researched and selected) claimants to discover their attitudes; and it included a visit to the Centre for Social Justice, the think tank most closely associated with the views and prejudices of Iain Duncan Smith, but no other organisation with a countervailing view – for example CPAG. As most of the controversial comments were made by Humphrys direct to camera, to claim that this was not a personal view is ludicrous. I cannot think that this conclusion is anything other than an attempt to draw a line to prevent calls being made for Humphrys to be sacked.

Based on watching the programme and reading the Daily Mail piece that launched it, I think that CPAG were spot on in their complaint:

"The programme explored the topic from within a partisan and politically interested framing that purports there to be a 'benefits dependency culture' and an 'age of entitlement'.

"This framing precluded the exploration of opposing views and relevant factual information, and led to the mischaracterisation of benefit claimants interviewed by John Humphrys as 'victims of the benefit system' despite their own focus on problems such as low pay and the high cost of childcare.

"The failure to include any expert voices from the UK with views diverging from those of the government compounded the inaccuracy and impartiality and prevented salient facts being brought to the audience's attention.

"These failings resulted in breaches of BBC Editorial Guidelines on both accuracy and impartiality.

"Furthermore, the programme gave the appearance of presenting the personal views of one of its senior news and current affairs presenters, in contravention of guidelines. This was compounded by the publication of an article in the national press, authored by the presenter, John Humphrys, and with the headline 'JOHN HUMPHRYS: How our welfare system has created an age of entitlement'."

This programme was indeed a biased, sensationalised and prejudiced attempt to portray people in receipt of benefits as undeserving scroungers. It was obviously a personal view developed by the presenter, who took a year to research and prepare the programme for broadcast. The BBC has admitted that it breached its standards for impartiality and accuracy. Their argument that it did not breach their standards relating to senior presenters, who normally have the trust of the public, is flimsy in the extreme.

John Humphrys should be sacked.

The role of new settlements

September 5, 2013

It's a truism that all current settlements were once new settlements. Were there NIMBYs when Gloucester was founded by the Romans, when Oxford was established in Saxon times or when Henry I established a monastery and a new settlement at a crossing of the Thames in what became Reading? How is it that people living in existing settlements feel so strongly that they have the right to veto anyone new coming along, when their own property was once a new one that might have infringed on someone else?

A new report from the *Building and Social Housing Foundation (BSHF)* examines what conditions are necessary to make it possible to create new settlements in England. The report is a good summary of the current, but decades old, problem of housing under-supply. It argues that there is a multiplicity of reasons for the chronic failure of housebuilding – not just planning, not just restrictive green belt policies, not just the profit-motivated policies of the volume housebuilders, not just local opposition, not just lack of effective demand, not just the petty restrictions on borrowing by councils to build new homes – but all of these things and more contribute to the problem. It reinforces my view that there is no silver bullet, and that undersupply can only be solved by a truly comprehensive and strategic approach. It often seems that those who obsess about any one issue seem to be doing so to divert blame from themselves (it's not us, say the builders, it's the planners; it's not us, say the planners, it's the lenders; and it's everyone but us, says the Government, because we've deregulated the system and cut red tape).

The report traces the story of new settlements over the last century and a half, from the imaginative interventions of philanthropists like Cadbury and Rowntree, to the inspiration of Ebenezer Howard and the Garden City movement, to the post-WW2 overspill programme, to the new and expanded towns movement, to the unfulfilled ambition of the Eco-town programme. Whether or not previous residents opposed the development of Letchworth or Welwyn Garden Cities I don't know, but it is hard to imagine them being built under current conditions.

To try to answer the question 'how can we create the conditions for new substantial settlements to be built?', BSHF's recommends better understanding of the impact of recent new settlements, especially in the overspill and new town periods, trying to develop political consensus, the creation of a single national strategic spatial plan for England, strengthening the 'duty to co-operate' in planning, establishing a powerful body with powers to manage disagreements between authorities, making sufficient public finance available for upfront infrastructure, setting up new settlement partnerships involving communities, clear Government messages to set the debate, and better communication of housing supply problems to the public.

Most of these things will help, but I was left with the feeling that the recommendations were rather anodyne and inoffensive, perhaps because such a wide range of actors, including Government, were involved in the BSHF's consultation. The report tiptoes around key issues like land prices, risk-averse profit-maximising builders and the Government's dilution of policies requiring affordable housing to be built. It acknowledges that more needs to be done at the 'larger than local' level but fails to identify the Government's abandonment of regional spatial strategies as an error. RSSs were not a roaring success, and there were major tensions around their proposals, but they held promise as a creative mix of top-down and bottom-up and needed another decade to be fully effective. They were far more likely to achieve something than the current confused approach that ranges from central Government hectoring, petty interference and expensive bribes to localism gone mad.

In city or in country, I would be inclined to be a NIMBY too if a modern developer package of expensive but profitable houses and a trivial amount of affordable housing for local people came my way. Under current policies, I would be concerned that any new settlements would be little more than a few acres of executive homes within reach of a fast train to London, unlike the genuinely mixed communities that were created in the Garden Villages or the New Towns.

Although the report is about new settlements, it would be wrong for anyone to see this area of policy as 'the solution', any more than the other current hobby horse, building on green belt land. The search for a silver bullet invariably ends in failure. We need policies that will tackle the shortage in all types of areas: intensifying existing cities and towns as well as expanding existing settlements, especially those with good communications, and building new ones. None of these is enough on its own.

Even in the most hard-pressed place, London, successive land capacity studies have shown more land to be available or potentially available than many thought possible. However it is often expensive or difficult to develop, suffers endless delays, or needs intensive work on site assembly. More imagination would also help: for example, London and other cities are replete with single storey buildings with nothing on top and tens of thousands of acres of car parks (I have never understood why cars need to be stored at ground level when people can be stacked on top of each other, it should be the other way round). Large retailers like Tesco and Sainsbury's are beginning to see the potential above their stores and this breakthrough could lead to thousands of new homes being provided.

As regional planning has been abandoned (except in London, where it has become a negative force under Boris Johnson), the BSHF's proposal for an English national spatial strategy is an intriguing idea. There is a strong case for a long-term national infrastructure plan, including housing, that looks 20 or even 50 years ahead. I might be more convinced by the case for HS2 if I believed the Government's claim that it will help reduce the gap between the north and south (rather than just making it easier to get to London). The answer to the questions 'how many new settlements do we need, and where?' may emerge from the bigger question 'what do we want the country to look like geographically in 50 years' time?'

The abominable yes man

September 19, 2013

Nick Clegg's rhetorical flourishes are quite clever until you ponder on them for a second or two. Then the argument falls to pieces. Yesterday's speech included a long list of things he'd said 'no' to within the Coalition. I suppose headlines like 'Dr No' and 'The Abominable No Man' were the desired outcome, supporting the line that the LibDems have been a brake on 'the nasty party'.

In housing they have been the Party that likes to say yes. Or, to put it another way, the Party that rolled over to accommodate every nasty Tory policy imaginable.

60% cuts in housing investment? Yes! End social housing? Yes! Put social rents up to 80% of market rents? Yes! Bedroom Tax? Oh yes please! Make large parts of the country unaffordable to people in and out of work who need housing benefit? Yes! A new housing bubble? Yes! End security of tenure? Yes! Increase homelessness? Yes! Slash the homelessness safety net? Yes! Let Boris remove all progressive policies from the London Plan? Yes! Vote against own 'Mansion Tax' policy? Yes! And on it goes.

As I've argued before, I have no real issue with the LibDems going into Coalition with the Tories. On the economic front, Plan A has been a natural home for them since they reverted to being a classically economic liberal party following the rise of the so-called 'Orange Liberals' like David Laws. Vince Cable may huff and puff but the LibDems are close to George Osborne on economic theory and reasonably comfortable with austerity. Nor do I complain that they negotiated a joint platform with the Tories in the Coalition Agreement, winning some things and giving way on others. What is so dishonest is that the policies they have actually pursued in Government were not set out in the Tory or the LibDem Manifestoes, nor were they contained in the Coalition Agreement.

The genesis of the Government's policies was the work of a little cabal of right-wing Tories supported by a small number of leading people in the housing world, working through the Localis_think tank. As yes men, Ministers like Andrew Stunnell, Don Foster and Steve Webb have been indistinguishable from their bosses, Eric Pickles and Iain Duncan Smith, as they laid waste to the decent tradition of providing affordable housing for the poor that was established post-War by Aneurin Bevan and Harold Macmillan.

The inability of the LibDems to bring any of their Party's policies into Government is what will condemn them in the General Election housing debate. On paper, their Party policy is very good and no doubt they will try to distance themselves from Government policy. They should be reminded, forcefully, of what they have actually done. The only consolation is that, if the next Election produces a Lab-Lib Coalition (perish the thought), it will be relatively easy to agree a common approach to housing in Government.

A false start

October 14, 2013

People in new jobs frequently make their worst mistakes at the very beginning. I am hoping this is the case with Rachel Reeves and her 'tougher than the Tories on welfare' message in the Observer yesterday.

I tried to think why she might have decided to take this line. Perhaps she thought that it was important to stake out this position at the beginning, to create space for more nuanced policies later – but all that does is encourage the Tories to challenge you to go even further. Perhaps she was reacting to the infamous 'boring snoring' Newsnight incident and decided to blast herself into a more interesting category. Perhaps she mistakenly thought this was the line having read a couple of Liam Byrne's earliest speeches.

Reeves has had some support from other commentators, including James Bloodworth on Left Foot Forward, who have argued that she represents the 'realistic' position that Labour needs to take to neutralise the Tories huge lead on 'welfare'. The dominance of the right-wing agenda on welfare and the filtering of information in the mainstream media are such that the public have a seriously distorted view of the facts. Alternatives to the conventional wisdom are hard to come by, one of the reasons being that Labour has been far too supine on the issue over the years. Weakness just emboldens the right, in Reeves' case to the point of being thanked for endorsing Iain Duncan Smith's policies – 'game set and match to IDS,' according to Fraser Nelson. Well, I hope one lesson of the last few weeks is that it is time to stop being pushed around by the Daily Mail.

I would like to unpick her arguments a little. First, Reeves is correct to emphasise the importance of Labour's compulsory jobs guarantee. The devil will be in the detail of delivery but it has to be right that Labour's central policy should be to do everything possible to get people into jobs. I have no problem with a 'carrot and stick' approach but it is the carrot that is missing at present, not the stick.

Secondly, her approval of the Tories' overall benefit cap, but with regional differences, is a re-interpretation of where Labour has got to on the issue. She puts too much emphasis on accepting the existing £26,000 limit and too little on the differences Labour would introduce. She failed to mention that it is effectively a brutal cap on housing benefit for large families in high rent London.

Thirdly, she is right to say that the charge that Labour Governments have been 'soft on welfare' is not right: the last Labour Government removed benefits from people unreasonably refusing to take jobs. And fourthly, she is right to focus on the extraordinary incompetence with which Duncan Smith has pursued his policies.

My main objection is around the use of language and the implied adoption of the Tory 'narrative' on 'welfare'. Saying you will be 'tougher than the Tories' when their policies are vicious and punitive is simply unacceptable and challenges my normally acute sense of loyalty. She reverts to using the Tories' favourite word 'welfare' rather than the recent front bench choice of the more neutral phrase 'social security'. And the word 'linger' is straight out of the Tory lexicon. Her statement that 'we will not allow people to linger on benefits' ignores all the evidence that, when there are jobs, people take them. Unemployment is primarily a structural economic issue and is not about personal pathology – why else would there be a sudden increase in the number of 'malingerers' during a recession?

By validating the Tory narrative Labour fails to challenge the propaganda that the 'cost of welfare' is mainly about the lazy unemployed and that unemployment is about personal failure. It ignores the real crises in 'welfare' – the ageing population and the growing cost of credits and benefits to 'hardworking people' who have very low or irregular earnings.

Finally, conceding the narrative makes it much *harder* for Labour to communicate a genuine alternative – for example cutting the costs of social security not by punishing the poor but by creating employment, by getting people into jobs, by promoting the Living Wage and by building houses rather than paying huge amounts of housing benefit to subsidise high rents.

That's the message we should want the public to hear.

2014

'An artificial and temporary recovery based on property inflation'

January 3, 2014

It's quite a long time, around 40 years, since I picked up an economics textbook. But the basic laws of supply and demand get lodged in your brain and help in the daily struggle to interpret what is happening in the world.

However foggy and distant these memories are, I seem to be better informed about the interaction of supply and demand than our Prime Minister. As the New Year breaks, David Cameron has been keen to make a big noise about his 'Help to Buy' scheme, which has now supported 750 households to buy a property. Yesterday he dismissed fears, expressed by almost every economic commentator, that it would create a new property market bubble. His argument was that property prices outside London and the South East are *'still way below the peak they reached in 2007'*. There is, he said, *'no evidence of a problem'*. He dismissed criticism of Help to Buy as *'London-centric'* (no hint of irony!), pointing out that prices in other regions have been relatively stable, failing to mention that one-quarter of the purchases so far have been in the London and South East.

Better versed in economics than Cameron, Business Secretary Vince Cable takes a diametrically opposing view from his boss. Cable has attacked the Help to Buy policy consistently, repeating his complaints at least twice over the holiday period, warning about *'a raging housing boom'* in London and the South East on the Marr Show and *'a recovery based on property inflation'* yesterday in the Evening Standard.

Cable argues that help should be targeted at areas where the property market is flat. *'Help to Buy is a good idea if prices are collapsing and development is stalled'*, he said, *'I'm sure it has a very useful role to play in Northern Ireland and parts of the North of England'*. He attacked the central economic policy of the Government: *'What I want to see is a real economic recovery based on British industry and exports of goods and services, not an artificial and temporary recovery based on property inflation.'*

So what does economic theory tell us about subsidies and how they might impact on the housing market? As a subsidy, Help to Buy works on the demand side, enabling people to borrow more to buy their property. Theory says that subsidy on the demand side puts prices up, which in turn leads to a responsive increase in supply. However, housing is an unusual product because the supply of it is *inelastic*. Price rises might encourage more existing owners to put their homes on the market but the speed at which the market can respond by building additional houses at the new higher price is extremely slow. The policy will potentially have a big effect on prices before it has any impact on supply. This is simply not what is needed.

The alternative policy of introducing subsidy on the supply side would have very different effects. It would reduce the market price at any level of demand, but also increase supply. Supply would still be inelastic, but the effect of the subsidy would be more direct and predictable for builders.

Currently we have no mechanism for introducing Help to Buy in some regions and not in others, so the impact on the housing market in London and South East, which is already drastically overheating, is inevitable and cannot be dismissed in the superficial way that Cameron has done. A further increase in house prices in London will have a wide range of economic effects and will push homes further out of reach of people on even good incomes.

Help to Buy is the wrong policy at the wrong time and acts on the wrong side of the supply/demand equation. In the words of the Institute of Directors, *'The world must have gone mad - the housing market needs help to supply, not help to buy'*.

This policy is not about housing affordability, housing supply, or pursuing the home ownership dream as Cameron would put it. It is a desperate attempt to boost the Tories' chances at the 2015 Election by creating the appearance of economic good times whilst the truth is less rosy. Nothing is more damning, or more accurate, than Vince Cable's description of it as *'an artificial and temporary recovery based on property inflation'*.

Squeezing welfare out of the system

January 8, 2014

by Monimbo

Shortly before George Osborne set out his alarming vision for public expenditure, James Meek asked whether government welfare and housing policy is a war on the poor. He begins his LRB article *Where will we live?* with the case of a 60-year old woman in Tower Hamlets, struggling to pay the bedroom tax, who has also been hit by loss of her incapacity benefit as she's now judged fit to work. As Meek says:

'What's being done to her is happening quite slowly, over a period of months, and is not the work of a gang of thugs breaking down her door and screaming in her face, but is conducted through forms and letters and interviews with courteous people who explain apologetically that they're only implementing a new set of rules. At the age of sixty, having worked for thirty years before being registered as too unwell to work, Pat Quinn is effectively being told that she's a shirker, and that the two-bedroom council flat where she's lived for forty years and where her husband died is a luxury she doesn't deserve. She's been targeted for self-eviction. Essentially, the government is trying to starve her out.'

Red Brick readers are familiar with such cases, but Meek's description cuts to the quick. He concludes, 'the government has stopped short of explicitly declaring war on the poor. But how different would the situation be if it had?' Here I beg to differ with him slightly: while the attacks on the poor haven't yet quite been described as a war, they certainly look very much like one. As Ken Livingstone said about Thatcher's assault on trade unions, in which three million unemployed was a price worth paying: 'Thatcher's great friend Augusto Pinochet used machine guns to control labour, whereas Thatcher used the less drastic means of anti-union laws. But their goal was the same, to reduce the share of working-class income in the economy.' Or to put it in Meek's terms, Osborne hasn't actually sent in a gang of thugs to drive Pat Quinn out of her house, but the goal is the same. It's to squeeze spending on welfare benefits, at least for non-pensioners, out of the economy.

Another parallel occurs to me, and this time Labour shares part of the blame. Both the current and previous Home Secretaries effectively believe that 'asylum seeker' is another name for an illegal immigrant and that, while still paying lip-service to UN conventions, life should be made so uncomfortable that they will stop coming here or go 'home'. The same panoply of weapons was used in the war against asylum seekers as is now being used against welfare claimants: placing negative stories in the media, cutting financial support to levels on which it is almost impossible to survive, vastly increasing the bureaucracy they have to cut through to get any help at all, moving them around so as to cut any community ties they may form, and finally handing over their accommodation to the likes of G4S and Serco.

OK, so the latter hasn't yet happened to welfare recipients, but the government has already resurrected the idea of outsourcing housing management and it will certainly do this if it gets the chance in the next parliament. We might also add that asylum seekers were prevented by the last government from getting jobs and supporting themselves, which made them easier to demonise. Osborne hasn't prevented the poor from working, of course, but by saying they *could* work when either realistically they couldn't, or there aren't jobs available, or the welfare system penalises them if they only work part-time, he achieves the same demonising effect. There's even a direct link to immigration in the weaponry deployed by Duncan Smith: benefit scroungers who won't work mean that employers look for immigrants who will. So as well as wrecking the economy, benefit claimants are also responsible for immigration.

There are now of course tens of thousands of cases like Pat Quinn's, many involving stomach-churning hardship. Osborne and IDS cannot be unaware of the damage they are causing, so the obvious conclusion is that it is not just a 'price worth paying' to squeeze welfare out of the system, but is actually an intentional part of the process. If poor people can be made to suffer sufficiently, some will indeed move into low-paid jobs; but most (like asylum seekers) will live on the margins of survival, even if a few will regrettably turn to crime, end up sleeping rough, commit suicide or simply die. Squeezing welfare out of the system isn't just about saving money, it's about changing minds. Welfare claimants have to learn the hard way that relying on the state is no longer an option, because the state is no longer interested in their survival.

To legitimise this cruelty, claimants are made to look like they're crooks or worse. As we saw in response to the Channel Four programme *Benefits Street*, there are plenty of real thugs with baseball bats (or at least with Twitter accounts) who'd love to sort Osborne's problem out for him. It's difficult to disagree with Pat Quinn's conclusions, based on her own plight: 'I'm sure if they had their way they would kill us. I really believe that.' Even if you think that she's exaggerating, you can't deny that Pat Quinn and other claimants are getting Osborne's message.

Rolnik and the Tories: The Truth Hurts

February 4, 2014

If you have ever wondered what an *'ad hominem'* attack is, then the Tory and right-wing media broadside against the UN special investigator on housing, Raquel Rolnik, is a very good example of it. (*Ad hominem* means rejecting an argument by referring to some irrelevant fact about the person presenting the argument.)

In Ms Rolnik's case, her gender, her nationality, her religion, and some gross assumptions about her personal politics have all been used to undermine the fact that she has written an exceptionally good report on housing in the UK.

Raquel Rolnik is the United Nations' special rapporteur on housing. She operates under a UN treaty that the UK has signed up to. She is one of 30 rapporteurs who visit UN member states and comment on various aspects of policy. Adequate housing is an element of the 'right to an adequate standard of living' and the 'right to non-discrimination'. Rolnik's record is impeccable: she has commented on many countries around the world without fear or favour, including Serbia, Cambodia, Israel, Italy, Panama, Portugal, Nigeria, Colombia, Egypt, France, Brazil, Turkey, Spain, Russia, India and Nepal. Her reports are all available on her excellent website. She has also produced a number of thematic reports, including one on security of tenure across the world. It is her duty to report when she finds that a country is not compliant with the international human rights standards that it has voluntarily signed up to.

Ms Rolnik visited the UK in August/September last year at the invitation of the British Government, and spoke to many people, ranging from community organisations to Government Ministers, about housing conditions in the UK.

Both her initial report and her final report are extremely critical of housing policy in Britain, recording decades of underinvestment but highlighting the 'despair' created by welfare reform and the bedroom tax.

Rather than try to deal with the content of her report, the Tories have gone into full attack mode about Ms Rolnik's background and lifestyle. When her initial report was published, Grant Shapps dismissed her as a 'a woman from Brazil'. Tory MP Stewart Jackson called her 'a loopy Brazilian Leftie'. The Daily Mail managed the headline 'Raquel Rolnik: A dabbler in witchcraft who offered an animal sacrifice to Marx'. On her final report, Housing Minister Kris Hopkins called it a 'misleading Marxist diatribe'. This time the Daily Mail surpassed itself by describing her as a 'Brazil nut'. Why we should want to be so offensive about Brazil is beyond me.

Her final report on the UK is a wide-ranging document. No-one in their right mind would consider it to be anything other than a well-researched and evidenced document that looks into the history of housing policy as well as current policy. I defy anyone to find a trace of 'Marxism' or even of eccentricity. It is close to the mainstream of opinion across the political spectrum in the UK.

As Patrick Butler in the Guardian put it: '*Sometimes you just have to sigh and lower your eyes in embarrassment. There is nothing in this well-mannered report that would be out of place in any mainstream political, policy and academic discussion of housing in the UK. Of course it is uncomfortable for ministers: the truth hurts.*'

Money should be no object for homelessness too

March 7, 2014

There can be no doubt that the flooding of your home is a dreadful and traumatic event and that Government should be doing far more to improve flood defences and to mitigate the impact of climate change on our homes.

But the most surprising statistic to come out of the floods since Xmas is that the number of homes flooded was less than 6,000 and that media attention escalated when it affected residents in the Thames Valley. There has been a feeling of outrage in some parts of the north where much larger numbers of homes were flooded last year but without the same amount of attention being paid to them by the media and Ministers. No-one said to them that 'money is no object'.

But there is a more astonishing comparison that can be made: with the number of families made homeless each and every year for reasons that are not as visually photogenic as the floods. You can't normally see the homeless from a helicopter. The latest figures, showing yet more increases, created scarcely a ripple on the media and there were no statements of intent by David Cameron to spend more money on affordable homes.

Under the Coalition, homelessness is again rising rapidly after many years of falling. In the first full year of the Labour Government, the inheritance from John Major meant that 104,000 families were accepted as homeless by councils in England. It took Labour six years to bring it under control, by which time the figure had risen to 135,000 (2003/04). Each year after that the number of acceptances fell, down to 40,000 in Labour's last year (2009/10). Since the General Election it has started to rise again, to 44,000 in 2010/11, 50,000 in 2011/12 and 54,000 in 2012/13. (*NB figures rounded – they count households who are deemed to be unintentionally homeless and in 'priority need', mainly households containing children or a member who is 'vulnerable' due to mental or physical ill-health or age.*)

The detailed homelessness statistics are remarkably consistent year by year (e.g. which regions are most affected, the reasons for homelessness, the size of households, and so on). But there is one significant recent trend that is noteworthy. Homelessness that is attributed to the 'end of assured shorthold tenancy', which was 15% of cases when Labour came into office and fell to 11% in 2009/10, is now on a steep upward curve, rising to 22% in 2012/13 and 25% for calendar year 2013. This is now the biggest single reason for homelessness. It illustrates the 'revolving door' of Government homelessness policy: the duty to homeless households is increasingly discharged by placing them in private rented accommodation, but the loss of a private let is the biggest single reason for homelessness.

One of the most controversial aspects of homelessness is the use of temporary accommodation for long periods prior to a housing solution being found. Labour's slow, but eventually effective, response to rising homelessness is again illustrated by these figures. The number of households in temporary accommodation stood at 47,000 when Labour came into power, but rose to over 101,000 in 2005. Following the implementation of a series of policies designed to meet a Government target to halve the number in TA, the figure began to fall, reducing each year to reach 50,000 when Labour left office (and thereby meeting the target). Since then the trend has been reversed and the number in TA has been rising again, standing just short of 57,000 at the end of 2013.

Households in temporary accommodation contain an astonishing number of 81,000 children. Everything that has ever been written about TA shows that it is bad for children. They become dislocated from school and child care, from friends and family, and from the place they identified as 'home'. Educational attainment and socialisation suffer and behavioural problems become more common.

Of the households in TA, 7% are in bed and breakfast hotels. 500 households, containing 1,550 children have been resident in B&B beyond the statutory limit of six weeks. The contribution of private sector leasing (primarily where the property is managed by a housing association) is waning, and the number of households placed directly into private accommodation on a temporary accommodation basis has grown – doubling from 6,200 at the 2010 Election to 13,500 at the end of 2013. This is a hugely expensive option in terms of housing benefit costs.

Some authorities have great difficulty in procuring temporary accommodation within their own district – which everyone recognises is the best option for families and individuals if they are to retain contact with their network of family, friends, schools, health services and other public services. Receiving authorities also often face additional costs of providing services to these families. Nearly 6,000 households were placed in TA in another district at the time of the General Election, this has now doubled to just short of 12,000.

The problems associated with homelessness and temporary accommodation are at their most acute in London – three quarters of the households in TA are from London – but they are certainly not restricted to the capital. There are hot spots all around the country.

High and rising levels of homelessness are an extreme symptom of wider levels of inequality in British society and our growing failure to meet basic human needs. Someone once said that the way we treat our most vulnerable people is the basic test of our civilisation. Quite.

Half a great housing strategy – unfortunately, the wrong half

April 1, 2014

The new London Housing Strategy from the Mayor of London is half a great document. The analysis is broadly sound and it is quite well written and clear. The critical weakness is that the policy prescriptions just don't match up to the problems identified and the proposals fall apart under scrutiny.

The strategy revolves around a classic Boris Johnson trick. As you'd expect, the document identifies the need for additional housing, concluding there is a requirement for market, intermediate and social rented homes. It estimates that just short of 16,000 homes for social rent are needed each year. Then it switches to how the Mayor will provide these homes. Now you see it now you don't, suddenly the phrase 'social rent' disappears and is replaced by 'Affordable Rent'. You want juicy apples at 40p each! I've got dry oranges, £1 a go.

Unaffordable 'Affordable Rent' is of little use to London. Under the current programme (2011-14) rents are far too high and the programme is partly paid for by selling existing social rented homes on the market and 'converting' many others from social rent to 'Affordable Rent' when they become vacant. The desperate attempt to keep up the headline number of 'affordable homes' being built is at the expense of ever more social rented homes being removed from the stock. It is a disgrace but it is also a con. What used to be called 'intermediate rent' levels under Ken Livingstone – sub-market homes targeted at key workers – is now the main offer to people on very low incomes in acute housing need (assuming they are not diverted into the private rented sector first).

Now, to give Johnson a little credit, he has realised the error of the Government's ways in relation to 'Affordable Rent'. So he has edged back towards the Livingstone categorisation of affordable rented homes into 'social rent' and 'intermediate rent' but without admitting it. In the new programme (2015-18) 40% of the affordable homes he hopes to provide will be shared ownership and 60% will be 'Affordable Rent'. But the AR component will be split into two: half of it (i.e. 30% of the programme total) will be capped at 50% of market rents and the other half will be pushed up to the top of the range, i.e. 80% of market rents. He regards the former as being targeted to vulnerable people, downsizers, tenants affected by regeneration, or people on benefits; and the latter towards people 'in work'. This division is a nonsense due to the very low incomes of many people in work. Rents at 80% of London market rates are so high that they push more and more people in work onto housing benefit, so they face very high marginal rates of tax and benefit withdrawal – the very opposite of 'making work pay'.

To be helpful in the extreme, it could be argued that the 'capped' programme is vaguely equivalent to social rent. Johnson's own analysis concludes that there is a need to build 16,000 homes for social rent a year for at least 20 years. So what will his strategy deliver? He claims it 'seeks to deliver 45,000 affordable homes over 3 years', or 15,000 a year. Of these, 30% will be at 'capped' rents, around 4,500.

So Johnson's strategy fails before it starts. Instead of the needed 16,000 social rented homes, on a generous interpretation he will provide 4,500 homes for 'capped affordable rents'.

The strategy makes much of how many affordable homes Johnson has delivered so far. And here lies the second trick. It takes a long time to finance, plan and build homes. Johnson inherited Ken Livingstone's 2008-11 programme, funded in full by Gordon Brown's Government until 2010. It was a big part of Labour's National Affordable Housing Strategy. This one Labour programme delivered a huge slice of what Johnson now claims as his achievement – 11,500 homes in 2008/09, 12,600 in 2009/10, 12,500 in 2010/11, 15,400 in 2011/12, and as many as 6,800 in 2012/13, five years into Johnson's mayoralty. Nearly two-thirds of these homes were for social rent.

Johnson's main programme, cunningly called the Affordable Housing programme, took three years to get running. It produced 265 affordable homes in 2011/12, 671 in 2012/13, and 1,582 in 2013/14 (11 months up to end of February). Around 560 of these were for social rent.

So there we have it. Johnson's fine strategy is a cover for a total failure in delivery. Most of his claims to have produced affordable homes turn out to be the achievements of Ken Livingstone and Gordon Brown. His own programme has been characterised by delay and confusion and failed delivery. When some supposedly affordable rented homes come through, we find that they are at unaffordable rents. And when he announces his new strategy, with a fanfare, a whole five years into his mayoralty, we find it plans for an even more serious deficit of homes at social rents or their equivalent into the future.

Fail, fail, and fail again.

Waiting lists are becoming political devices

April 27, 2014

By Monimbo

It's a long time since waiting lists did what they say on the tin. But the changes resulting from the latest DCLG guidance mean they will soon be more a barometer of local politics than of housing need.

Back in the good (or bad?) old days, anyone could put their name down on the waiting list for a council house and many people used to do so as an insurance policy. The last Labour government arguably had contradictory lines on this. In its quest to reverse the 1996 Tory homelessness legislation, its Homelessness Act in 2002 made waiting lists open to anyone (except those ineligible because of their immigration status). However, it later began to backtrack and encourage councils to adopt a 'housing options' approach to housing applicants. Some councils implemented this enthusiastically, notably Portsmouth who by reviewing old applications cut their waiting list from 12,500 to 2,500. Nevertheless, the 2002 requirements stayed in place.

The coalition saw the rise in waiting list numbers over recent years in England as resulting partly from these open lists, which in its view encouraged people to register even when they had 'no real need of social housing'. The Localism Act 2011 introduced the concept of 'qualifying persons' who would be eligible to apply for housing, and gave considerable discretion to local authorities to decide who they should be. That said, the initial guidance wasn't very different from the previous government's: both emphasised a 'housing options' approach.

This changed last December when the government more specifically encouraged councils to give preference to local people, or those who have 'a close association with the local area'. Its recommended 'residency requirement' is now two years. As a result of the various changes different councils have been trimming their lists (while equally some have done nothing). For example, Bournemouth seemed to follow similar practices to neighbouring Portsmouth in cutting its list from 9,425 to 3,177.

There is a difference between applying a residency test for entry to the list, and applying one before an allocation is made. It's relatively common, for example, to have a local connection test like Dover's which requires applicants who get an offer to show that they've lived there for three out of the last five years.

However, the changes seem to have launched a war of attrition in London, with various Boroughs implementing increasingly tough criteria before people can even get onto the list. Most now have a three-year test. But last year both Hammersmith & Fulham and Brent introduced five-year residency requirements for entry to the list. In Hammersmith's case, this enabled them to cut its numbers by a gigantic 90% to only 768 applicants. Then Hillingdon upped the ante by introducing a ten-year residency requirement. Barking & Dagenham have just followed on by also adopting a ten-year test.

It is interesting to read the paper to B&D's cabinet meeting on 8 April on its housing allocations review. Officers put forward options of having two-, five- or ten-year residency tests. In their assessment of the variable impacts, they judged even the five-year test would have a disproportionate impact on BME residents (they form three-quarters of those affected), with other affected groups being young people and those with jobs. Nevertheless officers recommended a five-year test.

They appeared very concerned about the impact of a possible ten-year test, because of those who would then qualify 80% would be white British – even though they now form only an estimated 40% of B&D's population. Their equalities impact assessment indicated that it would not only disproportionately affect BME groups, but that these are also (on average) in greater housing need. It concluded that there was a potential impact on community cohesion in the borough as well as risk of a legal challenge.

What did Barking & Dagenham's brave councillors decide to do? They went for the ten-year test. Facing UKIP challengers in all wards in the coming elections, they decided a policy change was needed which would (on the advice of their own officers) give clear preference to white British housing applicants over the majority of the borough's population.

We'll have to see if the more extreme residency tests remain in place after next month's polls. But whether they do or not, it's clear that housing need is again becoming a political plaything. Of course local politicians should be able to decide their waiting list criteria and allocations policies, but they shouldn't be able to throw objective tests of housing need out of the window. Surely the best response to UKIP is to get out the black, young and working voters who'll be penalised by the sort of policies they'll introduce if they get into power.

So what's not to like about social renting?

May 6, 2014

I have posted below my contribution to the CIH series of essays on 'Where is housing heading?', which is published today. It's therefore a longer-than-usual post.

*The essay presents the **core arguments in favour of social rented housing** and the urgent need to re-start a programme of building new homes which will be available at traditional social rent levels and with security of tenure. It is highly critical of the Coalition's so-called 'affordable rent' scheme, with its high rents and reduced tenants' rights.*

So what's not to like about social renting?

It is not possible to consider the role of social rented housing except in relation to the housing system as a whole. Previous essays in this series have shown how the tectonic plates of housing tenure have moved markedly over time in response to economic conditions, social expectations and political ideologies. Over the past century we have moved from a dominance of private renting towards a parity between home ownership and social renting and now there is a strong trend back to private renting, with the other two tenures in decline.

That the housing system is in crisis is hardly in doubt. Not so very long ago, when I started my local government career in housing in Camden in 1976, I well remember a senior professional telling me it was the wrong business to be getting into because 'the housing crisis is nearly solved'. It is hard now to imagine a time when it seemed possible to 'solve' huge problems like housing. At that time, mammoth strides were being made. Councils and housing associations were building large numbers of genuinely affordable homes, matching those built by private enterprise for home ownership. Intervention in the private rented sector was at its peak, with systematic inspections and assertive municipalisation tackling the worst landlords. A real safety net for many homeless people was on the horizon and allocations policies were being relaxed. Home ownership was rising and widening its appeal as mortgages were responsibly liberalised. Landlords and poorer home owners could get generous grants to repair and improve their homes. New forms of tenure, like part-rent/part-buy, were being discussed as new ways to offer variety and choice in the market.

There was genuine optimism. But in the years that followed it was all thrown away. Council housing investment tightened following the IMF crisis and its decline accelerated for ideological reasons under Thatcher after 1979. Councils were prevented from municipalising housing and both new build and rehabilitation programmes stalled. The much-heralded 'third arm' – housing associations – grew in status but crucially never came close to matching the number of homes that were previously provided by councils. Private enterprise continued to build in parallel with economic cycles. The pattern was set that has lasted since. The hole left by councils was never filled and the housing system could no longer respond to rising housing demand and need. Since that watershed period, we have failed to build enough homes of all types to meet the needs of the population and we have allowed, indeed encouraged, house values (and hence rents) to soar through successive bubbles, making homes increasingly unaffordable.

Although wholly discredited, the theory of 'trickle down' still infects housing policy – the belief that building executive homes in Cheshire or Hertfordshire will somehow eventually assist people in housing need in Manchester or London (in reality such additional supply leads to a more rapid rate of household formation before the trickle has got very far). For example, in the debate about building New Towns in the south east, the assumption is still made that somehow this additional general housing supply will benefit those in housing need in London.

We have failed to match the *distribution* of prices and rents in the housing system to the *distribution* of incomes. Inequality has grown and so has insecurity: the number of people with very low incomes in the 'flexible labour market' with zero hours contracts, casualised labour, irregular self-employment, and part-time work. The correct housing policy response to these changes is that homes need to be cheaper not more expensive.

For thirty years housing policy has suffered from the erroneous analysis that it is more efficient to let markets set rents and then to subsidise the individual household to find somewhere to live. Even worse was the growing belief that social housing rents should be closely linked to whatever the market comes up with. As a consequence, housing benefit has been rising and investment grants falling, to the extraordinary point where 95% of the money put directly into housing by Government is in the form of benefit and only 5% in the form of investment. People on low incomes, in or out of work, are charged increasingly high rents, making them more reliant on housing benefit and creating extraordinarily high marginal tax rates.

A rational housing policy would deliver homes in a way that is consistent with the income distribution and thereby maximises the advantage of working. Only a traditional form of social rented housing offers what is needed to people near the bottom, whether they are in or out of work.

Misguided policies have been compounded by the demonization of benefit recipients, including social tenants. The perceived wisdom that social tenants are 'subsidised' and that many of them live the life of Reilly on benefits is as dominant as it is inaccurate: but the prejudice is reinforced by the media, some politicians, and even some in the housing business, every day.

Better public understanding of the real pattern of flows of subsidies, discounts and tax reliefs (economically they are the same) in the housing system would transform the debate. All of the tenures are subsidised. One policy alone, the right to buy, has cost £50bn in discounts over 25 years. New social rented housing receives an initial grant per dwelling to enable it to be built but subsequently receives nothing towards running costs.

Different people draw different conclusions from each part of the patchwork of assistance to housing. But the most important lesson is that the system is expensive and incoherent, badly geared towards meeting primary housing objectives (increasing supply and making homes affordable), and detrimental to the wider economy. The narrative is even more damaging if you take a wider view of property and land taxation as a whole. Not fit for purpose is something of an understatement. In particular, the primary forms of support for home ownership over the past 50 years, from Mortgage Interest Tax Relief to Help to Buy, have bolstered demand not supply: they have been hugely expensive and largely counter-productive. In renting, we have stopped funding the most efficient and value-for-money sector, social renting, and instead expanded subsidy to the least efficient and lowest value-for-money sector, private renting, a policy change that is now driving a very rapid increase in the cost of housing benefit.

Of course, I do not argue that the world of social renting is some perfect nirvana. Many mistakes have been made in social renting over the past 50 years as well. I would name the failure of imagination in urban planning and its inability to create mixed neighbourhoods across the piece, the disaster of system-build and some gross errors made in the design and construction of large estates during the heyday of building in the 60s and 70s. And it is the case that social rented homes have often been badly managed both by councils and housing associations.

But my point is that *the model of social rented housing* has been tried and tested and it works. It is a wheel waiting to be reinvented. Targeting subsidy at building homes in the first place, with no subsidy for subsequent running costs: this is the most efficient use of resources. The focus is on construction and there are strong multipliers in the wider economy so that the Treasury gets a big slice of its money back. Rents rise over time while borrowing costs flatline, so the pooling of rents allows a cross-subsidy from older properties to newer properties, helping to keep them all affordable. Social landlords can borrow money to build at the best possible rates. Housing Associations get a return on their investment over the lifetime of the loans they take out; councils currently make a surplus on their activities with no general subsidy. Cost-plus rents mean there is a need for housing benefit but at much lower levels than that required for private rented homes.

So what's not to like about social renting?

Neo-liberals assert that markets lead to an optimal use of resources. Economic theory would tell us that high prices lead to more homes being provided so that an equilibrium price is achieved over time to the satisfaction of those providing and those buying or renting the homes. And the evidence is?

It is a particular nonsense to have a dysfunctional housing market, inflated by demand subsidies, and then to require social rents to be tied to it, whether at 40% or 80%. Once council housing started to make a profit, people hostile to any form of public housing provision switched from complaining about cash subsidies to claiming that it was subsidised simply because it was sub-market. Of course it is fair enough for economists to identify the 'economic subsidy' or 'opportunity cost' involved – i.e. how much you could get for it if you sold it in the market instead and applied the money to some other activity – but it is unrelated to the cost of provision. In the real economy, where there are tens of thousands of market distortions caused by taxes, tax reliefs, imperfect competition, and even geography, the notion of economic subsidy makes little sense. Staying in hospital, for free, involves a taxpayer subsidy for the cost of treatment and the cost of occupying a hospital bed. No-one goes to BMI Healthcare, asks how much they would charge, and then says the subsidy for an NHS bed is the difference between free and private fee levels.

Social rents should be linked to the net cost of provision of the stock, adjusted by local or regional variations in incomes. Hence rents in London would be higher than rents in Newcastle, which everyone would agree is fair.

Labour's social rent policy, introduced in 2001, followed a review which concluded that social rent levels were set at broadly the right levels but needed to rise gradually over time (in those days incomes tended to rise faster than prices) to help fund investment. The outcome was too formulaic and centralised, with little local flexibility, but was quite well accepted, predictable and stable.

Since 2010 rent policy has gone haywire, but the underlying principle is that social rents will be much higher than in the past. A rapidly reducing proportion of 'social housing' lettings have been for 'social rent' under Labour's policy and a rapidly increasing proportion have been tied to irrational and volatile market rents through the Coalition's 'Affordable Rent' regime. Actual rents vary between 50% and 80% of the local market rate as determined in negotiations between providers (when bidding for contracts) and the Homes and Communities Agency or the London Mayor. As the investment programme was cut by 60% during George Osborne's first spending review, it was always underfunded, so providers are required to help fund new build by selling some existing property and 'converting' a proportion of their existing social rented homes to 'Affordable Rent' levels when they are re-let. Councils building new council homes are charging a variety of rents to ensure that schemes are viable. The picture now is chaotic. A new 'Affordable Rent' tenant living next door to a social rent tenant might be paying as much as twice the rent, with less security of tenure.

The central argument deployed against an expansion of social renting is that it would require additional borrowing to fund a larger grant programme and that this cannot be afforded. Currently the programme is around £1.5 bn a year: chickenfeed in public expenditure terms, almost within the margin of error for housing benefit. Builders buy materials and newly employed workers spend their incomes. Tax revenues rise and benefit payments fall. Homes are let at rents that might be half the price of private lets, saving hugely on housing benefit in every future year. The net cost to the Treasury is significantly below the gross cost.

The new campaign group, SHOUT (Social Housing Under Threat), in its submission to the Lyons Commission, argued that half of Labour's proposed target of 200,000 homes a year by 2020 should be homes for social rent. They estimate that the cost of these proposals would rise to £6bn a year by 2020 (an increase of £4.5 bn over current spending plans). A proportion of the cost would be borne by the private sector through planning gain and some of the grant could come in the form of free public land. There would be savings in other programmes, such as health. It would be an ideal form of investment because there are no additional revenue costs - management, maintenance, renewal and debt servicing would be paid for out of rents.

This kind of programme is achievable if housing is a genuine political priority. Additional spending on grant would clearly be an extra public spending commitment. But the headline cost is, according to SHOUT, "*well under 1 per cent of planned 2013-14 spending; the equivalent of less than 1p on income tax, or just 13 days of welfare spending; and less than 15% of the planned cost of HS2*".

To achieve a new social rented programme of this size, changes will be needed to how both local authorities and housing associations operate. In the council sector there is considerable capacity for additional prudential borrowing within business plans following the reform of the housing revenue account subsidy system. Despite being a self-financed trading activity, borrowing by councils is artificially constrained by Treasury conventions which are different in the UK compared to the rest of Europe. By switching to international measures of public borrowing, it is estimated that councils could build an additional 12,000 homes.

For housing association programmes, additional private borrowing to match additional grant is already 'off balance sheet' and does not add to public borrowing. The issue here is a different one. It is hard to generalise because it is a more diverse sector than ever, but too many large housing associations have lost their way and have actively pursued a path away from social renting. They see themselves as large development and regeneration companies. They are not accountable and have lost sight of their mission to provide homes for the homeless and badly housed. Of course, their activities contribute to the overall supply of housing, but they detract from what should be their core product – social rented housing. Their mission should be rebooted.

Even if we begin to build many more social rented homes again, the gap between supply and demand will require a system of rationing and allocation. The question still has to be asked 'who is social housing for?'

The mix of tenants living in social housing has changed over the years. In the 1950s the rents of high-quality single occupation new council homes were often higher than in the multi-occupied poor quality private rented sector and were out of reach of the poorest. Many families were deliberately excluded by devices such as assessing 'housekeeping standards'. Council housing became focused on meeting the needs of the 'respectable' skilled and semi-skilled working classes rather than the unskilled. Homes were often allocated against unclear and unpublished criteria and frequently involved councillors making individual letting decisions. Judgemental attitudes, discrimination and favouritism were common. It was a long struggle to move to transparent housing allocations policies based on assessments of housing need, with no means test, with individual lettings decisions made objectively against public criteria by officers.

It is commonplace to be told that 'the problem' with modern social housing is that it is let on the basis of housing need and that too many poor and vulnerable people have been congregated together on 'sink estates'. Thatcher pursued a deliberate policy of residualisation and a shift towards the American model of a small welfare housing sector, turning off the supply tap and selling hundreds of thousands of the best homes to better-off tenants. No-one should be surprised that over time this obligated the sector to restrict access to the most desperate applicants. In my view it was right, and still is right, to prioritise housing allocations to those objectively assessed as being in the greatest housing need, and the length of time they have been in need, and not on income or employment or community contribution or other factors. In the circumstances of a sector forced into decline it was right to focus resources in this way.

It was also inevitable that residualisation would have implications for housing management down the track. In my view many landlords failed to identify the challenge or to rise to it. Better and more intensive management was required but blaming the people was easier than fixing the problem. It would be wrong to respond to difficult management challenges by housing even fewer people in the direst housing need, just as it is wrong to be reverting to the 1960s by excluding homeless families from social housing by recycling them back into insecure private renting. It is a worthy aspiration to want social housing to house a wider cross-section of society, but it is a pipedream in the current circumstances.

In this short essay I hope to have conveyed the view that social rented housing has been a huge factor in the improvement in housing conditions in our country and in breaking the automatic link between poverty and bad housing. Over the last 35 years it has had the life squeezed slowly out of it by ideology and bad policy. But it can be reinvented. And the benefits of doing so could be great.

Time for raised voices

May 22, 2014

An excellent opinion piece on 24 Housing last week by Tony Stacey reminds me just how supine – and in parts, complicit – the housing industry has become. From the off, Red Brick has objected to, criticised, parodied, and been outraged by the Government's 'Affordable Rent' scheme. And in equal measure we have tried to expose the deliberate attempt to reduce and, we think, eventually eliminate social rented housing.

Tony, who is Chair of the 'Placeshapers' group of medium-sized housing associations, says he refuses to use the term 'Affordable Rent' and describes 'the wretched thing' as 'AR'. He finds the few references to people speaking out against AR and in favour of social rent, including the important 'Just Say No' blog by Colin Wiles, which in turn led to the creation of the SHOUT campaign for social rented housing. Tony hopes that Boards and Chief Executives will 'find their voices' having 'sleepwalked into acquiescence'. He makes the simple but blinding observation that 'subsidised housing needs subsidy'.

The reason I use the word 'complicit' is that some in the housing world have been rather more than naïve people going meekly along with an externally imposed agenda. Quite a few were actively involved in creating this whole plan. There are of course many honorable exceptions, but over the years I have experienced a considerable number of chief executives and other senior people distancing themselves from social rented housing, travelling away from their associations' original mission to assist the homeless and people in greatest housing need, becoming obsessed with home ownership and equity stakes, prioritising what they called 'aspirational' people, and stigmatising people trapped in 'welfare dependency' in a way that would make even Iain Duncan Smith blush. In the words of one housing director, 'it's not the homes that need fixing, it's the people'.

And so they would rather build for shared ownership or even private sale than social renting, even when their business plans allowed for a choice between them. Promises of future cross-subsidy from surpluses – we should make shed loads of cash, then invest it in rented homes, I can remember being told - never quite materialise in the way promised. Just like developers, they don't want the value of their for-sale products diluted by having social housing mixed up with them. They are in awe of 'the market' and the magical importance of 'market rents' even when it is so blindingly obvious that the market is completely dysfunctional. They have changed the brand and image of their organisations, becoming 'developers' and 'regeneration agencies' rather than housing associations building homes to meet housing need.

I have heard chief executives complaining about having to house 'chavs', objecting to local authority 'dumping' of tenants and demanding that landlords should have more power to evict tenants and to end the tenancies of people they feel don't deserve them. Some even specifically advised the Conservative Party in the development of policies in favour of higher market-related rents and reduced security of tenure, which in turn mutated into the 'AR' policy. Too often they seemed obsessed with development, irrespective of what was being developed, and disinterested in existing tenants and housing management or old-fashioned concepts like meeting housing need. Strategy was a word they applied to their own organisational objectives and not to the needs of communities.

Be careful what you wish for. The scene was set, the monster was created and then incubated by a 60% reduction in investment in the Coalition's first spending review. The only way to build any new homes at all was to slash grant for each home and to massively increase rents – in new but also in existing homes. Now housing associations have to live with a product that is almost useless to their poorer tenants in high rent areas, stretches their own resources, and – what madness – costs more in the long term in public expenditure. And yet some of these same chief executives still sit smugly on CIH and NHF platforms telling the world what a wonderful job they're doing.

If associations had refused to play ball in the first AR round the product would have been dead in the water. Some were just toadies but the depressing fact is that others were getting what they had been seeking for years. I'm not normally a bitter and twisted person, but if I was in charge if Labour wins the next Election, some of these organisations would never see another penny of public money.

So well done Placeshapers and well done SHOUT for helping to change the tone of the debate. The housing industry must stop failing the people.

Regeneration or Gentrification?

July 13, 2014

How to improve housing conditions in an area whilst keeping the cost of living there within the reach of people on low incomes has been a key issue in housing for as long as I can remember, and especially in London. In the 1970s I was involved in campaigns to protect low-cost housing against gentrification in Paddington and then more widely. At that time a lot of social housing was being built (Tory Westminster alone was producing nearly 1,000 homes a year, mostly on former railway land), so the gentrification process was restricted to the private sector.

In the 1960s people like Rachman made huge fortunes by removing established tenants and packing houses with immigrants who could not get housing elsewhere, profiting from overcrowding. As market conditions changed, in the 1970s the practice of 'winkling' became common. Speculative landlords still bought run-down inner city property and shifted established tenants out, but now they were more likely to convert the houses for a newer richer group who could afford higher rents or to buy.

In Islington the campaign against the notorious estate agent Prebble became the focus of regular demonstrations outside their offices in Upper Street – and heavy-handed police action, it also has to be said. There were long campaigns to save traditional local communities across Inner London, including Barnsbury, Covent Garden and Pimlico. In some boroughs, councils and progressive housing associations intervened by buying out landlords, rehousing the tenants and improving the properties for future social tenants.

Thatcher ended council municipalisation programmes after 1979 but this was also followed by a major shift in emphasis amongst housing associations from the purchase and refurbishment of street properties towards new build. In turn this was followed by the deregulation of the private rented sector, leaving us with an unfettered market that has been busily gentrifying the capital as shortage has grown and values have risen. We have seen the gradual transformation of many of London's traditional working class communities into much more affluent and expensive neighbourhoods. The process is well known but, with a growing number of hotspots and the advent of the global super-rich, it is now spreading well into outer London. By restricting the ability of people on low incomes to live in more affluent areas, the welfare reforms are probably the final nail in the coffin of these historic communities.

The ability of poorer people to stay in affluent neighbourhoods has become more and more dependent on the availability of social housing in those areas, a big and hugely valuable legacy of generations of housing policy in inner London. In the 1980s the focus rightly turned to look at the quality of the many estates built between the wars and after WW2. Well-intentioned 'estate regeneration' schemes started in an era when the supply of social rented homes was sufficient to enable extensive 'decanting' to take place, and tenants were normally promised the right to local rehousing in a new or refurbished home at social rents. A succession of Government schemes brought estate improvements which benefitted existing residents.

The phenomenal rise in property prices in London brought attention to inner London estates because they sit on extremely valuable acres in good locations. If only their latent value could be released, whole areas could be transformed and new neighbourhoods created. In the most valuable places, like along the river, new 'quarters' could be created and profits could be used to build new social housing elsewhere. Government, national and local, realised that regeneration could be done with little or no subsidy as long as sufficient private homes for sale could be included. As public borrowing remained constrained, private borrowing by developers, including housing associations, became the natural model.

The politics of housing through this era meant that council housing had few friends. The new generation of Tories were mainly hostile and council housing was not quite a New Labour thing. Developers obviously wanted as much private housing as possible and many housing associations were transitioning away from social housing provision towards mixed tenure development with social housing a smaller and smaller proportion. The perceived wisdom was that council estates, even in otherwise rich parts of London, were drab 'monotenure' concrete monstrosities dominated by unemployment and criminality. It was obviously much better if they were replaced by bright new developments of 'mixed tenure' homes.

Of course some of the estates were shockingly built and many were also badly managed, but even so it has been rare for tenants to call for redevelopment rather than refurbishment. The normal call is for the community to be preserved, for refurbishment to take place and for better management and maintenance to be put in place.

Despite the appearance of being high density, many estates use land inefficiently. Spare land and rising values meant that opportunities for adding to the stock (or densification) began to open up, sufficient to finance and facilitate a wholesale regeneration or redevelopment. The finance tail was finally wagging the housing strategy dog. The bigger the scale, the grander the vision, the greater the planners' desire to sweep away nasty council estates and replace them with 'mixed communities', the less influence residents seemed to have. Big estate regeneration schemes in London involved the loss of tens of thousands of social rented homes that were replaced by more housing, but much less social housing. Regenerated estates contributed little to meeting the needs of the waiting list, often they were a net drain. In a borough like Brent, which has had four or five major estate regeneration schemes, the wider implications for supply have been felt for many years.

In recent years some Labour boroughs have insisted on the complete reprovision of the social rented housing involved in the scheme, but this has rarely been achieved. Despite often good intentions, rising costs during a scheme tend to create pressures to increase the number of homes for sale and to reduce the amount available for social rent. More recent, the obscenity of unaffordable 'affordable rent' has added another layer of confusion as promises focus on badly defined 'affordable homes' rather than social rented homes. Some developers think that the social housing element will depress private sale values and will do anything to wriggle out. And on top of it all, we now have a London Mayor who actively intervenes to promote 'regeneration' that has next to no social rented provision and who uses his powers to block or prevent Labour boroughs who wish to ensure a fair share of social renting in redevelopments.

Last week the Homes and Communities Agency and the Mayor launched the bidding process for the latest miniscule housing pot, this time it is the £150m fund for estate regeneration schemes to start in 2015/16. Some of the reasons for regenerating estates given in the prospectus sound ok: they include estates that were built at quite low densities that do not always use land well. And I would support the prospectus's statement that *'The best regeneration projects actively involve residents so that the new homes and area are re-developed to meet local needs, provide well-designed and high quality new homes and reflect a sense of community identity.'* However in practice it is hard to believe that this is what most estate regenerations are about.

The rules around the new scheme help explain why 'regeneration' has moved away from the aim of serving the interests of existing residents and people in housing need towards a corrupted vision of what a mixed London neighbourhood should look like. Despite all the talk about how poor these estates are, the Government money is delivered as loans not as subsidy. The Government's investment must be returned, schemes must 'work with the grain of the market', and total public funding will be required to be less that 50% of the total project costs. It says 'Funding will only be delivered to private sector partners' and the delivery body must not be classifiable as a public sector body.

It is a good thing therefore that the London Assembly's Housing Committee has launched an investigation into the 'Demolition and Refurbishment of London's Social Housing Estates'. I hope their work will focus on the loss of genuinely affordable housing through so-called regeneration over the past few years and look for improvements in future. I also hope that Labour London boroughs will take a stronger line – protecting existing communities and delivering social housing must be the top priorities.

Developers are eyeing up estates across the capital in the currently febrile property market. Council estates have been the bulwark against gentrification since the 1970s. They are the largest remaining pool of genuinely affordable homes and must be protected. Yet London Tenants Federation have estimated that more than one-third of new social rented homes built in London from 2007 to 2013 were just replacements for others that were demolished.

'Poor doors' and a 'failed brand'

July 27, 2014

By Monimbo

The Mayor of New York probably has enough on his plate without keeping up with Red Brick. But if he did, he'd find we are much bigger fans of his than we are of Boris Johnson. Told of the new practice of installing 'poor doors' in New York apartments, where providing a proportion of affordable housing has been a condition of their receiving building permits, Bill De Blasio said he intended to outlaw them. Back in Britain's capital, however, installing poor doors seems to be an established practice that fails to trouble his London homologue.

Are poor doors the ultimate sign that social housing is a 'failed brand'? The story came at the end of a week in which there was a live Guardian debate that saw the issue raised several times. A week earlier, Boris Worrall of Orbit Housing said that the social housing brand is 'broken', although he distinguished the brand from the product. Three weeks before that, Peter Hall's blog picked up a Red Brick article about 'the slow demise of social housing' and argued that it would be better to subject it to euthanasia than to try to revive it. Not surprisingly, our friends in SHOUT have been vigilant in defending both the brand and the product. Colin Wiles took part in the Guardian discussion (along with Steve from Red Brick) and went on to challenge the notion of social housing having 'failed' or being 'damaged' in his column for Inside Housing.

Where does this leave us? There is a suspicion that this 'failed brand' debate comes about because some in the sector are positioning themselves to abandon social housing all together. After all, Boris Worrall has elsewhere proclaimed that 'social housing is dead'. The NHF is hosting what it calls its HotHouse debate about the future of housing associations, one suggestion being that local authorities should be left to house those most excluded and vulnerable, perhaps predominantly in social rented properties. This would free up housing associations to cater for the more aspirational members of Generation Rent. Peter Hall's argument is that it would be better for housing providers simply to create good quality rented housing, charging discounted rents to poorer tenants and full market rents to those able to pay them.

Probably few would oppose the idea that building some houses for sale or market rent can be a useful way to cross-subsidise social rented dwellings, but can this be done on a big enough scale? In Peter Hall's example, only one third of the units are at social rents. Alan Holmans, the well-known expert on housing demographics, has pointed out that if we ever build 250,000 homes per year then indeed one-third of them will need to be at subsidised prices. But this means that for the Hall model to work across the board, we would need to capture all of the profits from the housebuilding industry. However tempting to Red Brick this might be, this simple calculation shows why we still need actual subsidy.

As Colin Wiles reminds us, another point that some would wilfully ignore is that both the need for and popularity of social housing are enormous. The Resolution Foundation's report Home Truths showed that some 1.3 million low/middle-income households face housing costs which take one-third or more of their income. So far, few of these are in the social sector. But in 2012/13 alone there was a net loss of over 40,000 units that would have been let at social rents, so already we are putting parts of the social sector beyond the reach of broad numbers of low-income households, when we should be doing the opposite.

Kate Davies has also entered this debate, from a slightly different viewpoint. She says she admires the aspirational tenants 'who get good jobs and go on to become homeowners', but at the same time says we do need social housing as a safe haven for vulnerable people. However well-intentioned, this serves to confirm rather than confront the failed brand argument. It moves us much closer towards the position that the sector is (as she puts it) for 'poor' or 'damaged' people who can't be self-sufficient. Ironically, this is the ambulance service view of social housing which persists in the U.S. and which De Blasio aims to challenge.

It's a regrettably short leap from describing tenants as vulnerable to telling them that it's all their fault. The media don't necessarily make that leap – they don't need to, there are enough viewers and below-the-line commentators who'll do that for them. Arguing for sympathy rather than condemnation won't work, especially when half those ready to condemn probably do so because they believe their own circumstances are more deserving of help from the state.

What's the way forward? As Colin did, we need to keep on banging on about the scale of need that exists and of the supply that's required. Given that we have an economy in which huge numbers on low and middle incomes find neither renting or buying affordable, low-cost housing is vital and only the social sector can provide the numbers of homes needed. Furthermore, if we were able to do this, we'd soon find that we were housing fewer vulnerable people and more who are simply working in low-paid jobs. (After all, those in work currently account for the fastest growing segment of housing benefit claims.)

But we also need to get a grip on our own perceptions of the sector we run. The fact that new lettings usually go to the most vulnerable applicants shouldn't blind us to the broad range of people who still live in social housing, even after 30 years of 'residualisation'. Kate Davies admonishes those who promote social housing as an 'idealised workers' paradise' but it's equally misleading to go to the other extreme. In my view, talking about 'failed' or 'broken' bands does just this, and undermines the case we need to make for massive investment so that the sector can properly cater for many more of those who need and want to live in it.

A small lesson can be drawn from a different piece on the Guardian Housing Network. Residents of the Aylesbury Estate objected to the way their homes have been regularly portrayed by Channel 4, including in the opening images of 'Benefits Street'. The short clip, called an 'ident' in the trade, shows a monochrome estate, apparently after a rain storm, populated by pigeons and strung with washing lines and bin bags. Residents helped produce their own, alternative clip, showing the estate in a very different light, featuring the varied groups of people who actually live there. Both the film and the fact that they did it should remind us that there are (still) plenty of vibrant people living in social housing who are getting on with their lives. They suffer much more than we do if where they live is described as 'failed' or 'broken'. Social housing pundits, please note.

Giving away council houses

August 17, 2014

By Monimbo

Next June it will be 40 years since it was first proposed that council houses should be given away to tenants. It was too radical even for Margaret Thatcher, but there is always someone who will resuscitate a daft idea. This time it's Paul Kirby, the erstwhile head of the No.10 policy unit, who has gone through the maths on his blog. What you can't do is find any notion that social housing has any value other than its sale price. Like right to buy (which presumably Kirby regards as a timidly unambitious policy), it ignores social housing as an asset: something that needs looking after and will serve future generations. I imagine that what annoys such pundits about the sale of the Royal Mail is not that it was done cheaply but that the buyers were forced to pay for it.

I also imagine that Eric Pickles would be happy to adopt Kirby's plan, but for the moment his hands are tied. He's doing his best, however, and in the last few weeks we have seen three further steps towards making the right to buy even more generous – to the buyers. First, in July, maximum discounts rose to £77,000 (£102,700 in London) and from now on will increase in step with inflation. Second, the maximum discount for a house, previously 60%, became 70% (in line with that for a flat). Third, this month, the government implemented what Eric charmingly calls 'Flo's law', which sets a cap on the service charges that councils can impose on leaseholders, most of whom are in flats bought via the right to buy.

All of these undermine the asset value of social housing but the third actually shifts costs from the right to buy purchaser back to the local authority. When the original consultation took place last year, CIH, London Councils and others warned that, effectively, council tenants would have to subsidise major renovations in blocks of flats where there are leaseholders, in order to keep service charges within the new limits. However, this government increasingly treats the consultation phase of its proposals as it would the Royal Assent to legislation: an unfortunate requirement that delays the outcome but is otherwise unlikely to change it. Councils have been left to work out whether they should forego government subsidy so as to continue to be able to apportion service charges fairly, or whether they should partly absorb them into their housing revenue accounts (which means tenants subsidising neighbouring owners who have already been subsidised once via the discounts they received when they bought their flats).

Pickles can't of course resist putting the blame for high service charges on councils and is 'appalled' by how they treat leaseholders. It's also true that buyers can find themselves landed with massive charges when roofs or lifts are replaced, and immediately blame the local authority for charging them while tenants get the work for 'free'. Pickles is keen to perpetuate this myth, even though achieving the Decent Homes Standard is government policy and, of course, tenants are paying for improvements through their rents.

What he doesn't say is that, when people exercise the right to buy, no one warns them about long-term repairs costs. Councils are limited to telling buyers what service charges will be for the next five years, and must be careful not to obstruct the sale process. The government's own web page for buyers who will be leaseholders restricts itself to mentioning the five-year service charge estimate, and only vaguely mentions the bigger charges that might come later. Of course, the dedicated government website, Facebook page and leaflets are aimed at talking up right to buy, not reminding buyers of the costs.

It so happens that the folly of right to buy (that would also result in spades if Paul Kirby's mad idea was ever implemented), was also beautifully illustrated this month. Harrow Council finds itself spending half a million quid leasing back 35 former council homes, sold at discounts of up to £100,000, so that it can provide temporary accommodation for the homeless. Councillor Glen Hearnden was quoted in Inside Housing as saying:

'We lose twice with the government scheme, we lose the property from our stock and then we pay to rent it back. It all adds up to our residents suffering. It feels like we are fighting the fires caused by an overheating housing market whilst the government is stood on our hose pipe.'

Paul Kirby doesn't so much want to stand on the hose as cut off the water supply. Naturally, his proposal to give away council homes is also given the hard sell:

'I would say to both left-wingers and right-wingers, it's not often that any politicians get the chance to do something dramatic to sort out poverty overnight, especially in a way that costs the tax-payer a lot less. Given that both Left and Right can win from this proposal, they only lose by doing nothing, leaving all that money tied-up in the 4m homes, the poor still poor and the welfare bill climbing every year. So why not do it? Unless, either of them has got a better idea?'

Monimbo is not so immodest as to speak for the whole of the 'Left', but I do suggest that, to see many better ideas than his, Paul Kirby could read through Red Brick.

That sinking feeling[1]

August 24, 2014

It would be easy to condemn this weeks' Policy Exchange report on 'turning round' Britain's council estates. But it is important to separate out the spin and editorialising from the evidence in the report. Published by a think tank with a less obvious agenda, Gavin Knight's report might have had something useful to say about reinventing the art of community development.

Regrettably the report trades in the usual stereotypes. It starts with a rhetorical flourish: *'The riots of August 2011 were an eruption from the violent underbelly of our inner cities.'* Then comes the statistical mirage. Step 1: 40% of those before the Courts were on a DWP benefit. Step 2: 'young rioters were more likely to be from deprived areas'. Step 3: 'many' deprived people live on social housing estates. Step 4: Many social housing estates are 'sink estates'. Step 5: the biggest leap of all – the riots of 2011 started on a sink estate, Broadwater Farm in Tottenham (I think they may be three decades out on that one). Step 6, Conclusion: The problem we must tackle is council sink estates.

Most of the 2011 rioting in Tottenham, and in other areas, happened in shopping streets, and in mixed areas. There is no evidence of any link to tenure. The excellent London Citizen's Tottenham inquiry identifies reasons for the riots, based on the evidence of hundreds of local people, and none have anything to do specifically with tenure or Broadwater Farm. Indeed, in their report the only mention of the Farm is to record the many contributions to the Inquiry made by residents in support of wider improvements in Tottenham, in youth services, in shopping, in police relations, and so on. Regeneration is supported but the emphasis is more on the High Street and on business start-ups, there is no mention of estates separate from the rest of the area.

The thought process leading from the riots to the description of social housing estates as 'a national embarrassment' is the usual lazy prejudice and stereotyping. It leads to newspapers like the Express talking about 'ghettoes' and the direct association of a tenure with poor education, single parents, child neglect, domestic violence, low levels of employment and gang warfare. Undoubtedly these are real problems on social housing estates but it is a parody and a caricature to pretend that these problems are not just as severe elsewhere and in other tenures.

Behind the spin and the usual Policy Exchange right-wing editorialising, I found some good points in the report and some good evidence to support a return to the community development approach, something of a lost profession. This approach is just as relevant in areas with a predominance of private renting or low income home ownership as anywhere else.

Knight is right to emphasise the importance of crime and police-community relations, although he ignores the point that the cuts are leading to a major reduction in the highly effective neighbourhood policing approach that brought about many improvements. He is right to see the need to support and back local leaders, especially local residents. He is right to argue for 'interventions' (e.g. to promote work and training) to take place in the heart of the area and not at service points well away from the area. He is right to say that communities must themselves be the agents of change. He is right to say that existing resources could be better deployed, for example by agencies working more collaboratively, although he fails to address the implications of the cuts to many services (e.g. youth) that are taking place now. And he is very right to emphasise the importance of supporting women, not only to improve their personal circumstances but also because they usually turn out to be the community leaders that are needed.

So some interesting stuff here, and in the case studies (although I don't know the local circumstances to be able to comment on the veracity of the text). But when we turn to the recommendations, the spin and political ideology of Policy Exchange take over again. Council estates undoubtedly need investment, and some need transformation, but the recommendations are once again about 'turning round' 'sink estates' by setting a 'National Estate Recovery Board' working closely with, yes you guessed it, the 'Troubled Families Team'.

Take out the stereotyping and demonization of council housing, and the highly political focus on one tenure, and I suspect there will be significant agreement around the author's broad conclusion:

Perhaps the most remarkable thing about the case studies in this report is how effective a series of very small-scale, very simple, very inexpensive interventions proved to be. By being locally-minded, determined and creative, individuals were able to catalyse huge change. Leaking, crumbling, gang-ravaged estates are a powerful symbol of inequality in Britain. All political parties need to offer positive, innovative and cost-effective solutions to the multiple, complex problems residents face every day. It is time to go into these estates and help these communities to rebuild themselves.

[1] *'That Sinking Feeling'* was a 1980 Bill Forsyth film about four unemployed Glasgow teenagers who steal stainless steel sinks from a warehouse and sell them on. The term 'sink estate' has no known derivation despite its common media usage.

The Right to a Home – 30 years on

December 16, 2014

30 years ago the Labour Housing Group, which had been founded in 1981, published its first book on housing policy[1]. It was 200 pages of tightly-argued analysis split into 18 chapters, each with a specialist author, forged into a coherent whole by the editing of Christian Wolmar, now campaigning to become Labour's candidate for London Mayor. Although circumstances have changed dramatically since 1984 – mostly for the worse, it has to be said – much of it stands the test of time and there are still lessons that can be learned for today.

The launch of LHG and the book – *Right to a Home* – came at a depressing time for housing. The Tories had stolen the whole debate with the right to buy, putting Labour on the defensive. Housing had slipped down Labour's agenda despite having been a quiet priority for the Wilson Government of the 70s (although much less so after the IMF fiasco in 1976). The aim of the book was to set out a new stance for Labour which also spoke powerfully about housing rights – but a completely different set of housing rights from the Tories.

The optimism of the 1970s – when it was widely believed that the housing problem was well on the way to being solved – gave way to Thatcher's single-minded pursuit of home ownership. Then as now huge cuts in housing investment meant that progress was reversed in terms of affordable housebuilding and the renewal of our oldest housing areas. Public sector starts (Britain) fell from an average of 135,000 in the 1970s to 36,000 in 1981 – the watershed leading directly to our modern catastrophe. Homelessness grew and there was an emerging crisis in the heavy use of temporary accommodation – especially bed and breakfast hotels in London but everything including caravans around the country. Conditions in the private rented sector were deteriorating, with several terrible fires in multi-occupied houses. As some housing areas began to gentrify, evictions became more common as landlords looked to sell out.

The core of LHG's argument was the principle of the right to a home – that everyone, irrespective of income or type of household should have a practical right to housing on a par with the accepted rights to health care and education. Arm in arm with this, housing subsidies should be redistributed away from those that already had good homes to those that did not, leading to greater fairness of housing costs in relation to people's incomes. Recognising that the withering of the private rented sector was leading to two relatively rigid (in terms of access) sectors (public housing and home ownership), the case was made both for new intermediate forms of housing and for greater parity of esteem between the main housing sectors. '*Whether people rent or buy their homes raises no issue of* principle for socialists,' wrote David Griffiths. *'A viable strategy has to move beyond a sterile confrontation between the tenures by accepting their long-term coexistence and seeking to ensure there is real choice between them.'* We would be in a very different place today if that advice had been taken then.

The book considered housing issues comprehensively, making proposals in relation to the reform of land taxation and housing subsidies, a better system of house buying and selling, the role of housing associations, housing allocations, and new forms of co-operative tenure. It broke relatively new ground by looking in detail at the issues of racial equality and gender equality in relation to housing policy. In one area the crystal ball failed spectacularly: it talked about 'the irreversible decline' of private renting and the need to plan for the removal of the absentee landlord from the housing system.

In my own chapter, on Planning Housing Investment, one paragraph I wrote has stayed with me ever since, featuring regularly as an argument on Red Brick: *'The monetary constraints on public housing investment are more imaginary than real. It is a nonsense to believe that an owner occupier borrowing money to buy a bigger house is somehow 'good' because it is a private activity, but that a council borrowing money, ultimately from the same sources, to build a new council house is an inflationary drain on national resources because it counts as part of the PSBR'.* Indeed, it made clear that the latter was a much more beneficial use of loan finance because it boosted economic activity, led to a permanent income, and by reducing social security costs and increasing tax revenue it almost became cost neutral to the Treasury. Ed Balls please note.

In the week of his funeral, it is poignant to read again the chapter by Chris Holmes on 'A Political Strategy'. He made the case for the central political demand to be for a Housing Rights Act *'which enshrines the legal right to a home within a comprehensive charter of individual and collective rights including the enforcement of minimum standards, security against arbitrary eviction, involvement in decisions and redress against grievance'*. He called for a *'vigorous attack on the acute inequalities which disfigure current housing provision'*. And, true even more now than then, he concluded: *'It would be naïve to under-estimate the difficulties of gaining political support for a genuinely socialist housing policy in the face of entrenched interests and deeply-ingrained conditioning…. We need new ideas but active support for a radical socialist housing strategy will only be won through campaigning.'*

So true.

[1]*'Right to a Home'*, published by Labour Housing Group in 1984, was written by Stewart Lansley, David Griffiths, Steve Hilditch, John Perry, Mike Gibson, Jane Darke, Bernard Kilroy, Tim Daniel, Richard Moseley, Nick Raynsford, Alan

Simpson, Geoffrey Randall, Bert Provan, Tristan Wood, Selwyn Ward, Marion Brian, Christine Davies, Chris Holmes.

The homeless are not just for Christmas

December 31, 2014

It probably has something to do with events in Bethlehem more than 2,000 years ago, but there is always an outpouring of concern for the homeless around this time of year. The compassion normally dissipates by New Year's Day. Many tens of thousands of people are homeless all year round, and it will be just as cold in January and February when the emotional and religious strings aren't being pulled. In the other months of the year, the shocking level of homelessness, like the shocking level of poverty, exposes our society to be lacking in compassion, preferring to blame the victim, and unwilling to tackle problems that are solvable with a bit of gumption.

Reflecting on the life of Chris Holmes, as I have been doing recently, makes me think that it is time for a new drive to build a genuine safety net for the homeless based on a basic right to a decent secure home. The first step would be to accept that homelessness is primarily a systemic issue, caused by housing shortage. It cannot be addressed by an approach based on personal pathology, as Iain Duncan Smith would have us believe.

At least this Christmas there has been some hard information around about who becomes homeless and why. For example, a survey of single homeless people for Crisis warned about 'the tragic waste of young lives' after showing that half of homeless people first experience it under the age of 21, and become vulnerable to violence, substance abuse and problems with physical and mental ill health. There has been extensive sympathetic media coverage of homelessness, including from newspapers that are normally hostile - including even the Mail. Others with a better reputation, for example Channel 4 News, put together the statistics in special briefings. The Labour Party collated figures which showed that nearly 61,000 families would spend Christmas in emergency accommodation, including more than 87,000 children. They estimated the cost of temporary accommodation over this Parliament to be £2.8billion – equivalent, in cash terms, to two years' worth of Government grant for new affordable homes.

Homeless peoples' rights have waxed and waned over the last few decades since the high spot of the 1977 Act. Labour's 2002 Act, which restored core rights taken away by the Tories in 1996, could have been revolutionary because it married stronger rights for individuals with new duties, in particular a requirement on councils to analyse the reasons for homelessness in their areas and prepare a comprehensive homelessness strategy to deal with the problems identified. Excellent in principle, the Act was destroyed by bad execution. Driven by a growing shortage of supply of social housing, and a well-intentioned but ultimately wrong-headed target to halve the numbers in temporary accommodation, many councils responded to their new duties by becoming more vigilant gatekeepers, finding new ways of 'diverting' people or turning them away. The revolving door of insecurity meant that many people were pushed back into the private rented sector, often many miles from their family and community. Bizarrely at a time when we're supposed to be saving money, the system that is now being operated is more expensive than the far better option of providing more homes at social rent. Labour is right to point out that numbers in temporary accommodation have grown by 20% since 2010, but the figure in 2010 was already a disgrace.

Under the Coalition, after many years of slow progress under Labour, all of the homelessness statistics are now rising rapidly. There is of course no reason why more people in the population should suddenly become more feckless or enter the ranks of troubled families – Duncan Smith's favourite pigeon hole - so it is glaringly obvious that the main problem lies in the lack of supply of genuinely affordable homes. To this can be added a general de-prioritisation of the homeless in the allocation of social housing. As a Government adviser on homelessness said when the latest framework for homelessness was introduced in 2012: *'The overall conclusion of introducing this framework is inevitably that new statutory homelessness applications will become minimal.'*

One person who was concerned about the homeless all year round was the actor Robin Williams, who sadly died earlier in the year. He always had a rider in his contract for any movie he made that the producers must employ a certain number of homeless people. This evidently compared with other actors wanting private jets, on tap champagne, and such like. One of his greatest and most testing roles was playing a homeless man in the 'The Fisher King' in 1991, with its sensitive portrayal of homelessness and mental illness.

Williams was a longtime advocate for Homeless Rights. In 1990, he testified before the Senate in support of the Homeless Prevention and Revitalization Act. In his testimony he said: *'The problem cannot be denied anymore... I do believe this can work in an incredible way, from a grassroots level, that the money can get to and prevent, truly prevent, homelessness. That's where it lies. You can't keep picking people up; you have to stop them from falling. That's what I hope. Thank you.'*

Let's hope 2015 is a much better year for housing than 2014. As Williams also said, *'You can't keep picking people up; you have to stop them from falling.'*

2015

Selling the family silver

January 19, 2015

One of the key themes on Red Brick over the years has been the importance not only of building more social rented housing but of protecting the stock we already have.

Evidence to be published in the upcoming 2015 Chartered Institute of Housing UK Housing Review shows just how much stock is being lost.

The bald facts are these:

- In 2012-13 the stock of social rented homes in England fell by 19,189. In 2013-14 this figure more than doubled to 43,850. The loss over two years of over 63,000 homes compares with additions to the social rented stock (eg through new build) of a mere 28,000 homes.
- Of these, more than 36,000 of the losses have been housing association homes. The biggest factor has been the 'conversion' of homes to so-called 'Affordable Rent' when they are re-let or their sale on the open market - arrangements which are driven by the need to cross-subsidise the new development of other 'Affordable Homes'.
- Right to buy is the biggest factor for local authorities, with 17,000 sales over the two years.

John Perry of the CIH says *"On present trends, the record loss of social rented homes in the year to April 2014 will be exceeded in the current year, as right to buy and conversions accelerate and new build for social rent declines still further. **By April 2015, we can safely predict that over 120,000 homes will have been lost to social renting over the three years** in which the government's Affordable Rents programme was being fully implemented."*

It is hard to exaggerate what a disaster this is for housing in England. The stock of social rented homes is the most precious housing resource we have – already built, mostly in good condition, available on good terms and at genuinely affordable rents. It is like, as Harold Macmillan once said, selling the family silver.

It is increasingly clear that the Government's unstated strategy is to gradually remove social rented housing from the system altogether, to be replaced by so-called 'Affordable Rent' at up to 80% of local market rents and by an increasing reliance on private renting. We have argued before that the real agenda for the Tories in Government (and therefore for the uncomplaining Liberal Democrats) was set by the infamous *Localis* report before the 2010 Election which advocated the 'marketisation' of all social housing.

Although 'Affordable Rent' levels have been mitigated for a proportion of new homes in London (even Boris Johnson appears to realise that 80% of market rent in London is hopelessly unaffordable), the average rent is still in the region of 65% of market, much higher than social rent levels. For tenants who need support from housing benefit to meet the rent - increasingly people in low paid employment - this high rent strategy is to all intents and purposes funded by making poor people poorer or through the back door by the State. In the greatest of all contradictions, it is Government policy to both increase and decrease housing benefit at the same time.

The pressures on the social rented stock, a vicious combination of the lack of new provision and the loss of existing stock, is the direct result of a range of government policies, which together mimic the Localis agenda:

- The removal of social rented housing from the Government's main funding programme - the 'Affordable Homes Programme' - which only supports homes made available at 'Affordable Rent' levels and other products like shared ownership.
- Conversions and sales undertaken mainly by housing associations as part of their deals with the Homes and Communities Agency to get a degree of grant for new homes under the AHP.
- Voluntary sales – Labour MP Karen Buck recently revealed that Genesis Housing Association had sold 200 homes in one borough – Westminster, where her constituency is - over the past few years.
- Right to Buy – where discounts have now reached over £100,000 in London and the Government has totally reneged on its clear promise that RTB homes would be replaced 'one for one' – currently estimated to be about one-in-seven.
- Going soft on Planning Gain – where so-called 'viability tests' are being used by developers to get out of making affordable housing provision in new developments.
- In London the Mayor's London Plan excludes almost any reference to social rented housing and expectations of provision are entirely in terms of 'Affordable Rent' or intermediate housing.
- Misguided 'regeneration' schemes in many places where redevelopment leads to a huge loss of social rented homes and their replacement by much more expensive homes, even if they are termed 'affordable'.

In some places, like for example Islington, there has been a real determination to focus on social rented housing, including a new council housing programme, refusing to support housing associations unless they provide social rented homes, and insisting on full replacement of social rented homes in regeneration schemes involving redevelopment. More could be done in many other places to protect social renting, but nothing should divert attention from the main cause – a Coalition Government that is determined to bring social rented housing to an end.

Social housing is worth its weight in gold

February 12, 2015

Regeneration sounds like a good thing. Who could be against it?

Today's report *'Knock It Down Or Do It Up'* from the London Assembly shows why many people, and especially tenants on large estates, have come to see it as a dirty word.

The report looked at major regeneration schemes in London over the last ten years. It found that, although the total number of homes in the defined regeneration areas had increased significantly – in this sample, from 34,000 to 67,000 homes – virtually all of the increase comprised homes for sale at market prices – up from 3,000 to 36,000 – and 'intermediate' homes, including shared ownership – up from 550 to over 7,000.

In comparison, the number of homes for social rent declined from 30,000 to 22,000 – a loss of 8,000 genuinely affordable homes.

And to add insult to injury, recent regeneration schemes have added to the number of so-called 'Affordable Rent' homes (at up to 80% of the market rent), which have increased from virtually zero to over 7,000. Even if they are promised homes in the new development, tenants in the latest schemes are likely to find that it not 'like for like'.

This outcome puts figures to a view that residents on many estates have had over the years: despite all the warm words, the hidden aim of the scheme is often to gentrify the area, to remove stigmatised social housing and replace it with a shiny new development that meets the needs of an entirely different group of people. Far from turning 'mono-tenure' estates into 'mixed communities', they marginalise and displace those who need genuinely affordable rented homes in favour of those who can afford to buy a new, and inevitably expensive, home. For too long the 'mixed communities' argument has only concerned changing existing estates: in housing strategy terms it only bears scrutiny if there is also a sustained programme of providing more social rented homes in predominantly private housing areas.

The justification for sweeping tenure change is normally financial. The private homes are needed to cross-subsidise the affordable homes and to pay for the physical improvements which normally accompany the scheme. But in some cases, refurbishment of the existing stock for the existing residents would be significantly better value.

There is also the question of 'drift': the initial promises about the proportion of social housing in the final scheme and the ability of tenants to be rehoused back on site, are 'revised' as costs rise. Inevitably, the social housing is squeezed and the share of private housing is increased. Although almost every council says that the interests and views of residents are paramount, they become less so as the scheme progresses and pragmatic variations are made to keep it on course. Two other tricky issues also arise as the scheme is designed in detail: to maximise the value of the final property, the private homes have to be in the best locations, and the social homes in the poorest, and the issue of high service charges in private blocks, which social tenants cannot afford, leads to segregation, with the social tenants accessing their homes through 'poor doors' as they have been dubbed.

This is an important study based on the reality of what actually happened on 50 council estates around London. It is a warning to residents as to what to look out for when a proposal comes your way, and it offers a clear guide to councillors who think regeneration is a good way forward for one of their estates: think it through, consult properly and transparently, do a thorough appraisal of all the options, be sceptical about developers and financial models, and keep control of the project from beginning to end.

And finally, don't let the value of social housing be assessed merely in financial terms. It might be cheap, its value might not look much to an estimator, but it is a hugely vital and unreplaceable community asset and it is worth its weight in gold.

City Villages or ghettoes for the rich?

March 26, 2015

I have a bright idea. London has a terrible housing crisis. There is a general shortage of homes of all kinds and a specific shortage of genuinely affordable housing. So, let's sell off the only genuinely affordable homes we already have and 'redevelop' large estates containing concentrations of the only genuinely affordable homes we have, replacing them with a mixture of much less affordable and downright unaffordable homes.

Doesn't work for you? Well, actually, it doesn't work for me either. But this is exactly what a large number of housing people are doing in London today. And they want more. With developers all around London eyeing up estates for their next big killing, egged on by the mayor and councils like Barnet, it is a good time to have a hard think about what public policy should be.

A timely set of essays published this week by the Institute of Public Policy Research looks at the possibilities of transforming London's, and especially Inner London's, council estates into 'City Villages', with higher densities providing many more homes. There are lots of good ideas here, and a brilliant historical piece by the late Peter Hall, summing up in a few pages the successes and failures of London planning over 70 years. There are several interesting case studies from around the London boroughs. But two things got my goat.

First, in what at first I thought was a joke, they have a chapter by a representative of Capco about their Earls Court development. A city village (if 7,500 homes is a village) of rich people replacing long-standing social tenants with virtually no new social housing is not my idea of progress and has no place in such a report.

And secondly, some of the essays are littered with casual prejudicial statements and phrases. Council housing estates are 'mono-tenure' (no such thing exists in London anymore, if anywhere) and lazy descriptions like 'dysfunctional' are used. The worst examples are exploited to generalise and condemn all estates. London's housing market is indeed dysfunctional, but council estates are not top of my list for reform. Some authors seem to operate on the assumption that there is no community on estates because the people are poor; I wish they would look around at some of the campaigns going on in London now (for example in Barnet). Amazingly, when the surface is scratched you find estates are full of gifted people doing all kinds of great things in their communities. And when it comes to it, they can fight and organise!

The chapters in IPPR's book are diverse and come from different standpoints. In some of the chapters there is recognition that a clear aim of regeneration should be to protect the existing residents and to replace the social rented housing like for like. In their case study, Jules Pipe and Philip Glanville, writing about Hackney's Woodberry Down, make it clear that this was an explicit objective that seems to be being achieved. But in others there is the usual lack of definition of 'social housing' and what is being discussed is the 'Affordable Rent' model, which is often not affordable at all. If people like Capco are not to be trusted, then neither are some of London's biggest housing associations, who are switching as fast as they can from traditional social rent to 'Affordable Rent' at much higher rents. It is the central nonsense of housing policy: cut the upfront investment that would keep rents low, creating a commitment to pay higher housing benefit for ever.

Stephen Howlett of Peabody goes with the grain of the National Housing Federation's calls for more 'freedoms' for housing associations by proposing 'more flexible rents'. He says: *'To increase affordability in London, a new, more flexible rent model that is based on a combination of the market rent and the tenant's ability to pay, including the ability to move to shared ownership and/or outright ownership when appropriate, might offer an affordable solution for Londoners.'* Of course, the model is one thing: what matters is how many £££s people are going to be charged. To my mind, the only likely outcome from such new formulations would be rents that are significantly higher than social rents; landlords would have a direct incentive to find higher income tenants to get more rent (as is already happening with 'Affordable Rent'). It is only social rents that produce quality homes that people on low incomes can afford.

Lord Andrew Adonis, who put the book together with IPPR's Bill Davies, describes the need to more than double the rate of housebuilding in the capital. He has a nice vision of 'hundreds' of properly planned, mixed-tenure, socially mixed City Villages replacing existing estates. No-one doubts that there is a lot of potential to build extra homes on local authority land within estates, and that long-term comprehensive regeneration is the best answer in some cases, but I find the overly-grandiose vision unconvincing; the existing estates also had beautiful masterplans published before they were built with famous architects pointing to the parks and community facilities. The problem is that so much gets lost in the delivery, and these days social housing is the first to go when costs rise as they invariably do. My instinct is to prefer the approach of Islington Council, looking estate by estate for development opportunities to add vital social rented homes to the stock. I do not share the authors' view that it is somehow wrong for Islington to have so many council housing estates using up some of the most valuable land in the country.

Adonis tries to contradict the 'assumption' that existing residents will be displaced by wealthier incomers. *'This need not, nor should it be, the case, since redevelopment will usually mean a much better use of land with typically around twice the density of the existing estate'.* But the proof of the pudding is in the evidence. A recent well-researched report by the London Assembly on regeneration in London discovered the huge scale of losses of social rented homes over the past decade – more than 8,000 in a relatively small number of comprehensive schemes. When you look around London now, things are getting worse: the political and financial drive behind development is to create ghettoes for the rich and profits for the developer. If that doesn't change, City Villages will not become the cohesive mixed communities that Adonis dreams about.

The other issue that is critical to the regeneration of large estates is the problem known by the unpleasant name of 'decanting'. Even if genuine commitments are made to existing tenants that they will be rehoused back in the new development on like for like terms, they often have to be rehoused elsewhere for a number of years. The normal solution is an alternative social rented unit provide by the council or a housing association – and 'decants' often have power to get what they want. Flats let to decants are not available to rehouse others on the waiting list or parked in temporary accommodation. In some boroughs the opportunity cost of the decanting programme has been huge. The impact of a major redevelopment on the flow of homes for new lettings is rarely recognised, and the IPPR report envisages redevelopment on a huge scale.

The issue of tenure is central to the consideration of major regeneration or redevelopment of existing estates. It is not just a matter of crude numbers of new homes – what is built at what rent and for whom matters just as much.

Social housing is our most important housing asset. Losses through regeneration and continuing losses though right to buy, 'conversions' to unaffordable 'Affordable Rent' and market sales to bring in the cash to pay for new build, create major questions which those in favour of the new City Villages need to answer – and don't in these essays. If these questions can be answered and the provision of rented homes at genuinely affordable social rents becomes a **primary** objective in such schemes, then the proposed intensification and better optimisation of land use might be more of a runner.

The super rich push out the rich push out the middle class push out the poor. Welcome to London the Global City.

April 28, 2015

Attending Hustings meetings in and around the area where I live - central and inner west London - is a depressing business. The fact that the meetings I have attended are in marginal seats tells me that the population there is more mixed than is commonly supposed. The statistics show that there is a lot of deprivation in the area, children living in poverty, and poor standard housing. There are lots of these meetings, but they seem to be dominated by a certain type of punter. Mansion Tax is raised a lot; Bedroom Tax doesn't get a mention. I doubt if this is true anywhere else in the country.

Savills estimate there are 76,000 properties in London liable for Mansion Tax and all their owners seem to have been to a Hustings in the last few weeks. Two of the meetings I have attended have been organised by faith groups. In one case Mansion Tax was raised by the priest, in the other it was the first pre-arranged question asked. In both cases some people got really hot under the collar about it. Poverty and homelessness didn't get a look in.

People who are quite well off by any definition see themselves as victims, and they see Mansion Tax as the last straw. They see themselves as being punished for working hard and buying a property in the area on a big mortgage when houses were just very expensive not mega-inflated like now. They have mixed feelings about what is happening to their community: their properties are valuable because they have been virtuous but they resent the fact that their areas are now falling prey to 'bankers and foreigners'. Gentrification should only go so far: barristers good, bankers bad, foreigners worst of all. They have no concept that their riches are a windfall gain, an unearned bonanza, visited on them by stupid housing policies over a generation. They feel they deserve it but they seem to have no awareness that it is much worse for many others.

Some of them are undoubtedly 'asset rich but income poor'. Partly as a result of Tory propaganda they believe they are going to be taxed out of their family home and out of the area, and are not mollified by the policy allowing deferment for those not earning enough to pay the higher rate of tax: it seems £42,000 is not that much.

It is undoubtedly the case that people are being pushed out of most areas close to the centre of London. It is a process that has been going on for 40 years but it has greatly accelerated in the last few years, especially in the era of London as 'The Global City'. London property is now one of the favourite places to put your millions for hundreds of thousands of rich people, especially Chinese, looking for a safe haven and a potential home to emigrate to if the going gets tough at home.

The fact that the feeling of victimhood stretches to people who are merely rich living in £3m houses is an extraordinary realisation. What hope does it offer for people on low and moderate incomes who have never been able to afford to buy anything at all?

An excellent article on the CityMetric website by the Chartered Institute of Housing's John Perry describes the ways in which people on low incomes are being banished from central London. He identifies five:

1. Welfare reform means people on low incomes can't afford to rent: since the caps were imposed, people in receipt of Local Housing Allowance has plummeted, by as much as 30-35% in Westminster and Kensington and Chelsea. Young people fare worst.
2. Homeless families get a tougher deal in London: homelessness continues to rise rapidly in London, increasingly because people have had their private tenancy ended – 38% of the total. Use of temporary accommodation is rising rapidly and is likely to be offered outside London.
3. Council housing is being sold off: twice as many homes were sold by London boroughs in 2013-14 as the year before. One-third of right to buy properties are now rented out privately.
4. Social lettings are going down: the consequence of losing stock is falling lettings, down to a mere 21,400 by councils and housing associations in 2013-14. Waiting list restrictions are also now commonplace.
5. Social homes are more expensive: housing associations have gone for so-called 'Affordable Rents' big time, rents are on average £60 a week more than social rents.

These are the pressures that are leading to an almost un-reported clear-out of people on low incomes from central London. Areas that have been genuinely mixed communities for generations are being changed rapidly. And when people living in £2-3m houses feel that change is happening too fast and are fearful (justified or not) that they might be pushed out as well because of the new Tax, you really do have to wonder what kind of city we are creating.

Be wary of those who say they already know why Labour lost

May 12, 2015

Those who have been quickest into print or on to the airwaves after the awful defeat on 7 May are not to be trusted. For them there is no period of reflection, no attempt to consider their own fixed views in the new context. Their ready solutions could have been written at any time in the last few years; they have said what they always say and have nothing new to offer. Their purpose is either personal advantage, because they are likely to be candidates, or to rubbish Ed Miliband and in particular his decision to move on from New Labour.

I defy anyone at this stage to have a genuinely rounded analysis, especially those who have already boiled it all down to simple solutions. Stella Creasy's Guardian piece on Saturday argued that we have to deal with the grief first and go through the grieving stages, and I'm probably somewhere between denial and anger, moving into depression. Half of me wants to sound battle cries and the other half wants to give up and quietly slip away. Half of me sees the mayoral contest in London as the next great challenge, half of me thinks it's not worth the candle because a Tory Government will be ruthless in controlling a Labour mayor.

Some people who were obviously not tired enough after Thursday have had a lot to say about reaching out to middle England, being 'business-friendly' and speaking to 'aspirational' people. But, when pressed, where are their policies different from what Ed Miliband has been saying these past few years? Labour was spun as anti-business because it wanted to tax the rich a bit more and because it attacked the big corporates, not because it had weak pro-business policies. Should we have dropped the tax proposals or the energy price freeze to reduce the damage? Of course not. Nor did Labour focus on the poorest 10% as is alleged, for example by Alan Milburn today, and it did not ignore middle England. In housing, the emphasis was entirely on first-time buyers and people who have good incomes but are still forced to rent. Apart from Bedroom Tax, hardly a word was said about social housing in the whole campaign.

Quite a few mistakes were made after 2010. We did not defend the record of Gordon Brown in saving the global financial system, which he did, because we were embarrassed by him. We didn't build on public anger about bankers by setting in concrete the link between the global banking crisis and the recession. We allowed the Tories to blame Labour's spending for the crisis despite the fact that the Tories supported Labour's spending plans up to the banking collapse. We were never comfortable with austerity nor brave enough to oppose it, and it showed.

So of course there are lessons to learn but I do not accept the view that our policy offer and post-New Labour positioning was all wrong. We were blamed for the recession and could not restore our reputation for economic competence, but we still made net gains in England. The result in London was patchy but it became even more of a Labour city. We were punished in Scotland and the Tories fed and exploited unpleasant anti-Scotland feeling in England which helped them win but could break up the Union. Labour was squeezed between two nasty nationalisms.

But it is vital to remember that 2015 was nothing like 1997. Then the big crisis, falling out of the Exchange Rate Mechanism, happened on the Tories' watch. This time it happened on Labour's. Then Scotland remained safely Labour, this time the referendum and rampant nationalism happened.

More than anything I feel that the defeat was the revenge of Murdoch and the other newspaper-owning billionaires. Can Labour ever win in the face of their dominance and hostility? Perhaps Ed Miliband's greatest mistake was to take on Murdoch and to show integrity over phone-hacking and Leveson. He did not play the game according to their rules and he did not travel around the world to dance to Murdoch's tune as Blair once did. Should Miliband have been more accommodating on policy to keep them onside? Was that possible? Could we have won the Election that way?

I do not accept that the papers have diminished influence these days: they set the tone, and the lazy broadcast media simply follow their lead. Their front pages are blazoned across every TV public affairs programme and their journalists populate programmes like Question Time. Miliband eating a bacon sandwich was repeated thousands of times – on the BBC as much as in the Sun – and was one small part of a deliberate strategy to undermine and ridicule him. The fact that he nearly rose above it is a remarkable tribute to him and I resent the fact that some people have now turned against him. Cameron's gaffes were mentioned but washed over. Miliband would not have survived leaving his child behind in the pub or being a Bullingdon boy or forgetting which football team he supported. Will any new Labour leader suffer in the same way?

It will be the same again next time, newspapers will still be owned by the same people and have the same bias, and the broadcast media will be no better – indeed the BBC will be much worse. One other lesson this time is that, in politics rather than celebrity, social media is not yet as powerful as everyone involved with it pretends it to be.

The depressing reality is that negative campaigning and propagandising worked. No amount of navel-gazing and blame-gaming will change that. The Tories are much better at it than us. Without hiring a Lynton Crosby, can Labour retain its integrity whilst being stronger in attack and much better at rebuttal? Are there ways of working round media bias without giving in to it?

So was Miliband 'too left wing'? It is the media message and some people's mantra. I can't see it myself. He wanted to regulate markets a bit more, spend a bit more public money, and tax the rich a bit more, but it was all incremental and at the margins. The Tories managed to align in the public mind the interests of the rich with the interests of business. In fact they are very different, and the behaviour of the rich over the past 20 years is the antithesis of a successful long term economic plan. They also managed to make welfare cuts popular – Labour must remember that you cannot overcome huge prejudice and the stigmatization of 'scroungers', built up over many years and fanned even by some in the Labour party, in a single Election campaign.

So, like everyone else, I have some views on why Labour lost but they are not necessarily well-formed. We need to debate the pros and cons so we can be better next time. But a false analysis based on pre-determined views that Labour was 'too left wing' or 'not left wing enough' will get us nowhere.

Talking aspiration

May 27, 2015

The most over-used and least defined word of the moment is 'aspiration'. Some Labour leadership candidates use it in almost every sentence. Not understanding it cost Labour the election says Alan Johnson and many others, including Alan Milburn, who must by now have met every one of his monetary aspirations several times over.

Of course, the Tories use it a lot, it is part of their lexicon. They use the word in inverse proportion to the ability of people to achieve their desire for a better life. The flatter the wages, the more they claim to support aspiration in work. The faster home ownership falls, the more they use it to describe their housing policies. The new Communities Minister, Greg Clark, said yesterday that their new right to buy for housing association tenants (RTB2) was driven by the Government's desire to meet the 'aspiration' of 86% of the population to own their home – before admitting that there is a huge gap between their preference and the reality of housing affordability.

I come from an 'aspirational' working class background, brought up on a Newcastle council estate. My parents wanted their children to succeed and do better than they had. For my Dad, that would have meant a real apprenticeship and a trade. For my Mum, it meant staying on at school and trying for College. She got her way, at the considerable cost of me not bringing in a wage, and I got into University. My fees were paid by the council, and I got a grant, enough to live on. It led to a decent career, good pay, and home ownership. So, I think I understand aspiration and social mobility, how it works, and the kind of Government policies needed to make it happen. But for my parents the top priority in their list of aspirations was the advancement of their children. Becoming home owners was a secondary consideration.

By the time I was in my 50s I was a board member at Notting Hill Housing Trust and the word 'aspiration' was used almost as often as the dreaded phrase the 'housing ladder'. Whenever I heard either of these, it would be followed by a proposal to reduce the amount of social rented housing in the development programme and to increase the amount of shared ownership. Shared ownership was evidently 'aspirational' and social rent was for people who were part of the 'dependency culture' (or 'chavs' as they were called once). It seemed to me to be a perversion of the idea of aspiration to link it to one of many possible ambitions and a single tenure. People's aspirations are their own affair, not restricted to the definition imposed by Iain Duncan Smith or housing association bosses. It is a complex concept, and it should not be reduced to the simplistic idea that people only want to be richer or own a specific asset.

If you are one of the millions who are homeless or overcrowded or living with parents or living in a hugely expensive but crap private flat, you may well aspire to a decent, genuinely affordable, secure social rented home where you can begin to build a better life for yourself and your family. The first rung on the housing ladder is somewhere you can genuinely call home, a place you can afford where you cannot be turfed out on someone else's whim. You might see it as your home for ever, the foundation for everything else you want to do, the bricks and mortar blanket that keeps your children safe and warm and allows them to settle in one school. It might lead to you getting a job or a better job or a training place or you might have a mission to improve your community and not just your personal finances.

Whenever I have worked on delivering social rented homes, I have always felt that I was also delivering on aspiration. I should make it clear, because annoyingly I always have to make it clear, that supporting a much bigger supply of social rented housing does not mean that I am against home ownership or shared ownership. It means I believe in a rounded balanced housing policy which aims to meet the needs and desires of everyone. I am against policies which assist better off people *at the expense of* poorer people – like subsidising home ownership whilst removing subsidy from social housing, or denying people access to council housing so homes can be sold to pay for RTB2.

In housing policy terms, when I was helping write the draft London Housing Strategy, this involved finding the right balance – ultimately a political judgement but based on huge amounts of evidence about affordability - between market and sub-market housing, and (within sub-market housing) between social rented housing which would be allocated on the basis of need and intermediate housing which was aimed at people on bigger incomes who still couldn't afford to buy outright. Ken Livingstone instinctively understood this need for balance.

To the complete contrary, Tories, and in particular Iain Duncan Smith, think that social housing tenancies 'stifle aspiration'. Back in the day, his Centre for Social Justice working group, chaired by the Chief Executive of Notting Hill Housing Group, started the argument for shorter social tenancies and selling off the most valuable social homes, perversely all in the name of aspiration and social mobility. Duncan Smith said that social housing was no longer the 'tenure of choice for the aspirational working class'. In practice, his policies force more and more people into the very inferior option of private renting, at hugely greater cost to the state. I am absolutely certain that these policies meet the aspirations of no-one.

The logical extension of his thinking is to accelerate the sale of the housing association stock through RTB2. 'Here, have £100,000 and become a Tory' is their real slogan. They also hope to obscure the basic fact of the modern housing market: home ownership is declining, and private renting is taking its place. The Tories do not want people to understand this.

If, like so many commentators, some Labour Party leadership candidates explain the election defeat as a failure to understand aspiration, it is time for them to turn the word into policy and to offer a bit of definition. I cannot for the life of me see the point made by one candidate that the Mansion Tax was anti-aspirational. The policy had its problems, especially in my bit of north-west London, but I simply can't see that taxing the most valuable 0.5% of properties has anything to do with blocking aspiration. If that is the case, the USA, which has much heavier property taxes than us, must be the most anti-aspirational country in the world.

I suspect the reality is that 'failing to understand aspiration' ranks with 'being anti-business' and 'spending too much' as a totally unconvincing explanation of Labour's defeat.

The economic and fiscal case for social rented housing is unanswerable

June 17, 2015

SHOUT, the campaign for social rented homes, has stolen a march (together with the National Federation of ALMOs) by commissioning the global macroeconomic research company Capital Economics to undertake independent research into the fiscal and economic case for building 100,000 new social rented homes each year.

This was inevitably something of a risk. Could the case for a major programme of building social rented homes be made under rigorous scrutiny and analysis?

SHOUT's core argument - that a major programme of new social rented homes offers not only the best housing solution for people on low incomes but would also be beneficial for the wider economy, reduce the requirement for housing benefit, increase work incentives, and be positive fiscally - needed to be tested in a robust way. The key question: should building 100,000 new social rented home a year not only be a flagship housing policy but also a central component of the Long Term Economic Plan?

The Capital Economics report, published today, is unequivocal. **'The economic and fiscal case for building new social rent housing is unanswerable'.**

If the trends over the last Parliament were to continue into the future – building almost no social rent, a modest amount of 'affordable rent' and becoming increasingly reliant on the private rented sector to house people on low incomes – *'the overall bill for housing benefit is set to accelerate – worsening the government's structural deficit now but also into the longer term'*. The trends, say CE, are unsustainable, as the cost of housing benefit (UK) can be reasonably projected to increase from around £24 billion today to almost £200 billion a year by 2065-66, with households in the private rented sector accounting for 63% of the total, up from 37% today. Building 100,000 social rent homes would reduce public sector net debt as a share of gross domestic product – the holy grail of the Chancellor. A long time frame? Certainly, but this is the horizon for the Office for Budget Responsibility's long-term fiscal projections. And the point of a Long Term Economic Plan is to make decisions that are, well, long term.

'Investment in new social rent housing offers a solution that is fiscally sustainable and economically efficient'.

CE make the key point about social rent: it requires both investment, financed by private borrowing, from social landlords, underpinned by a level of upfront contribution from the state. Once built, the servicing of the debt, management and maintenance of the properties and other costs can be covered by rent. Once built, no further subsidy is required. Over an even longer time scale – as homes have to last for even longer that the debt – the homes make a return. *'A social asset is created which will endure for decades, if not centuries'*.

Not only does the equation work in terms of the fiscal trade-off between bricks and benefits, it also works as an economic stimulus. Each pound of investment is estimated to stimulate an extra £2.84 of economic output through the supply chain and the extra spending of employees. Each £1 would stimulate an additional 56p of new tax revenues for the exchequer.

It would also have other beneficial knock-on effects that are harder to estimate and have not been included in the fiscal arithmetic. They note savings that could be made due to improvements in health, well-being, education and energy efficiency. They note possible improvements in policy towards children, due to the security of having a stable home, and to older people, who will have the greater possibilities of living in a suitable home rather than expensive residential care.

CE model the effects of building up gradually to 100,000 social rent homes a year by 2020-21, to enable the commissioning agencies, the construction industry and the supply chain to adapt. So where is the downside? At the start of the programme, the welfare savings and new tax receipts will be less than the money needed in grant to fund the new homes – so initial additional public borrowing is required. CE estimate that this would peak in 2019-20 at no more than 0.13 per cent of GDP. The policy would be creating a net surplus to the public finances by 2034-35. Taking a long term approach to controlling the deficit would, say CE, be welcomed by financial markets.

The report can only be briefly summarised here. It has a wealth of detailed material and many sophisticated calculations to demonstrate the case. It can be pored over by other macro-economists and fiscal experts. But it will become the core text for all of us who care about housing and want a balanced housing policy that encourages both sustainable home ownership and high quality affordable renting. Housing policy is off the rails; it is totally ineffective whilst at the same time being hugely expensive. 'No direction home' as Bob Dylan would say.

There is a solution. I have waited 30 years for the case to be made as well as it is in this report. Just a little political bravery could put us on the genuine path to solving the housing crisis in a generation. It is a policy that could be adopted by any and all political parties because it works, fiscally, macro-economically, and in social policy terms.

Because, as Capital Economics say, the economic and fiscal case for building 100,000 new social rented homes a year is UNANSWERABLE.

The Tory message on social housing: it's for 'losers'

July 9, 2015

By Monimbo

Social housing is 'subsidised' to the tune of £13 billion annually said George Osborne in his Budget. So 'it's time to act' on the higher earners who use these taxpayer-funded subsidies. In the Guardian, Zoe Williams says that his message is that the state is for losers. In the Sun, Osborne retorts that it's a simple matter of fairness.

Let's deal first with the dubious claim that social housing costs the taxpayer £13 billion per year. This calculation is based on social rents being on average £3,500 below market rent levels. But calling this a subsidy is to assume that it would make economic sense to raise rents to market levels. Not only would much of the saving be absorbed by increased housing benefits, but there would be a severe work disincentive effect. In other words, the potential savings are fictional. That this is obvious is clear from another Budget measure, to bring down social rents by one per cent per year. On the same logic as the 'subsidy' calculation, this should require even more tax-payer subsidy. But it turns out that the Office for Budget Responsibility thinks this will *save* money: indeed it will be 'the largest single measure' in savings in the housing benefit budget apart from the overall benefits freeze. What it will do, of course, is deter social landlords from building, but perhaps we are meant to be grateful that the threat of even more 'tax-payer subsidised housing' has been successfully thwarted by the Chancellor.

The pay-to-stay measure has another particularly nasty twist: while housing associations will be able to keep any extra income they collect, councils will have to pay it to the Treasury. While this may well be chicken feed, along with the enforced sale of high-value properties it is yet another way in which councils are being undermined. It adds another point to the list of government threats to social housing. Indeed, it also directly undercuts Grant Shapps' council housing finance reforms of three years ago, when he promised that from now on council housing would cease to be controlled by central government, and that councils would have the freedom to make local decisions and no longer have to 'pay their council house rents to Whitehall'. Even the coalition's official announcement on self-financing said that 'councils are best placed to make decisions about how they spend money they raise locally'. Can promises made while in coalition now be broken with impunity by the new government?

But Zoe Williams puts in the wider domain a thought which must preoccupy all those who support SHOUT's campaign for social housing: that the government's aim is to whittle away at the sector until only a rump remains, fit only for 'losers'. Under this scenario, better housing association property will be let at near-market rents to those who are earning half-decent incomes, but council housing that hasn't been sold off will be let at low rents aimed at those who will never learn their lessons from Iain Duncan Smith on how to stop being feckless.

One respected housing policy commentator said immediately on hearing Osborne's proposals that if we were going to adopt means-testing for social housing, the logical next step would for rents to be set as a percentage of incomes as in Canada and other countries where social housing is a residual sector. He added: '...which is also where we now look to be heading'.

In a prescient article on the role of social housing back in 2008, Mark Stephens described it as providing a 'safety net' in England rather than having the wider 'affordability' role that it has in several Northern European countries. While many housing professionals wanted social housing to cater for a broader range of income groups, the threat was a move in the opposite direction, to provide only an 'ambulance service'. As he pointed out, in several English-speaking countries (USA, Canada, Australia and the Republic of Ireland) the social sector is much smaller as a proportion of the stock, is specifically aimed at low-income families (often with some degree of means-testing) and may even cater especially for those with support needs (e.g. what the Tory government calls 'troubled families'). As the name suggests, the aim of an ambulance service is to move the patient on as quickly as possible, in this case into the private sector. Of course, in England such an aim is undermined by so-called 'lifetime' tenancies, which is why another of Osborne's proposals is to look into how they can be scrapped.

When pay-to-stay was originally proposed there was an excellent analysis of its effects by the Swindon Tenants Campaign Group. They called it a 'petty and stupid proposal' which would turn social housing into a tenure *only* for the poor'. Tenants don't want this, nor do councils or housing associations. Creating a totally false label that it is 'tax-payer subsidised housing' when other housing sectors are all subsidised is not accidental, it is a deliberate step towards reducing social housing to the 'ambulance service' that Mark Stephens warned us about. If less than a month ago it looked like social housing as we know it might be faced with either a slow death or a killer blow, after July 8 the prognosis looks even worse.

Jeremy Corbyn MP on Housing

August 4, 2015

London Labour Housing Group (LLHG) sent a questionnaire on 15 key housing policy issues to each of the four Labour Leadership Candidates and to each of the Deputy Leadership Candidates. We published all the responses on Red Brick. The response from Jeremy Corbyn became our most read blog post by far, a sign of the victory that was to come.

Jeremy Corbyn MP replies to LLHG's questions

LLHG: Britain is only building half of the homes we need annually. What specific measures will you take to increase house building?

JC: The key is to get local authorities building again. In the post-war decades they used to build approximately half of our homes until they were prevented from doing so – and it was then that we saw the gap between supply and demand opening up and reach its current crisis. Through local councils, regional government in London, devolved administrations and the Homes and Communities Agency a structure already exists that can deliver a large-scale council house building programme. Public investment to make this happen is vital; and would be a social and economic win-win. For every £1 spent on housing construction an extra £2.09 is generated in the economy, and ensuring we have a supply of homes for social rent is the only way in the long run to keep the housing benefit bill down. Lifting the borrowing cap in the Housing Revenue Account would mean local authorities could borrow up to the prudential limits and thereby build more homes. Returning to having regional home building targets is needed to ensure homes are built in every area, so that our rural areas benefit from building social homes as well as our urban centres.

We also need to look at bringing in a Land Value Tax (especially on undeveloped land with planning permission) and other 'use it or lose it' measures to act as a strong deterrent against land banking.

LLHG: How would you reform the private rented sector to make it more stable and affordable for tenants? Do you support: a. a national register of landlords; b. some form of rent regulation?

JC: Yes, everyone should have a decent home that they can afford. It is currently the case that we have one of least regulated private-rented markets in Europe and spiralling housing costs.

Private landlords should be nationally registered and locally licensed, including a 'fit and proper' persons' test, making sure that tenants' rights are respected and ensuring that decent homes standards – such as minimum safety standards, and being damp and pest free – are adhered to in the private rental sector. Licensing and registration should be administered and enforced by the relevant local authority. Some London Labour councils have already done some positive work in this area with the powers currently available to them, and it has been effective in moving against some of the worst offender landlords.

Regulation of private rents should be linked to what determines whether something is affordable – average earnings levels and increases, not the local market rate for housing. We need this, alongside large-scale house-building, to stop the social cleansing of London and other major cities. We should cap rents not benefits.

LLHG: Will you support the proposal, backed by former Labour Housing Minister John Healey MP, that we should aim to build 100,000 homes a year for social rent?

JC: We should invest in a large scale house building programme. We should be aiming for at least 100,000 homes a year available for social rent. We need to build an additional 240,000 homes a year just to meet current demand – and we know we have a long waiting list for social homes. If we tackle our housing crisis it would help address health, education and other inequalities, strengthen local communities and naturally lead to a fall in Housing Benefit expenditure. The recent report by Capital Economics for SHOUT made the unequivocal economic and financial case for building 100,000 homes a year for social rent. We can and must be ambitious.

LLHG: Will you support the removal of the HRA borrowing cap, to allow councils to borrow prudentially for investment in housing?

JC: Yes.

LLHG: Do you agree that estate regeneration schemes should involve no net reduction in supply of social rented homes?

JC: Yes. Estate redevelopments have led to an increase in housing units overall, but as your question highlights, those available for social rent have fallen in almost all schemes. Recent research published by Unite highlighted a loss of 8,000 social rented homes already through such schemes in London alone. This, along with Right to Buy eroding our social housing stock, and the government's plans to force councils to sell 'high-value' council homes on the open market when they become vacant, will effectively social cleanse whole areas of London and other cities. Estate redevelopments should instead be done for the benefit of existing and future residents, and local communities.

LLHG: Do you support the Right to Buy for council tenants and if so what reforms, if any, would you make to it? Do you support the extension of Right to Buy to Housing Association tenants?

JC: Right to Buy (RTB) has eroded our social housing stock, and directly contributed to the current housing crisis. If we are publicly investing in building much needed social housing then this shouldn't be converted to private wealth - one-third of all council homes are now owned by private landlords. We need to maintain the public investment in council housing for future tenants. We used to have security of tenure for council home tenants, meaning that despite not owning the property it was very much their home – in many cases for life. We should return to that.

I will vote against extending RTB to housing association properties, and would favour ending RTB full stop.

LLHG: Will you sign up to LLHG, Unite and the GMB's joint Our Homes Our London campaign against forcing councils to sell off properties in high values areas?

JC: Yes. It is important that all those who care about the future of social housing come together to oppose this policy. London needs mixed communities where low and medium paid workers can afford to live too.

LLHG: Do you support the Chancellor's decision to cut social rents by 1% per year?

JC: Cutting social rents by 1% a year will undoubtedly help many with low incomes who are struggling to make ends meet. But I don't believe that was the motivation for Osborne introducing this policy - otherwise he would impose such a regulation on the private rented sector too. It also is completely at odds with the government presumably continuing its policy of increasing rents for many new tenancies to so-called 'affordable' rents at up to 80% of the market rate. The Chancellor's move is a crude attempt to say they have 'cut' Housing Benefit expenditure, and distract from the policy of asking those with household incomes of above £40,000 in London (£30,000 elsewhere) to pay market, or near market rents. This will have a devastating impact on people, particularly in London and other inner city areas – forcing people from their homes just for earning over a certain amount, or possibly giving people a perverse incentive not to earn more if they have the option. It will undoubtedly come at the cost of building more homes for social rent in the current climate. It does nothing to address the underlying cause of the housing crisis.

LLHG: Do you support policies to switch resources rapidly from meeting the benefit costs of high rents to investing in new homes at genuinely affordable rents?

JC: Yes. The majority of spending on housing in this country used to be investment in affordable housing – now the vast majority is spent on housing benefit. We need to reverse this by investing in a large scale council house building programme which will bring rents and therefore housing benefit down overall. This will require upfront investment in new affordable homes – and as the Capital Economics report set out, investment in assets that will reduce housing benefit expenditure in the future is likely to be welcomed by financial markets. . We also need to look at reducing the £14 billion tax breaks going to private landlords, and redirecting that to fund house-building.

LLHG: Do you agree that affordable housing definition should be based on households not spending more than 30% of net income on housing costs?

JC: Yes, this links housing costs to what determines if something actually is affordable – peoples' incomes – rather than the wider market rates.

LLHG: Would you relax restrictions on building on the Green Belt?

JC: I would be very cautious about doing so. Developers will nearly always argue for the release of green belt land because it is easier for them compared to developing brownfield sites. But we don't simply want our towns sprawling outwards with reliance on cars growing – and the green belt has prevented that to a certain extent. Any widespread relaxations would also risk inflating the land values of green belt sites, without careful planning requirements being set in place first.

LLHG: Would you reverse permitted development rights allowing offices, shops, and other employment spaces in dense urban areas to change asset class and be converted into flats without planning permission?

JC: Yes. By not needing planning permission there cannot be an assessment and provision for the wider facilities and infrastructure that communities need. In residential conversions this of course includes affordable housing. It also includes transport, education, health facilities, leisure centres, green spaces, community centres, libraries and entertainment – all the things that bring people together in local areas to create sustainable communities.

LLHG: How would you secure more affordable housing contributions from private developers through the planning system? How would you change the current approach to viability?

JC: Viability studies are being used by private developers to evade their responsibilities to build more affordable housing. Especially in London these developers and particularly landowners are making extremely large profits from the building and selling of properties. At the moment, local authorities are faced with a large imbalance of power and resources when faced with a private developer who is determined not to include affordable housing in their build. In London, there is a role I believe for the GLA to have a central resource that local councils can call on to support them when faced with a private developer wielding viability studies that say affordable housing renders a whole scheme 'unviable'. This could include specialist support that is currently out of the reach of local councils.

LLHG: Would you support devolution to the Greater London Authority and city regions of control over: a. private rented sector regulation; b. Housing Association regulation; c. Right to Buy?

JC: As outlined above, I think that there needs to be a national framework for regulating our private rented sector, both landlords and rent, our Housing Associations and a national drive to increase house-building; council housing in particular. The implementation and enforcement of these schemes would then have to be done at city region and local council level. On Right to Buy, I think we should end it altogether but I recognise that there is very broad support for ending it as a mandatory right for tenants and instead for local authorities to be given the power to suspend or end Right to Buy in their local areas.

LLHG: Will you commit to restoring the previous Labour Government's homelessness safety net for priority groups and to improving support for single homeless people?

JC: Yes. Rough sleeping has increased by 55% in England since 2010, and by 78% in London. Evictions of private tenants are also at record levels.

There is no excuse for anyone to be homeless in one of the richest countries in the world – and we should restore access to housing benefit for all adults.

A bitter pill to swallow

December 11, 2015

I had intended not to write any blogposts during my extended visit to the antipodes this winter. But the addition of new clauses at very short notice to the Housing and Planning Bill which introduce 'mandatory fixed term tenancies' of 2 to 5 years and end security of tenure for new council tenants touches a raw nerve for me. This is a smash and grab raid, stealing a core right from tenants with no real opportunity for debate outside the Bill committee. I am delighted Labour has opposed the change forcefully.

The policy, and the stealth with which it has been introduced, is symbolic of the contempt and loathing this government shows for people on low incomes. They can be moved around like pieces on a chess board to suit the convenience of the government and landlords, or at least be kept in a state of uncertainty as their ability to stay in their home while they are 'reviewed' by a housing officer in what will feel like an arbitrary manner. They must not be allowed to settle, to integrate into communities, to put down roots, to provide stability for their children, to build successful lives for themselves.

For people like me, who associate our own 'social mobility' with the platform of security and stability achieved by our families due to living in council housing, this is a bitter pill to swallow.

The Tories are not the only people to blame, of course. During her short period as housing minister, Caroline Flint flirted with this idea as well, and plenty of housing 'professionals' have made the case for ending what they like to call 'lifetime tenancies' – an invented term, quickly picked up by Grant Shapps to make the whole business seem unreasonable. Even now the ethically impoverished National Housing Federation can't bring itself to defend what remain of tenants' rights: their argument is that housing associations should be able to let 'their' homes to whoever they like and on whatever terms they like. At present they have got their way: the new fixed term tenancy model will apply only to councils while the government continues to work out what to do about the reclassification of housing associations as public sector for the purpose of defining public borrowing.

The story of security of tenure for council tenants is one of bitter struggle. Councils have not always been benign landlords. Even when they wanted to build a lot of council housing to help emancipate the working class they often managed the homes with a rod of iron. They never really shed the mantle of Octavia Hill and consumer rights were a foreign land. Some used the threat of eviction to exert social control and to separate the deserving from the undeserving poor. Labour eventually listened to the case for a charter of tenants' rights and the Callaghan government sought to enact security of tenure, balanced by strong grounds for possession. Unlikely as it now seems, it was the Thatcher government that put 'secure tenancies' into law in the 1980 Act, picking up the Labour legislation and realising quickly that secure tenancies were a necessary foundation for the 'right to buy'. Thatcher had an ulterior motive, but the tenants' charter came into existence and brought with it a profound change in the style of housing management, more considered, more balanced, more respectful, more participative, and, when eviction was thought necessary, more evidence-based requiring a judgement in a court of law. Secure tenancies underpinned the modernisation of the social housing sector, even leading eventually (and regrettably) to tenants being called 'customers'.

Social rented housing is our most precious housing asset. It's existence broke the historic inevitability that people on low incomes and vulnerable people would also endure homelessness and dreadful housing conditions. It removed the blight of bad housing from generations of children. In my view it was the strongest mechanism of all to achieve genuine social mobility and to give children born into poor families similar opportunities to those enjoyed by better-off families. Many of the key tensions around social housing – the most controversial being who gets it, and who doesn't – arise not from failure but from its success and popularity and the shortage of supply.

Of course the government and big parts of the housing industry will seek to pacify opponents of the change. It will be helpful to tenants, they say, to have their tenancies reviewed every 2 or 5 years. Most will be renewed, they say. Well, what is the point of that? The policy fails in either direction. If non-renewal is the primary outcome, the vast majority of tenants will end up in private renting, far less suitable for families and more expensive for tenants and the state. If most fixed term tenancies are renewed, the policy will not achieve its purpose of getting more turnover to create more space for new tenants. The argument that the government is trying to make that people will be helped into owner occupation is, well, pants. A few more will exercise the right to buy, but where is the justice in that? Remain a tenant and get kicked out, buy and you can stay.

We now have a sector that, instead of managing estates effectively and helping tenants to progress in their lives, will be collecting vast quantities of data about their incomes in case they are 'high earning' (£30k per household), monitoring what they get up to so they can review their tenancy every few years, and of course checking the immigration status of new tenants to boot. The new Victorians are firmly in charge.

There is an old saying that to incentivise the rich you have to make them richer, to incentivise the poor you have to make them poorer. This is now writ large in housing. If you are or are able to become a home owner, all manner of gifts – let's call them subsidies – will be showered on you. The Prime Minister will talk endlessly about the important security and stability that being a home owner gives you, and that this in turn creates the conditions for social advancement. Meanwhile, if you are a social tenant, you will be accused of being subsidised even when you are not, your ability to pay your rent will be constantly threatened by bedroom tax or benefit caps or benefit sanctions, you will be denigrated and demonised in the media, and your ability to stay in your home will be subject to the whim of a landlord even if you meet all the terms of your tenancy.

Security for me and not for you. Subsidy for me and not for you. Social status for me and not for you. Insecurity at work and now at home. A two nation government without a doubt.

2016

Land ahoy!

February 25, 2016

Radical solutions to the housing crisis must focus on land

A new report from the London Assembly[1] has taken a good look at the question of land and has recommended a clear route forward for the next London mayor to move towards introducing a Land Value Tax (LVT). The report proposes a step by step approach with an initial review of the powers that would be necessary for LVT to replace council tax, business rates and stamp duty land tax; an economic feasibility study to model the likely yield of LVT compared to the other taxes; and, if the study is positive, a trial of LVT in a geographically defined area of London.

The report rehearses the reasons behind the need for a radical new departure that has the potential to release far more land for productive use to meet the needs of a city that is growing rapidly in population and requiring the regeneration of many of its older neighbourhoods. It argues that new mechanisms are needed to fund London's growth – which will continue to feed land and property inflation under current policies. And it argues that LVT would match the current appetite for devolution – with even the current mayor arguing for London to have considerably greater tax-raising powers and the Government already agreeing to devolve business rates by 2020.

As others have before, the report illustrates how the existing structure of property taxation encourages inefficient use of land and deters development. Council tax fails to deal with high value land, business rates fail to address unused land and taxes productive enterprises instead, and stamp duty is a disincentive to land sales.

LVT is defined by the report to be *'a tax on land, payable by the landowner, at a rate of tax which is determined by the value of the land in its 'optimum use' (as decided by a public authority) as opposed to its actual or current use'*. There would be a clear incentive to bring forward under-utilised land and the tax has the potential to reduce reliance on Whitehall funding and could lead to substantial community benefits when land values increase following public investment.

There is considerable public support for stronger action to be taken against land banking and against corporations which hold land simply to let it accrue in value without penalty. The report estimates that there are around 2,000 brownfield sites in London that may be available for development, comprising about 2% of the land area. It also comments that almost half the notionally available sites in London were held by those who had no incentive or intention to build. Based on the GLA's Strategic Housing Land Availability Assessment (SHLAA) in 2012, land classified as 'potential housing land' could accommodate 276,000 new homes, equivalent to 7 years extra housing supply.

The theory behind the merits of land taxation is straightforward. Unlike other assets, land has borne no cost of production and it only has value because of its scarcity. As the report says, *'land value owes nothing to individual effort and everything to the community at large'*. The tax is transparent and the asset it taxes is unmoveable – it cannot be shifted to the Cayman Islands!

The report notes that the modern case for a land tax can be traced back to Winston Churchill in 1909. He argued that landowners should be taxed on the benefits they accrue from external developments, which have been provided by the labour, investment and tax payments of others, often through public investment. Although developers do make section 106 and Community Infrastructure Levy payments, these represent only a small fraction of the uplift gained, for example, by new transport infrastructure. If owners of underused or vacant land paid more through a more broadly based land tax, ordinary taxpayers would be required to pay less.

The GLA report is frank about the objections that have been made about LVT. There are significant challenges in introducing any new tax and making it operationally workable. Many of these are practical around identifying ownership but the idea of 'optimum' land use is new and potentially complex, and existing land value is often a moveable feast depending on the variable potential value of different developments. It is also frank about the political challenge, pointing out the ridiculous position where council tax is still based on 1991 values due to the perceived political risk of revaluation. The switch would create substantial winners and losers, and the losers will be able to afford lawyers and lobbyists! It therefore identifies some alternatives that have been suggested such as a specific derelict land tax and a system based on incentives rather than taxation, as well as better use of the mayor's existing powers, including the power to set up area development corporations like for Old Oak and Park Royal.

The approach recommended is therefore gradual and based on a series of investigatory steps, clarifying issues and working towards holding a pilot. But it concludes that the political context is right – a desperate housing shortage, housing becoming a serious brake on growth, and a strong move towards the devolution of powers to elected mayors. For those like me who have long supported the idea of land taxation whilst being doubtful about its political deliverability, this report and its careful approach makes a lot of sense.

[1] *Tax trial: A Land Value Tax for London?, published by the London Assembly Planning Committee in February 2016*

Harold Wilson – a housing hero

March 11, 2016

Today is the centenary of the birth of Harold Wilson, winner of four General Elections and Prime Minister for eight years in the 1960s and 1970s.

So why would we celebrate Harold Wilson on a housing blog?

The answer is simple: as PM in the 1960s he achieved the best housebuilding figures in the last century. He achieved that rare double: hitting a peak in both public and private housebuilding at the same time. The outcome – over 400,000 new homes in one year – is enough to make the modern housing enthusiast's eyes water.

Housing was a big deal in Wilson's 1964 and 1966 administrations. The 1964 Manifesto was replete with housing proposals. Development land would be publicly owned and profits retained by the community. Interest rates for housing borrowers would be subsidised and councils would be able to make 100% mortgages available. The Rent Acts would be repealed, old houses would be modernised, and if landlords failed to do so they would be purchased by the council. The 1966 Manifesto set the target of 500,000 houses a year – sadly 'only' 400,000 was attained.

It was not just about housebuilding; the Government was committed to encouraging home ownership, and introduced the Option Mortgage Scheme to enable low income households to benefit from the tax relief policy that benefitted other home owners. There was a new departure in terms of area improvement of older housing: the introduction of General Improvement Areas. One policy that I would see as an error in the subsequent highly inflationary era is that an attempt was made to stimulate the housebuilding industry by exempting house owners from capital gains tax.

Harold Wilson Speech to party Conference 1965:

"We had promised to repeal the Tory Rent Act, to provide new machinery for fixing fair rents, and to give Government and all others who required them, the powers they needed to fight the evils of Rachmanism. That Bill is through the Commons despite Tory obstruction. It is in the Lords - within a week of Parliament meeting again, we intend it to become law.

"It was on the Bill to restore security of tenure, and it was on the Rent Bill that our new Members, not I imagine to their surprise, saw the full virulence of Tory Opposition tactics when the Tories were fighting for something near and dear to them, the rights of landlords and property interests."

By 1974, when two elections were won in a year, the economic prospects were much reduced. The February Manifesto however repeated the radical approach to housing: promising to repeal the Tory Housing Finance Act (which had led to rent strikes), to control rents and introduce protection from eviction for furnished private tenants, to start the 'municipalisation' of private renting, and to significantly increase subsidies to all housebuilding.

At the time I was working with tenants in Paddington, and I recall the short minority administration in 1974 for being remarkably radical: it felt that the Government was really taking the issue seriously. For example, in that one year it increased subsidy for council housebuilding by £350million – curiously the same cash figure suggested this week – more than forty years later - by the Kerslake Commission on housing in London (how small our ambitions are these days!). It also introduced a rent freeze and created Housing Action Areas – thereby keeping me busy for the following few years!

The Manifesto for the October 1974 election contained the commitment to give security of tenure to council tenants – a huge advance but not actually enacted until after Labour went out of office in 1979 when the Tories found that a stronger definition of a council tenancy was a helpful platform for the introduction of the right to buy. It also repeated the promise to introduce land reform, essentially the 'nationalisation' of development land, and this time it was enacted, in 1976 along with the Development Land Tax legislation, but critically, by the time it was on the statute books it was much watered down and we had entered the more austere late 70s economic climate, and it was never really implemented.

Wilson's resignation in 1975 came before the 1976 'IMF crisis' which put many progressive policies, including housing, into reverse. I see 1976 and not the usual

1979 as the watershed year in the UK when sound progress on most fronts was no longer to be achieved.

Of course, Wilson should not get all of the credit for the good things or all the brickbats for the bad – there were a succession of Ministers who did the detail. But he set a tone for Government, he oversaw radical commitments in manifestoes and he worked diligently to deliver them. Both the commitments and the delivery put our current politics to shame.

Wilson died in 1995 suffering from both cancer and Alzheimer's disease. He was the iconic figure for me growing up and developing an interest in Labour politics and housing – indeed I joined the Labour Party in response to his defeat by Heath in 1970, which was a devastating blow.

Government support for the private market is more than double its spending on affordable homes

March 20, 2016

By Monimbo

The new UK Housing Review 2016 puts together figures you won't find anywhere else: the government's investment plans for housing and how they split between supporting the private market and building affordable homes. They show that the different market-support packages like Help to Buy and starter homes now total £43 billion, whereas affordable investment totals only £18 billion. The CIH concludes that, as a result, investment in affordable renting 'will fall to its lowest levels since the Second World War'.

Red Brick has already picked holes in the Chancellor's 'long-term economic plan'. Insofar as he has one, it seems to be unravelling before our eyes. But if at last he's being criticised for robbing the poor to pay the rich, the criticism hasn't yet affected his housing plans, where the shift away from affordable renting towards helping builders and would-be home owners becomes more marked each time one of his 'long-term plans' is scrapped and another put in its place. As the UK Housing Review reveals, whereas the current Affordable Homes Programme, that began last April and extends to 2018, was originally to have invested £2.9 billion, this has now been cut back to just £1.8 billion. The promises made in the 2013 Spending Review (another one of Osborne's 'long-term plans') have been ditched, and what's left of the programme is confined to schemes already committed by the HCA and GLA. The rest of the money has been scooped into the Chancellor's pot for supporting home ownership.

One effect of past policies has, of course, been a remarkable shift towards homes let at so-called Affordable Rents. By April last year there were 123,264 of them, almost five per cent of housing association stock, of which less than a third were newly built and the rest were conversions or acquisitions. This has inevitably produced a big shift away from building homes to let at social rents. The result is that while in England there were 4,063,000 social rented homes in 2012, by 2015 this had dropped to 3,967,000, a fall of two per cent. CIH projects that by 2020 the loss will have reached 350,000, a nine per cent fall since 2012. This will be a result of further conversions, right to buy sales, demolitions (due to be ramped up estate regeneration plans if they come to fruition) and sales of 'high-value' stock. Of course, the scale of some of these changes can, as yet, only be guessed at, and the figures will be refined as more details are revealed.

The odd thing is that, if Affordable Rent was a key part of an earlier 'long-term plan', it's now been ditched. With the curtailing of the current Affordable Homes Programme, there is likely to be a drastic fall in output of sub-market rented homes over the next couple of years: Affordable Rent is due to follow social rent into the housing policy dustbin. The main replacement policy is, of course, the promotion of starter homes. The image of the 'subsidy sandwich' provided by Inside Housing earlier this month nicely captures how various layers of government money are being put together to construct this huge stimulus to developers and to house prices, all justified by labelling £450,000 starter homes as 'affordable'. As Nicky Gavron commented recently, the Tories have made 'affordable housing' a meaningless term.

Unfortunately, the effects are not just rhetorical: starter homes and shared ownership properties can be substituted by developers for social and Affordable Rent dwellings when negotiating 'section 106' agreements as part of planning permissions. It so happens that section 106 is one of the last remaining sources of funding for new homes at social rents: even that source is now to be cut off.

Although 2,410 social rented homes were started on site in 2014/15, it's likely that starts in the year now ending will be lower and in the next year lower still. Soon, any production of homes let at social rent will depend on social landlords' own funding – which is just being reduced as a result of the one per cent cut in rents that starts next month. If Osborne stays in charge, it seems his latest 'long-term plan' is not only to stop providing sub-market rented homes, but to get rid of those we still have as quickly as possible. As the UK Housing Review's analysis and projections show, a dramatic shift in housing policy is about to begin.

Is this how to deliver a 'One Nation' housing policy?

July 24, 2016

By Monimbo

Will Policy Exchange still be the go-to think tank for housing policy under this government as it was for Cameron's? The latest contribution to the post-Brexit housing debate comes from Alex Morton, formerly of PE and behind several of the ideas that the last government adopted, notably the sale of high-value council houses. When he left PE in 2013 he moved to No.10 as housing adviser, until April this year when he jumped ship to become a lobbyist.

His advice to Theresa May on delivering her One Nation housing policy will, however, probably be ignored. In a rambling piece that's riddled through with his distaste for local government, Morton offers few new ideas and is largely negative. His first point, that 'the key structures are broken' is hardly an inviting one, especially as it turns out that the main villains of the piece aren't (say) developers who build at a pace that suits their profits but are – yes you guessed it – local authorities. And their main failure is to create over-elaborate local plans that are invariably behind time and fail to prioritise housing. He claims that 'over 300 councils failed to oversee delivery of housing need', which means there are precious few that do.

This obvious exaggeration ignores the dual pressures that council planning departments face – to deliver plans and to administer development control – with steeply falling resources. In 2009/10, councils spent £2.3 billion on planning: spending is now less than half of that, at just over £1 billion. It is hardly surprising that many councils – particularly smaller ones – struggle to provide even the minimum service expected of them. Of course there is underperformance, and some councils have no doubt cut planning staff more than they should so as to maintain spending on, say, homelessness. But no government can expect to have a first class planning system when its resources have been decimated.

Morton's ire is then turned on central government, for failing to introduce the reforms he thinks are needed. He offers grudging praise for some of the changes to the planning system 'since 2015', but doesn't acknowledge that planning policies about housing (especially affordable housing) have been the subject of constant tinkering for the last five years, which has hardly helped to achieve consistent decision-making. In any case, firing random shots at the planning sector is hardly helpful to a government looking for 'One Nation' policies.

Morton's dislike of councils extends, too, to housing associations, who are said to gobble up twice as much grant to build rented homes as the government now spends on shared ownership properties. He ignores the savings in housing benefit this achieves, despite there now being plentiful sources of research to remind him. But he gets his sums wrong anyway – the government is planning to spend £4.1 billion to build 135,000 homes for shared ownership, that's an average grant of £30,000 a piece compared with £27,800 for Affordable Rent dwellings in the current programme that's being run down.

To be fair, he makes the worthwhile point that stoking up demand (as the previous Chancellor did) is unlikely to stimulate more supply. But he seems to think that councils could secure much more private development even though there is little plausible evidence that councils in general (as opposed to specific cases) are frustrating developments that would otherwise take place.

At this point, Morton's argument gets confusing, because although he seems to be opposed to measures that stimulate demand (like Help to Buy, presumably) he's all in favour of more home ownership. This is because it is a) popular, b) what voters worry about and c) necessary for the very survival of the Conservative Party. He's no doubt right about all these points. But a 'One Nation' policy surely (by definition?) has to be directed as much at those who can't buy (however much they might like to) as to those who can, albeit with some help. The current policy is hugely unbalanced, as Red Brick has pointed out regularly, including as recently as last month. If Theresa May genuinely wants a policy that addresses a wide spectrum of needs, she needs to change the government's priorities and recognise that many young households aren't able to buy in any conceivable circumstances, in part because they have to spend so much on rent that they'll never have the necessary deposit.

It just so happens that the new communities secretary, Sajid Javid, has the perfect excuse to reappraise the investment programme, given the likelihood of a post-referendum recession which will make it harder to sell market-oriented products and in which the construction industry may hit the doldrums. He's just been sent detailed recommendations from the NHF and CIH on what could be done. Let's hope he pays more attention to some of the advice he's getting from those who want a more balanced programme and have experience of delivering one, even though their views are dismissed by Alex Morton as belonging to 'vested interests'.

Troubled families: a tale of Cameron's prejudice and hubris

October 18, 2016

Back in 2012 Red Brick dubbed the Government's **'Troubled Families'** programme *'policy-based evidence making'*. The newly-released (and sneaked out) evaluation[1] of the billion pound programme proves our point. Despite constant claims by Government that the programme was 'turning round' the lives of hundreds of thousands of families – to the point that they massively expanded the scheme after a couple of years – the much-delayed evaluation report says the programme had *'**no measurable impact**'*.

This is no surprise – if you set something up on a completely false premise you get the wrong outcomes. To justify the policy, Government took a range of statistics that reflected the disadvantage suffered by some families and misrepresented them as showing that the families were dysfunctional – not the victims of economic and social reality, or mental incapacity, or disability, or abuse, or bad housing, or poverty, but to blame for their own social pathology. They were feckless and the Government was going to force more feck on them. It enabled the Tories to stigmatise and demonise a group of families as being responsible for social breakdown and even for the riots.

Much as the media are intrigued by the unusual (for a senior civil servant) personality of the 'Tsar' appointed to run the programme, Louise Casey, the Troubled Families policy was another catastrophic failure by David Cameron.

Cameron was an extremely judgemental man, and many of his judgements were plain wrong. *'You're talking about blame'*, he said, *'about good behaviour and bad behaviour, about morals.'* He called it the *'Shameless culture'*. His launch speech was full of stereotypes ripped from the pages of the Daily Mail – sink schools, sink estates, choosing to live on the dole, rampaging teenagers. And the big lie: these families had been subjected to *'compassionate cruelty, swamped with bureaucracy, smothered in welfare yet never able to escape.'*

I wrote on Red Brick at the time: *'Ultimately (it) reads like a script from the loathsome Jeremy Kyle Show: pointing at the Chavs and moralising about their sub-human behaviour.'* And it achieved one of its early aims: good media coverage, with the Daily Mail of course talking about the *'Criminal culture at the heart of feckless families: Shocking report lifts lid on incest, abuse and spiral of alcohol abuse'*.

"The fundamental flaw in the analysis – that the government was taking a set of families who were undeniably poor and disadvantaged, and redefining them – without a shred of evidence – as dysfunctional and antisocial." - Jonathan Portes

Of course, there were good points about service delivery which will strike a chord with anyone who has been worked with 'multiply deprived' families. Too many agencies, too little coordination despite too many meetings, a failure to work with each family holistically, family plans that never get delivered, bizarre rules to access services. And the central solution – a key worker for each family – offered some hope that the system, if not the family, could be turned around.

The failure of the original analysis, and the use and abuse of statistics, was compounded by setting up the project on a 'payment by results' basis and an extraordinarily low threshold for allowing councils to say that a family had been 'turned around'. If a child attends school a bit more often, probably coincidentally to any intervention, and the Government gives a cash-strapped council some money for it, guess what the outcome is? Yes, the headline claim that the Government turned round more than 105,000 troubled families, saving taxpayers an estimated £1.2 billion. And as Jonathan Portes of the NIESR, part of the evaluation team, says: *'This was untrue: the £1.2 billion is pure, unadulterated fiction.'*

Desperate for cash, councils ran rings round a complicit Government, and a programme with no measurable outcomes was deemed a success by all involved. Like Boris Johnson's Garden Bridge, this was David Cameron's vanity project designed to sort a problem that was defined by his own prejudice. We all pay and no one benefits. And just like Boris, not one word of apology: in the post-truth world one Government Minister even had the audacity to write an article over the weekend claiming that the programme had worked.

The real failure was that Cameron's politics and his hubris meant that a large sum of money that could have been used to genuinely help families facing real problems was squandered.

Search the Red Brick site for 'troubled families' and see the full series of five articles on this programme as the story unfolded: Eric's Troubled Families, Policy-based evidence making, Jeremy Kyle and the Zombie statistic, I'm troubled and I don't know why, and this one.

[1] *National Evaluation of the Troubled Families Programme: Final Synthesis Report, published by the Department for Communities and Local Government in October 2016*

Still '500 miles' from home, today it is 50 years since Cathy

November 16, 2016

The film **Cathy Come Home***, directed by Ken Loach and written by Jeremy Sandford, is highly recommended if you have never seen it. The credits track was* **'500 miles from my home'** *by Sonny & Cher, hence the title of this piece.*

50 years ago today the BBC screened 'Cathy Come Home' as one of its series of Wednesday Plays.

I remember it as if it was yesterday. I was 16 and I have more memories of 1966 than of any other year of my childhood or youth – the World Cup, 'O' Levels, Aberfan, the escalation in Vietnam, the first General Election I paid attention to, the Moors murder trial, the Rhodesia crisis, Revolver by the Beatles (Dylan's Blonde on Blonde was also released but I wasn't aware of it at the time). **And Cathy........**

I have seen the film dozens of times (it was a regular feature when I used to give talks while working for Shelter in the 1980s) but it is hard to explain the impact the first showing had. Years later it was voted the 'best single television drama' and 'the UK's most influential TV programme of all time'. Twelve million people watched it that first night, about a quarter of the population. No-one had ever seen anything like it, it was so realistic. And genuinely shocking. It felt like everyone had watched that Wednesday Play, and everyone talked about it the next day. No single TV programme could have that kind of impact today, with hundreds of channels and many other distractions.

My Dad was a plasterer, in work nearly all the time, my Mam a part-time cleaner, and we could hardly be described as well off. We lived in a council house – a Bevan house – on the large Montagu estate near what was then the northern city boundary of Newcastle. The house was of an amazingly high standard, front and back gardens that were my Dad's pride and joy, and at the top of the road the Kenton Bar was the last building before open countryside stretching all the way to Cheviot. It could be tough, but it was a great place to grow up. Until I saw the film it was unimaginable to me that people like Cathy could exist or that stories like hers were possible. All she ever needed was the one thing we had – an affordable council house, a secure and comfortable base on which to build a life.

There was little public consciousness of homelessness prior to the film, and the revelation that homelessness could lead to children being taken away from their family was shocking. It is so shaming that the number of homeless people is vastly bigger now. Ken Loach's latest film, 'I, Daniel Blake', is also having a serious impact and shows how little some things have changed. Its theme has echoes of Cathy. The circumstances are different, but the core story is the same: a decline from a contented and stable life into poverty, caused by ill health (Daniel's heart attack and Reg's accident at work), the experience of state institutions that punish rather than support, ending in destitution and total break-down.

I met Ken Loach when I worked at Shelter in the 1980s, I think introduced by Des Wilson, the founding Shelter Director. I tried to interest him in doing another film on housing and showed him around the sights of Paddington, the dozens of bed and breakfast hotels housing homeless families in Bayswater, the huge and squalid multi-occupation terraces of Sutherland Avenue and the rapidly deteriorating Mozart Estate, then only 10 years old but already neglected by Westminster Council. He didn't bite but proved to be both charming and quite hostile to the very idea of soggy liberal housing charities (something that made more sense as his own political position became better known). There ended my career as the second Jeremy Sandford.

50 years since Cathy means that the 50th anniversary of Shelter is imminent. The two were widely assumed to be linked but in fact it was just a remarkable coincidence that Shelter was launched a few days after the film was shown. It still gave Shelter huge impetus. Now a large organisation providing vital advice services, it seems to have lost some of its campaigning edge and punches below its weight in terms of influencing public attitudes and Government policy.

Cathy was the start of my political awakening, an event in my teens only matched by reading Robert Tressell's 'The Ragged-Trousered Philanthropists' and being exposed to 'ideas' at University that converted my working class chip into a vague leftish philosophy. I have suffered periods of optimism since – 1974 especially, and 1997. But the 50th anniversary of Cathy, the resurgence of homelessness matched by the apparent indifference of much of UK Housing, Labour's divisions and ineffectuality, all in the context of a global resurgence in nationalism and intolerance, make me feel that I have been deluded for fifty years in thinking that, as day follows night, each generation will do better than the last.

2017

Trump will be bad for housing too

January 1, 2017

By Monimbo

If social housing provision in the United States is already highly marginalised, it's due to get worse under the next president as budgets are hacked back. And the appointment of the new secretary for housing could be the worst news of all.

Social housing in the US caters for barely one per cent of households, and is disproportionately occupied by the very poor, with one-third earning less than $10,000 per year. Nearly half of tenants are black, even though black people make up only 19 per cent of the population overall. But the Housing and Urban Development department, HUD, has a budget of $47 billion overall, because its housing voucher programme assists millions more poor households in the private rented sector. With the focus of its spending so strongly on the poorest and on black communities, it's easy to see it as a potential target for Trump's budget cuts.

Traditionally HUD has been a low-key cabinet post awarded to a competent administrator (the incumbent is Julian Castro, a Clinton supporter and former city mayor). Even previous Republican presidents usually put it in safe hands. But Trump has appointed the uniquely unqualified Ben Carson to be the new secretary, a man whom even his friends describe as having 'no government experience' or ability to run a federal agency. However, Carson does have one characteristic that may have suggested to Trump that he was right for the post: he's black, and originally from a poor background. Perhaps because of this he was initially thought to be the only pick for the HUD position who had actually lived in a public housing scheme (it later turned out he hadn't).

What he does have, apart from his 'gifted hands' as a highly competent brain surgeon, is a strong commitment to small government that means he's hardly likely to fight for the bigger budget that HUD badly needs. At present, almost all new rented housing is created for middle-income earners and above. Despite being a person of colour, Carson's on record as opposing Obama's attempts to get HUD to put more social housing in wealthier neighbourhoods and to challenge discriminatory practices that the agency has tolerated. Obama, according to Carson, is guilty not just of social engineering but of failed socialism. In the UK we would call it trying to create mixed communities. In the US the principles are enshrined in the Fair Housing Act, and it would be an extraordinary irony if it were a black housing secretary that had to be taken to court for failing to observe this particular law, because of his belief that poor people must continue to live in poor areas.

Indeed, Carson's priorities, if he follows them when he takes up the HUD post later this month, could hardly be more misplaced. Federal housing policy has in key respects been a disaster for the poor and for minorities in particular. The failed, state-backed mortgage giant Fannie Mae was guilty of leaving many poor households destitute as a result of the crisis in and collapse of the 'sub-prime' mortgage market in which it had had a major role. Empty homes that have been foreclosed (repossessed) are often mismanaged, especially those located in poor areas, making it more likely that the former owners are still in debt and unable to obtain new credit. Homelessness has surged: more than half a million people are living on the streets, in their cars or in official shelters. Several cities, such as San Francisco and St Louis, seem to have decided to launch a war on the homeless rather than on homelessness. At the same time, social housing is far too small a sector to cater for the millions in need who are, of course, now much less likely to ever become home owners. New housing policies, like those which Bill de Blasio is pushing in New York (as covered by Red Brick in 2014), are needed across the United States.

The incoming housing secretary, however, believes that 'poverty is really more of a choice than anything else'. Oh, and he doesn't believe in evolution either, or that abortion should be permitted in any circumstances, and he thinks that gun control in pre-war Germany may have fostered the rise of Hitler and produced the holocaust. He was also the would-be presidential candidate with an unusual theory about the origin of the pyramids, leading one person to tweet that 'it's amazing how one can be a neurosurgeon and a dimwit at the same time'. Welcome to the Department of Housing and Urban Development, Ben Carson.

Radical solutions to the housing supply crisis – or just common sense?

February 16, 2017

Duncan Bowie displays his encyclopaedic knowledge of planning and housing in his excellent new book *'Radical Solutions to the Housing Supply Crisis'*, much of which is derived from the work of the *'Highbury Group'* of planning academics and practitioners that he convenes.

Bowie takes a long view of the housing supply crisis, looking back at the inadequate policies of governments of both persuasions over several decades. He sees 'ideological continuities' in policy since the 1970s but reserves his particular ire for the current Government's policies as contained in the 2016 Housing and Planning Act. He criticises all governments for giving over-riding priority to the promotion of home ownership at the expense of a broader and deeper housing strategy. Even in its own terms the fixation with home ownership has failed over the last dozen years, as home ownership has declined, but this has brought about little apparent change in thinking. He criticises the long-term switch from subsidising bricks and mortar (investment) to personal subsidies (housing benefit) and, even worse, to self-defeating subsidies designed to stimulate demand for home ownership. He criticises government approaches to the planning system for making private capital more powerful and the public sector weaker and more reactive and argues that 'localism' cannot deliver social justice. He traces the growing abuse of the term 'affordable', which has been taken to Orwellian levels in last week's White Paper ("War is peace. Freedom is slavery. Ignorance is strength. Unaffordable is affordable." he might have said.)

Bowie's book is an interesting read from the start, full of policy scrutiny, but the book comes alive when he moves on to make a passionate case for a wholly new strategy. Based on a set of principles derived from the historical analysis, he makes the case for a much larger number of new homes, but he puts the strongest emphasis on homes being genuinely affordable. The first action of a new government should be to switch subsidies from market or slightly sub-market provision to social rented homes at 'target' rents. In the long term, over a period of thirty years, funding should be switched gradually from personal subsidies to investment subsidies, providing housing that is genuinely affordable. Instead of counting anything which is in the slightest sub-market, as the White Paper does, Bowie reverts to the definition contained in the first (Livingstone) London Plan that housing costs should not exceed 30% of the net household income of the lowest quartile households. However, his central case is for a new spatial planning system with a National Spatial Plan and effective structures at regional, city region and local levels, with significantly stronger requirements for collaboration between authorities - effectively allowing a 'right to grow'. He argues for a much clearer relationship between local plans and neighbourhood plans, avoiding the latter becoming a mechanism by which wealthy residential populations protect themselves from development that might benefit disadvantaged people. He also makes the case for councils taking an equity stake in larger new developments, looking to benefit from long term capital appreciation rather than initial levies.

As you would expect, Bowie does not duck the question of land. He supports Labour's Lyons Commission proposal that there should be a cap on the value that can be gained by a landowner, for example when agricultural land is rezoned for housing, with the land coming into public ownership where necessary (eg if it remains unused). Published planning policies and conditions should aim to minimise land price inflation based on 'hope' value. Viability assessments, where needed, should be fully transparent, and he argues that taking development taxes (whatever system is used) at the point that the increased value is realised rather than when schemes are started would help developers to bring forward more schemes. Public land should be released for housing on the basis of meeting defined public objectives rather than just being put up for market sale, and councils should have far more flexible powers to undertake prudential borrowing for their own developments. Property taxes generally, he argues, need urgent reform, especially the hugely out-of-date council tax valuation system. Stamp duty hits households when they are at their most extended and there is a much stronger case for a tax on capital gain on disposal, starting at a high threshold to avoid penalising people on the margins of home ownership. Reforms to other taxes that impact on property, like inheritance tax, are also considered.

The current chronic lack of housing provision has been four decades in the making and will take many years to put right. Bowie's central case is that wholesale radical reform is essential which will bring about an integrated approach between housing, planning, land, taxation and social security. It will be possible to argue about the nuances of every point, but it is rare to see such a clear programme of action proposed in one slim volume (and there isn't space in a short review to mention many important points).

The book could be called 'common sense solutions' rather than 'radical solutions' because almost everyone knows that these issues must be tackled at some point. But can they become a winning programme for a future Labour Government? Proposals like applying capital gains tax to first homes would meet a hysterical reaction even if there are clear offsets like abolishing stamp duty. Council tax reform has been avoided by every party for the last thirty years due to fear of adverse reaction (even if gainers and losers cancel each other out). The housing supply problem will not be solved by a cautious approach, but our political and media culture induces panic unless proposals are carefully worked out and presented convincingly and with enough conviction to overcome the inevitable reactionary storm. After Lyons, and with contributions like this one, Labour now has an excellent stock of possible policies to put together into a strategy. The earlier that task is undertaken the more time there will be to convince the public. A bold approach to housing could be key to turning Labour's fortunes.

A basic right of citizenship

February 23, 2017

This week saw the 40th anniversary of the death of Anthony Crosland. *He served as a Cabinet Minister in the 1960s and 1970s Labour Governments, including as Foreign Secretary (dying in Office in 1977), President of the Board of Trade, Environment Secretary, and Education Secretary, where he made great strides towards comprehensive education.*

Normally regarded as a Gaitskellite revisionist, Crosland's famous book The Future of Socialism, published in 1956, had a great influence on me when I read it in the 1970s. His central contention was that socialism should be about 'ends' not 'means'; it should not be equated simply with the ownership of the means of production but should be judged by its contribution to ending poverty and improving the lives and prospects of ordinary people through the provision of the high-quality public services across the board. His beliefs were put into practice as Education Secretary through his determination to replace Grammar Schools with a system of properly funded local Comprehensives, and as Environment Secretary in the 1974 minority Labour Government when he pursued a progressive housing policy.

Crosland also wrote a seminal Fabian pamphlet in 1971 called *'Towards a Labour Housing Policy.'* (Herbert Morrison Memorial Lecture, Fabian Tract 410, available in the LSE Digital Library). This pamphlet was hugely influential at the time, but it also has many resonances today.

Writing more than a year into the Heath Government, Crosland reflected on the 1964-70 Labour Government's record – a huge building programme achieved, with increased subsidies that *'helped keep council rents at reasonable levels'*; increased help for new home owners through the Option Mortgage scheme and 100% mortgages, taking home ownership above 50% for the first time; increased help through improvement grants and the 1969 Act's general improvement area programme; greater security of tenure and fair rents for private tenants under the 1965 Rent Act.

Yet, he argued, these achievements did not mean that Labour had solved the housing problem: far from it, major changes were needed to future housing policy. He referenced homelessness, overcrowding and insecurity; the too-slow action on slum clearance (despite also saying that *'we have had too much of the bulldozer'*); housing subsidies that *'did not reach down to the poorest families'*; and inequity between tenures: home owners received indiscriminate tax relief, council rents were a muddle with inconsistent practice around the country, there was little help with rent for private tenants, and furnished tenants remained outside the Rent Acts.

He started his assessment of future policy needs by stating the duty of government: to make sure needs are met and to tackle poverty and squalor:

'It must be possible – indeed it is in our view **a basic right of citizenship** *– for every household.... to have a minimum civilised standard of dwelling adequate for a decent comfortable and private household life.'*

He then sets the need for government action against the failings of the free market:

'(Our objectives) will not be met by the free play of market forces. A free market is wholly irrelevant to the most urgent problem, since the homeless and the over crowded are generally poor people who could not conceivably afford the market price of decent housing.

'So we cannot have a market solution to the housing problem. Some part of the building programme must be public: some part of the housing stock must be leased or owned at less than the economic cost: and the government must bear a final responsibility for the overall housing situation.'

So, what did he advocate? Here are some of his practical policy proposals:

- A third force between councils and owner occupation and a less marginal role for housing associations;

- A strategic role for councils as well as their traditional role of building and managing homes, together with stronger metropolitan and regional planning for new homes;

- Stronger default powers when councils fail to deliver homes;

- A reorganisation of finance so that the most hard-pressed areas receive the greatest aid;

- Greater involvement of community and neighbourhood organisations in the design of urban renewal;

- Bring housing together with other aspects of urban poverty and deprivation.

- Resist the Heath government's plans to increase council rents: Labour should end the relationship between public rents and private rents – *'there is no analogy here'*; low rents essential to keep the pressure off the rebates system, otherwise the rebate scheme will have to cover even those on average earnings; Tory rents will lead to council housing making a profit and subsidising the Exchequer.

- Welcome the extension of rebates to private tenants, but there should be strict regulations over the fixing of rents and the state of repair. Furnished tenants, excluded from the Tory proposal, should be fully included.

- Tackle the unfair and indiscriminate subsidy to home owners through mortgage interest tax relief.

It was a strong programme then, and Crosland later went some way towards delivering it during his time as Secretary of State for the Environment. Extraordinarily, it has many echoes now 45 years later. And the fundamentals on which his policy platform was based – government subsidy to ensure many more homes are built, housing costs that were affordable without means testing, linking housing to other policy areas like social services, the economy and the physical environment, and the principle of equitable treatment between tenures – stand the test of time.

As a supposed revisionist in the 1960s and 1970s Crosland would probably be denounced as a leftie now, such is the distance that the political centre has moved in the meantime. But his practical and fair policy proposals, with just a little updating, were sufficiently prescient to guide us now.

The mother of all monopolies

March 1, 2017

Even with the most knowledgeable of housing audiences, eyes tend to glaze over whenever the issue of land is raised. To most it is just a huge expense and a barrier to building more homes. Not many people understand how the land market in the UK operates and how it impacts not only the housing market but also the wider economy. I studied the 'economics of location' as part of my degree but I still put this issue in the box marked 'too difficult' or 'might try to understand that one day'.

Fortunately, more housing people are looking at the issue these days and there is some hope that an effective land policy might emerge as a result. Last week I reviewed Duncan Bowie's new book, which has a lot to say about land and planning for housing, and this week another highly relevant new book is published '**Rethinking the economics of land and housing**' by Josh Ryan-Collins, Toby Lloyd and Laurie Macfarlane with the New Economics Foundation.

It's good to know from some of the early reviews that the book is highly accessible given the dryness of the subject – and Toby Lloyd has written an excellent taster for the Guardian.

Toby starts by recounting the many housing policies that have failed to meet the promise of solving the housing shortage and traces their failure back to our inability to address the role of land in the economy.

Land is obviously important for housebuilding, but the land problem goes much deeper than our housing shortage. It lies right at the heart of many of the economic problems we face today. Financial instability, mounting inequality, debt overhangs and the puzzle of stagnant productivity are all direct results of our failure to properly account for and manage land in the modern economy.

He traces the history of land ownership and the role it has played in impoverishing people as any additional value that they managed to create from the land was quickly absorbed by rising rents. He looks at the various attempts to justify private land ownership as the driving force transferred from agriculture to housing and notes the importance of partial public ownership in maintaining land supply. He traces the development of boom and bust in housing and the importance of financial deregulation in creating the over-investment in residential property that we suffer from today.

Lloyd argues that land is inherently scarce and its control inherently political: the normal rules of supply and demand are inoperable and the market is inevitably both dysfunctional and volatile. We therefore have *'to break the positive feedback cycle between the financial system, land values and the wider economy, and to capture more of the unearned windfalls private landowners currently pocket at the expense of society at large.'* That can only come through financial regulation, tax reform and more direct intervention.

Lloyd ends with the famous description by Winston Churchill of land ownership as *'the mother of all monopolies'*. Churchill's speech – delivered in 1909 – is one of the great reads, hugely ahead of its time and still relevant today.

Churchill complained of the *'enrichment which comes to the landlord who happens to own a plot of land on the outskirts or at the centre of one of our great cities, who watches the busy population around him making the city larger, richer, more convenient, more famous every day, and all the while sits still and does nothing.'*

'Enrichment without service' is still a primary feature of land ownership. More than a century after Churchill's prescient analysis, the time has come for all of us to get to grips with the issue, and this book will help us do it.

Why I care so much about housing associations

April 27, 2017

While Boris Johnson mutters inanely about mugwumps, Jeremy Corbyn has tried hard to raise the housing issue in the election over the last couple of days and has started to trail Labour's manifesto commitment to build a million homes.

Despite the media fascination with Johnson's clowning, I think Jeremy's core point – Labour will build more homes and more social rented homes – has come across well. It was good to see his real passion for the subject during his visit to Harlow today.

It seems any debate about housing during elections – the same happened in 2010 and 2015 – is dogged by deliberate obfuscation about what is being discussed. At PMQs on Wednesday, Corbyn's question to Theresa May was met by the well-rehearsed stock answer that Cameron delivered so many times before – the Tories have built more council houses than Labour did when it was in office.

It happens to be true, but what does it tell us? It tells us that the Labour Government didn't want councils to be major builders – it's one of my main beefs with Labour during the Government years. Instead, the money was put into housing associations to provide social rented housing and shared ownership. Mrs May never addresses that. The only comparison that matters between the two governments is how many homes for social rent were provided by councils AND housing associations together. Here the Labour Government wins hands down and many times over.

Sadly, the same confusion dogged the interview at lunchtime between Andrew Neil and Jack Dromey on the Daily Politics. Neil is just about the only interviewer who asks intelligent questions about housing because he has bothered to look up the figures and learn the difference between starts and completions. But even Neil compared apples and bananas in his questions. Mr Corbyn, he said, has committed to 500,000 new council and housing association homes over a Parliament but the only evidence we have to go on is Labour's record in office. And then, the switch – he quoted the figures for council homes only. And he repeated the point a few times – the Tories build more council houses than

Labour, so why should we believe Corbyn's commitment? And that was followed by another confusion, as Sayeeda Warsi started quoting housebuilding figures for the UK while Neil was talking England (or was it England and Wales?).

The viewer sadly must be left completely bewildered, and I hope Andrew Neil will return to the issue again.

Fortunately, Jeremy Corbyn managed to be very clear in his speech in Harlow that the commitment is to build **500,000 new council and housing association homes over the next Parliament**. I know it's a mouthful but truncating the commitment to 'council houses' removes the meaning. Most people involved with housebuilding know that it would be virtually impossible to reach a target of completing 100,000 council homes a year even by the end of the Parliament, and certainly impossible to do it each year starting this year. Even if the resources and borrowing powers were available, it would take several years to gear up, to assemble the land, design the schemes, procure the building contracts, and get started on site. **It would be a very good thing to do, but it would not produce the homes fast enough.**

So, meeting Labour's target will be dependent on getting housing associations to provide the homes. They are in a much stronger position than councils to accelerate housebuilding and have a track record of being able to produce homes for social rent and for shared ownership. To meet the target, councils will need to be the planners and the strategists and housing associations will need to be the primary deliverers.

As readers will be aware, I have my criticisms of housing associations. But if a new Labour Government had a clear direction and policy, and made the resources and powers available, I believe housing associations would respond. Most will do so with great enthusiasm, but even those associations who (shall we say) aren't keen 'to do social rent' anymore would follow the money.

GE2017: At last someone talks seriously about housing

June 6, 2017

There may be good reasons - in particular murder and mayhem on our streets - but another Election has passed in which housing has been the dog that didn't bark.

Sadly too late to have the impact it deserves in the Election campaign, Labour yesterday published its Housing Manifesto, enlarging on and extending the housing section of the main Manifesto put out a couple of weeks ago.

References to housing in the campaign so far have mainly consisted of the bandying about of some impressively large numbers. The LibDems played their trump card with the biggest housebuilding offer (300K a year), although their promise has been inflating as fast as their support has been falling. It quickly became apparent that the Tories have spent the last seven years muddling up their housing target (hundreds of thousands) with their immigration target (tens of thousands) and just promised again what they failed to deliver in the past.

The housing section of Labour's main Manifesto was quite well received, and this fuller version deserves praise for tackling the issues in a comprehensive way. When it comes to housing policy, the word comprehensive is important: it's not just a numbers game, it's about getting lots of elements of policy right, so it adds up to an effective strategy.

The document covers all the tenures. In home ownership it focuses help specifically on first time buyers, following up on the Redfearn review. It makes the important proposal to remove stamp duty on homes of less that £300K for two years, introduces permanently discounted FirstBuy homes, and restricts Help to Buy to first time buyers only. It implies that developers will qualify for Help to Buy only if they enter agreements on their building rates, which could be a game changing idea. And it borrows from Sadiq Khan in giving 'first dibs' to locals when homes go on sale.

Labour will also back existing home owners with a range of new initiatives. The safety net for low income home owners will be strengthened, long forgotten leaseholders will get new rights, and there will be new controls on variable rate mortgages. A new housing renewal programme is signalled alongside a new drive to insulate existing homes. There will be a review of housing options for older people wishing to downsize.

Building on the solid base of the Lyons Commission report, major changes to the operation of the housebuilding industry are proposed. The role of the Homes and Communities Agency will be strengthened, as will be the powers of local councils to assemble land at closer to existing value. We are promised the biggest council housebuilding programme for 30 years. Help to Buy will be used as a bargaining chip to secure a wide-ranging agreement with the sector on output and standards in design and quality. There will be a review of the post-Brexit capacity of the construction industry.

To my great relief, Labour unambiguously promises a new programme of affordable *homes for social rent*, and the target will be to achieve 100,000 'genuinely affordable' homes to rent or buy by 2022, which we have argued before on Red Brick is a sensible and realistic gearing up from the current abysmal position. Long term tenancies will be unbanned and right to buy will be suspended – to be reinstated only where full replacement can be guaranteed. More affordable housing will lead to housing benefit savings, which will be ploughed back to ease the worst aspects of the Tories' benefits policy – like ending the Bedroom Tax.

There is a promise of a 'consumer rights revolution' for private renters. There will be new legal minimum standards with stronger enforcement and an extension of licensing. Three year tenancies will become the norm, with inflation-controlled rent rises. Lettings charges for tenants will be banned and councils will be encouraged to set up local lettings agencies in their areas.

Homelessness is seen as the most visible sign of the Tories' failure. A target will be set to end rough sleeping in a campaign which will be led by the new Prime Minister in a Labour Government. There will be a gradual shift to a 'Housing First' policy seen to be effective in other countries. They will halt the plans to change funding for supported housing to avoid the closure of homeless hostels.

All in all, this is a decent attempt at a comprehensive new housing policy in less than 20 pages. It has gaps, undoubtedly, in particular it could have said much more about planning and it looks at homelessness almost entirely from the perspective of rough sleeping – only one element of the growing problem. It has weaknesses – for example not addressing the long term balance of tenures and glossing over regional disparities, and it has a touching sense of confidence which I don't share that the Homes and Communities Agency can become the driving force behind housebuilding delivery. And there will be many detailed financial questions that need to be considered and answered.

Whether the document could have sparked a real debate around housing if it had been published earlier is open to question. Regrettably, I can see very little coverage of it today except in specialist media. It is an area where Labour is strong - Jeremy Corbyn and John Healey in particular - and the Tories weak and threadbare. I guess we will never know, but win or lose, Labour has at least got its housing policy into a good place.

Tenants and the homeless must not be made to pay for the tower block fire safety crisis

June 23, 2017

I have found it hard to comment on the Grenfell Tower disaster. Words cannot convey the horror of it, and everything I tried to write felt hopelessly inadequate. Others succeeded where I failed, and I would recommend thoughtful pieces penned by Chris Creegan, Municipal Dreams, and Giles Peaker amongst others.

I was so angry at the ineptitude of the council's and the government's response and so in awe of the magnificent response of the emergency workers and the local community. They are in total contrast to each other.

I was also stunned that within hours some people started to use the fire to attack social housing. One tweeter said: 'The nature + quality of social housing is probably the single biggest post-war British policy failure' and there were plenty of a similar ilk. Others reverted to well-worn dystopian myths and Clockwork Orange imagery about council estates. Yesterday, first Theresa May and then Sajid Javid said we should pay more attention to social housing, but I found that menacing rather than reassuring. The dreaded Iain Duncan Smith called for tower blocks to be flattened and replaced by nice houses with gardens, presumably without the council tenant tag.

Grenfell does not tell me that we should have less social housing, or that private housing is somehow superior, or that tower blocks are bad – on the contrary we need more social housing of all types and, whatever its height, it should be of a highest possible standard. And it should be better resourced and better managed.

"The best memorial to all those who have lost their lives in Grenfell is that we as a nation choose collectively to invest in safe and secure public housing for all who need it." - Municipal Dreams blog

I do not know if cuts in spending on fire services and deregulation of some aspects of fire safety contributed to the Grenfell fire. But after a long period of decline, fire deaths have been rising again, and fire chiefs have put this down to cuts of up to 50% in some places. The fire statistics do not help us understand if there is a specific problem in social housing, but it seems highly unlikely. In the vast majority of cases, fires in towers are contained and the building does what it is supposed to do. The social factor that seems to have the biggest correlation with death by fire is age, with people over 80 particularly vulnerable. They live in all tenures. In the 1980s at Shelter I spent a lot of time working with the Campaign for Bedsit Rights trying to get standards in multi-occupied property raised after many fire deaths in such properties, including the appalling fire in a rabbit warren terrace of bedsits in Clanricarde Gardens in 1981, where eight people died a mere mile from Grenfell Tower.

"Will the Prime Minister today guarantee that local authorities will be fully funded for an urgent review of tower block safety and all remedial action that is necessary, including the installation of sprinklers when appropriate, so that they can proceed in a matter of days with that comfort? Does she agree that regulation is a necessary element of a safe society, not a burden, and will she legislate swiftly when necessary to ensure that all high-rise residents are safe?" - Karen Buck MP, House of Commons, 22 June.

Heightened concern about fire safety in towers can be traced back to the previously worst tower block fire at Lakanal House in Southwark in 2009, when six people died. Exterior cladding panels were identified as having helped the fire to spread fast both laterally and vertically, as with Grenfell. Yesterday Mrs May said "All recommendations from the coroner on the Lakanal House inquiry have been acted on" but this was strongly disputed by the local MP, Harriet Harman, and others. It is clear that the requested review of building regulations has not been concluded and published.

Even more damning of government is the lack of action in response to a series of letters from the All Party Parliamentary Group (APPG) on fire safety, chaired by the Conservative Sir David Amess, which included calls for sprinklers to be fitted in all towers. And the Tory obsession with deregulation was highlighted by the Guardian yesterday, reporting that the government-connected Red Tape initiative has been discussing how to reduce 'the burden' of fire regulations post-Brexit, including for external cladding.

I have spent much of my working life defending both social housing as a housing model and social tenants as an unfairly derided class of people. Rather than the stereotype of chain-smoking can-carrying foul-mouthed council tenants, after the Grenfell Tower fire a succession of residents described the events in the tower, the failings of the council and the TMO, and the strength of their community with extraordinary eloquence. As their back-stories emerged, we learned of the remarkable range of people living in the tower, people of all faiths and none, often with amazing and sometimes horrific histories. Their common point was that by some chance they had ended up in the cosmopolitan community of north Kensington (David Cameron's Notting Hill is a few streets but a world away). In the aftermath of the fire we learned of the extraordinary compassion and dedication of ordinary people willing to help each other.

The surviving residents and those evacuated from surrounding homes were initially treated with callous disregard until the community stepped up and stepped in as the death toll rose. Some of the stories of neglect and indifference by the council tell me that rather more than the chief executive of Kensington and Chelsea should resign. It was the council's job to organise the non-uniform response and they failed miserably and absolutely. They evidently turned down offers of assistance from neighbouring boroughs and the GLA, arrogantly assuming they could do the minimum required. They appeared not to understand the extent of their duty to all residents in an emergency under the homelessness legislation. Above all, they did not seem to care much. They were overwhelmed and it took days before more competent people were brought in. I am not alone in thinking that a civil emergency on this scale required military expertise: I am sure the army could have sorted communications and logistics in hours especially with so much community help. Traumatised victims could and should have been helped much faster with a range of services to meet both their physical and emotional needs.

Responsibility for the fire will continue to be debated, not least in the House of Commons as it was yesterday. As the Guardian's John Crace pointed out, Theresa May has had legal advice, but has been found to be *'morally wanting'*, and during questions *'the sound of backs being covered was all too audible'*. Fingers are being pointed, and I suspect responsibility will be located at several stages in the very long chain from building regulations to contractor. The specifics may have to await the criminal investigation and the public inquiry.

We also have to wait to see how many other towers are dressed in flammable cladding, it is possibly quite a few, and not all in social housing. Some Councils, like Camden, have already started removing suspect cladding, and it is hoped that blocks can be made safe quickly without rehousing becoming necessary.

Grenfell Tower alone has required between 100 and 200 replacement homes to be found from a diminishing stock of social housing. Attention has focused on one block of 'luxury flats' being bought by the City of London, but it turns out these were always destined to be some form of social housing. No information has been made available on the rents and service charges that will be levied, what form of tenancy will be offered and for how long. The first principles are that residents should be suitably rehoused and not be out of pocket.

As the supply of new genuinely affordable social rented homes has collapsed to a little over 1,000 homes nationally last year, from 36,000 in 2010, most of the homes that are likely to be available will be at so-called 'affordable rents' at up to 80% of market rents. Rehoused tenants must not be expected to pay those rents, the difference should be made up by the council. Some DWP rules have been suspended for these residents, but it has also been said that they would have to pay bedroom tax if they ended up with a spare room. That is grotesque.

The numbers matter. Unless **extra** social housing is provided in total then the people who will actually pay for this crisis will be those homeless families or people on the housing waiting list who will not be rehoused as a consequence. One way round this would be government to fund the purchase of an equivalent number of homes on the open market - as happened in the early 1990s to mitigate the housing market slump.

Theresa May was as slippery as can be when challenged about how the works to blocks like Grenfell will be paid for. It could be hundreds of millions. This should be a central government commitment, a new fund provided by the whole country to avoid another tragedy. May wouldn't commit, just saying it will be done. What is most likely is that government will allow councils to borrow more to pay for the works, with the cost falling to the housing revenue account. And there's the rub: unless there is specific subsidy or grant, extra borrowing on the HRA will be funded in the long term by tenants through their rents. Tenants will pay for a fire safety crisis that is not of their making.

It is absolutely right that the victims of the fire should have top priority and should be rehoused as quickly as possible. No-one will disagree that similar panels should be stripped from other blocks. No-one will object to an extensive programme of fire safety improvements, including for example sprinklers, in all towers currently without them. But, whoever is found to be responsible, it is not right that the actual burden of putting things right should fall on existing tenants and homeless people waiting for a home.

Central government should foot the bill, sharing the load. That's why we all pay taxes.

Not much controversy here

September 28, 2017

Jeremy Corbyn's speech to Labour Party Conference on Wednesday has caused a bit of a stir, notably his comments on regeneration and rent control. So, what did he actually say and are they new departures?

He said a lot about Grenfell, focusing on the fact that it was an avoidable disaster and looking at events from the tenants' perspective. He said it indicted 'failed housing policies... and yawning inequality'. I don't disagree, but I would repeat my warning that we have to be careful how we talk about the disaster. Grenfell does not tell us that social housing is a bad idea. When the Tories say 'we must now talk about social housing' I don't think they want to have more of it and to make it better.

The most important announcement in Corbyn's speech was that there would be a Labour enquiry into social housing policy – parallel to the government's – with Shadow Housing minister John Healey looking at its **building, planning, regulation and management**. He promised that Labour would listen to tenants across the country and bring forward a radical programme of action.

In support of his core contention that 'a decent home is a right for everyone whatever their income or background' Corbyn listed a number of policies which I don't think are controversial within Labour:

- insist that every home is fit for human habitation (which the Tories have consistently voted down).
- 'control rents' – despite much of the comment since the speech I suspect this is not a major new departure but a reiteration of the Manifesto commitments, possibly with some strengthened 'Berlin-style' delegated powers for large cities, and perhaps more interventionist policies like the London controls on Airbnb – which is of course a form of rent control.
- tax undeveloped land held by developers - using the Ed Miliband formulation of "Use it or lose it".

Corbyn's most significant area of new policy, and possibly controversy, concerned regeneration, where his comments mirrored a resolution passed by Conference. He said 'Regeneration is a much abused word. Too often what it really means is forced gentrification and social cleansing, as private developers move in and tenants and leaseholders are moved out.'

He established a basic principle: Regeneration should be for the benefit of the local people, not private developers. So, people must get a home on the same site and the same terms as before with 'No social cleansing, no jacking up rents, no exorbitant ground rents'. And there should be a ballot of existing tenants and leaseholders before any redevelopment scheme can take place.

I thought Aditya Chakrabortty, in an otherwise interesting column for the Guardian, over-egged the new policy by claiming that Corbyn had declared war on some Labour Councils. Personally, I think Corbyn's requirements are the minimum and I would go further. It is not enough simply to offer a new home to those who wish to return after regeneration – and some councils have had to be dragged into doing that - with the majority of new homes being for private sale. Regeneration – where it involves providing more homes in total - must make a net contribution towards meeting the housing needs of the district in question. Homes taken from the pool of rented homes to 'decant' residents from the area to be regenerated must as an absolute minimum be replaced in number and in kind within the completed scheme. Otherwise it is the homeless and badly housed who pay the real price of the regeneration scheme. There should be no dodges like replacing social rent with so-called 'affordable rent' or even 'affordable home ownership' – there should be a requirement that new social rent homes will replace those that have been lost. If that cannot be achieved through comprehensive redevelopment, then other options should be pursued, including partial redevelopment and infill. Many perfectly good estates are being proposed for redevelopment when what they need is better management and some investment to make them better places to live.

It was good to see Jeremy focus on housing in his speech, but all I see are sensible pragmatic policies that are a million miles better than what we have to suffer now. Not much controversy here. It is the review of social housing policy that carries most hope of future radical steps.

Will Haringey's HDV tackle homelessness?

December 20, 2017

It may be a fool's errand to join the argument about one of London's major 'estate regeneration' schemes. In most of the big schemes it has been almost impossible to distinguish fact from fiction amongst the contradictory claims made by proponents and opponents with equal belligerence. But this time it is Haringey, where I worked for many years in Tottenham, so this one feels personal.

The passions unleashed by Haringey's decision to set up (with *LendLease*) a 50/50 joint venture development vehicle (known as the HDV) have left the sides poles apart; they have become vituperative, and seem to have different facts let alone opinions.

Not just in Haringey, 'estate regeneration' is becoming the trickiest political issue for Labour in London. On the one side there is a genuine argument (articulated by Shelter amongst others) that national policy means there is a dearth of options, and that redeveloping lower density and 'worn-out' estates on council land to create additional and better housing at much higher densities, mostly at market prices, is the only way of providing sufficient cross-subsidy to enable some social rented and other 'affordable' homes to be built. The argument goes that this is better than nothing and that we can't hope and wait for a Jeremy Corbyn government to come along to get more resources.

On the other side are those who see the policy as an echo of David Cameron's clarion call in 2016 for the redevelopment of 100 council estates, places he called 'sink estates', 'bleak high-rise buildings' that 'are entrenching poverty... isolating and entrapping many of our families and communities', ending with his ominous sentence 'I believe that together we can tear down anything that stands in our way'. It is axiomatic that any policy initiated by David Cameron won't be good for the poor. But Labour councils are accused of adopting similar attitudes, wanting to build glossy new 'quarters' and failing to protect their vitally important social rented stock and working-class communities. There are now believed to be well over 100 potential schemes around London. In London housing terms, this is huge.

In Haringey, two polarised sides line up behind the conflicting perspectives – but all councils setting up joint venture or Local Housing Companies face similar predicaments (as discussed by Ross Fraser on Red Brick recently).

Proponents see the HDV as a transformative investment vehicle that will create jobs, fund a range of community facilities and services, transform the council's commercial portfolio, and directly tackle the housing crisis, homelessness and bad housing – whilst making big money (profit from development, increased council tax and New Homes Bonus income) for a cash-strapped council.

Opponents see a fundamentally gentrifying process that will knock down thousands of genuinely affordable council homes and build thousands of additional homes that will be mainly unaffordable to existing Haringey residents, adding up to the destruction of communities and 'social cleansing'. The argument goes that adopting regeneration/redevelopment as a means of coping with huge cuts in revenue support grant means that councils are effectively mortgaging the future by making a profit from the land they own, rather than maximising its use for genuinely affordable housing. The opportunity cost is that the land, once developed for this purpose, will no longer be available for a better purpose in the future. The alternative would be to develop more modest and less grandiose plans to build homes on spare land and invest in the existing estates.

Leaving aside the political controversy over councillor selections in the borough and whether a 50/50 joint company is privatisation (about which I have opinions but not for this piece), what are the likely outcomes of the HDV in housing output terms?

The council has made big claims that the HDV will tackle homelessness and waiting lists. Its HDV webpage starts 'Our residents need new homes to tackle the rising cost of housing and increased homelessness'. The council seeks the higher moral ground. The Cabinet Member for Housing and Regeneration responded to opposition from local MP Catherine West by arguing 'We need action now to help the three thousand families in Haringey in temporary accommodation, and the thousands more on our waiting list' and there have been attacks on opponents for not caring about delivering homes to the homeless for ideological reasons.

It is incumbent on the council to demonstrate that the HDV will achieve these aims, not merely to assert that it will. There certainly seems to be a weakness in the evidence. I have read most of the confusion of documents that make up the HDV proposal, and I am none the wiser on this central question: how *exactly* will the HDV aid homeless people in Haringey, and how many? Thousands of mainly social rented homes will be knocked down and thousands of mainly private homes will be built. There will be many more homes overall, but how will the proposed mix of market and sub-market homes tackle homelessness and the needs of people on the waiting list?

The missing number is how many social rented homes there will be at the end of the process. It has been a constant refrain on Red Brick that the type and tenure of new homes is as important as how many homes are built in total. Social rent remains the only truly affordable option for many people on lower incomes, a line of argument that, after a barren few years, is once again becoming common currency in the housing world. Of course, other forms of housing are needed, because housing unaffordability now stretches a long way up the income scale, but in my contention housing policies are **unacceptable** if they do not improve the chance of a decent home for people in the bottom 10-20% of the income distribution.

Haringey's own housing market assessment illustrates the point. 30% of the borough's households have incomes below £20,000 per annum, 50% below £30,000 and 65% below £40,000. Market housing does not meet their needs, and sub-market options only help at the edges. Only 4% of households have incomes above £100,000 per annum. Haringey is not a borough of affluent people just waiting for someone to provide a £700,000 flat for them to buy. Mean household income levels are highest in the West of the Borough and lowest in the East – where most of the estates to be regenerated are situated.

Whatever the wider benefits of HDV, in housing terms the council has not committed to the full replacement of all its social rented homes, let alone a much-needed increase. They have committed to providing existing tenants with a right to return on the same terms as now (rent and security of tenure) but no estimate is made of the number of homes needed to achieve this. I would have thought it was crucial to model this before decisions were taken – some people are keen to return but others prefer one-off permanent rehousing or choose to stay where they have gone temporarily and do not return.

The council's housing strategy sets an overall aim that 40% of new homes should be 'affordable' and it has adopted income-related affordability measures. That is across all development on private and public land and across the whole borough. On council-owned land the proportion of 'affordable' homes should be highest, but there appears to be no explicit aim or target or even expectation as to how many of the new HDV homes will be for 'social rent' or even 'similar to social rent' on an income-related calculation. The council also has a policy (misguided in my view) of not maximising the number of homes for social rent in the east of the borough, in Tottenham, on grounds of achieving a better social and tenure mix. This also has the effect of depressing the number of homes for social rent.

The evidence available suggests there will be fewer homes for social rent at the end compared to the beginning. Surely it is a basic principle that there should be full replacement of all social rented homes knocked down? Sadiq Khan's decision to refuse permission for Genesis's Grahame Park regeneration in Barnet due to the loss of social rented homes demonstrates two points: first how unambitious social housing agencies have been in trying to build for the poorest, and secondly, that the mood is shifting against them. Khan described it as "how not to do estate regeneration" and his own London Plan policies indicate that he would also turn down Haringey's plans as they stand.

There is a further impact on those in housing need waiting for council homes that is not assessed in any of the HDV documents I have seen. The regeneration process is long and complex and involves rehousing ('decanting' in the jargon) all existing tenants (temporarily with a right of return or permanently for those who do not wish to return). Demand from decants restricts the flow of social rented homes from the general pool to those in housing need, even if the redevelopment programme is carefully phased (eg by building on spare land first). Because they are on the critical path of a major development where delay is costly, decants tend to receive high priority and get first pick. Not only do fewer other people get rehoused, they also tend to get homes which are poorer quality.

Haringey's housing vulnerability is demonstrated by its own Annual Lettings Plan. This shows that the borough had 3,158 households in temporary accommodation at March 2017 with a further 9,220 households on the housing register. The number of new lettings available to the council has been falling for many years: in 2016/17 it achieved only 522 lettings to meet all forms of need and in 2017/18 only 490 lets are anticipated, with 60 'regeneration decants' amongst those afforded highest priority. The Plan already foresees the share going to homeless households declining from 62% to 34% in a single year.

Supply and demand in future years is not projected, but the number and share going to decants is likely to rise rapidly with the HDV. Far from improving, the prospects for homeless households and people with other urgent housing needs being rehoused will diminish sharply. It will be many years before the regenerated estates make a net contribution to the lettings pool, and it may never happen. I would hazard a guess that Haringey, like some other boroughs, will decide to discharge its homelessness obligations through the private rented rather than the social rented sector. Far from helping the homeless, **the homeless will be the primary victims** of the decant programme required for the HDV.

As we have seen, so far Sadiq Khan is sticking to the line that projects on this scale must not lead to the loss of social rented homes (although there are still concerns about the definitions that Sadiq is using in the new London Plan). There will be pressure on him to back off, but I hope he sticks to his guns, based on past evidence.

A 2015 GLA study of **what actually happened** in 50 past regeneration schemes found that they achieved more homes, more market homes, more intermediate homes, but a reduction in social renting.

The Housing Committee's report – *Knock it Down or Do it Up? The challenge of estate regeneration* – found that the schemes doubled the total number of homes in the regenerated estates – from 34,213 to 67,601 (nb the final numbers were not all built out at the time of the research) BUT there was a huge shift in tenure, with 'social rent' declining from 30,431 to 22,135 – a loss of 8,296 or 27%; 'affordable rent' increasing from 46 to 1,832; 'intermediate homes' (for rent or part-sale) increasing from 550 to 7,471; and 'market homes' increasing from 3,186 to 36,163.

It is clear who has benefitted from a doubling of density. Not people on the lowest incomes, but people wishing to rent at higher but sub-market rents and, overwhelmingly, people able to pay the full market rate. From the evidence of the GLA report, it is hard to avoid the conclusion such outcomes constitute 'gentrification' – ie on average the people residing there after regeneration are significantly richer than those who lived there before – and poorer people are both fewer as a proportion and in number. Some people think this is a good thing, often on a 'social mix' argument that I find wholly spurious. In the schemes looked at by the GLA, over 8,000 social rent homes were not replaced, meaning that 8,000 other households (homeless and waiting list) did not get a home at all. The real housing cost of the schemes was borne by these families – regeneration has been paid for by the homeless and badly housed.

Whatever view you take about development vehicles like Haringey's, in simple housing terms the claim that it will help meet the needs of homeless and waiting list households does not bear much scrutiny. The housing case for the HDV has not been made.

2018

Right to buy is not the biggest reason for the fall in social renting

February 5, 2018

By Monimbo

Why did the number of homes let at social rents fall by 150,000 in the last five years? Surprisingly, although right to buy was a big factor, it wasn't the biggest. From April 2012 until the same month in 2017, right to buy led to 55,000 council houses sales and 20,000 by housing associations (the latter is because of the 'preserved' right to buy kept by tenants if their homes are transferred to a new landlord). So half the net loss can be explained by such sales.

But there were two much bigger factors behind the recent assessment by the Chartered Institute of Housing of the losses in social rented stock. First, new build would easily have offset right to buy sales if output of social rented homes had continued at the same rate as in the previous four years: from 2008/09-2011/12, thanks to the investment made under Labour's National Affordable Housing Programme (NAHP), 142,000 social rented homes were built, over 35,000 per year. Had this continued, social landlords would have built two new homes at social rent for every one sold, even after right to buy was 'reinvigorated' with bigger discounts from April 2012. As it is, the Tories are clearly poised to fail in their much more limited promise to replace the extra houses sold as a result of the right to buy being 'reinvigorated', and of course the replacements are all likely to be let at higher, 'affordable' rents.

Nevertheless, *some* new homes are being built for social rent. Adding together new homes built by housing associations and by local authorities, these total just over 50,000 over the five years. Not only is this far lower than achieved under Labour's NAHP but numbers are now down to only 5,000 per year, with little prospect of their being revived. So in mathematical terms the biggest reason for the loss of social rented homes is failure to build: if Labour had still been in power, continuing a similar programme to its NAHP, around 125,000 more social rented homes would have been built than has been achieved by the coalition/Tory governments.

So, selling off the stock wasn't the biggest reason for the loss of social rented homes, it was the failure to build. Oddly enough, right to buy wasn't even the *second* biggest reason. From 2011 onwards, the coalition government set out to make a heavy dent in the provision of social rented housing in two ways. First, as we have seen, it built homes for 'affordable' rent instead of social rent, constructing about 90,000 up to April 2017. But second, it *converted* homes from social rent to 'affordable' rent at an even faster pace, with 102,000 conversions in total by the same date (shown purple in the graph, the green columns show the total AR stock from conversions plus new build). It forced associations to do this to give them extra rental income, to offset the loss of government grant (it fell from around £60,000 per new home built under Labour to less than £20,000 under the Tories). This is therefore easily the second most important factor in the decline of social rent.

Right to buy, whether for councils or housing association properties, is therefore the *third* biggest factor. But even this isn't the whole story: both councils and housing associations have been *demolishing* social rented stock (for example, in regeneration schemes), and these losses run at around 4,000 per year.

In addition to these recent attacks on the social rented stock, it faces two more potential dangers: the new right to buy for housing association tenants, and the enforced sales of 'high value' council properties. At the moment, the first of these is only going ahead as a pilot scheme in the West Midlands and will be funded by government. But the prospect of enforced sales of council houses, now less likely after the Grenfell Tower disaster, is still 'on the books' and is inhibiting many councils from taking on more ambitious investment plans. If right to buy for association tenants were to go ahead across the country, someone would have to fund the discounts and at the moment the only money potentially available is from forcing councils to sell off their better stock.

In this situation, Labour's priorities should be clear: not only does it need an even more ambitious new build programme than it had when it was last in power, but this needs to focus strongly on building for social rent, as John Healey has promised. And the haemorrhaging of the existing stock must be halted too.

This will mean, first, either suspending council tenants' right to buy or at the very least making the discounts they receive much less attractive; second, rescinding the promise to housing association tenants that they can buy their homes and calling off 'high value' council sales; third, ending the conversion of properties to higher rents and, finally, ensuring that any regeneration schemes provide for at least one-for-one replacement of any social rented homes that are to be demolished.

So how should we set social rents in future?

February 22, 2018

Today saw the launch of research on **social rent policy** commissioned by the SHOUT campaign for social rented homes, the Association of Retained Council Housing (ARCH) and the Local Government Association (LGA) and undertaken by the independent macroeconomic research organisation Capital Economics.

The idea of the research was to get an expert assessment of the options available for setting social rents in the future - so there can be a proper debate given the chaotic position of the current government, which first decided to cut rents for five years (designed to reduce the housing benefit bill, but only in the short run as more people are pushed into private renting) then decided to increase them by more than (consumer price) inflation.

There have been very few attempts to take an overview of all the implications of rents – to tenants, to the social security bill, and to the ability of providers to invest in the existing stock and new homes. There are even fewer attempts to examine the implication of rent policy at regional level – one size does not fit all and it is time rent policy reflected the very different conditions that apply in the different parts of the country.

The report sets the context for social housing in this country, contrasting the social sector 'target rent' regime that has been in place for 15 years with the current government's 'affordable rent' regime which sets rents at up to 80% of local market rents. It emphasises why rents matter:

- to the disposable income of tenants (linked to benefits policy) whether in work or not, to future investment where rent income has a surprisingly large impact on the ability of landlords to invest.
- to the government's fiscal position because significantly less housing benefit is needed to support a tenant living in social rented accommodation compared private rented housing – where a large slice goes to the profit of the landlord rather than being recycled into investment.
- to the business plans of social landlords because rents not only pay for management and maintenance but also service existing debt and underpin future borrowing for investment.

Capital Economics considered the long term impacts of various policy options taking account of the above factors and concluded that a policy of raising rents by CPI plus 1% is broadly appropriate across most of the country, but that no single policy is optimal across the whole country. It is important to note their caveat – the modelling depends on various assumptions coming to pass, notably that the benefit cap and local housing allowance rates increase in line with rents. Under such conditions, tenants on benefits will suffer no loss in disposable income due to the proposed 'optimal' rent increases, although tenants who are not in receipt of benefit would see a negative impact.

London and the south east, where private rents are highest, would see the largest fiscal saving from being able to move tenants from private rented housing to new social housing. They calculate that a real annual increase of 1.9 per cent after 2020 would enable sufficient social homes to be built to house all housing benefit claimants in private rented accommodation.

The report includes a detailed assessment of the position in each region. For example, for the north east, higher social rents would facilitate greater house-building, enabling 4,000 private tenants to move to social housing at 'CPI +1%', rising to 48,000 at 'CPI +3%'. However, the increase in the cost of benefits to cover these higher social rents would largely offset this, and the overall impact of different policies on government finances would be minimal.

So, the overall conclusions reached by Capital Economics are:

- It was right to conclude that an annual cut in rents was unsustainable;
- A single national policy should be replaced by regionally-based assessments, with different rates of increase in different areas;
- A rent increase policy is only sustainable if there are corresponding increases in benefits and cap levels;
- And finally, that rental income is only part of the story in terms of generating more investment – it is vital that government resumes grant for social housing and allows councils to borrow for HRA development, subject to the prudential code.

The report raises some crucial issues for the sector, and it is rare to see anyone try to link the issues of tenants' disposable incomes, benefit costs and investment together in such a coherent way. I would have liked to have seen more consideration given to the implications of 'affordable rent'. Although social rented homes remain the biggest segment of social housing by far, that is not true of the additions to the stock over the past few years, and the process of 'conversions' (switching homes from social to 'affordable' rents when they become vacant) has had a huge impact over the past few years. As more than 100,000 homes have been 'converted', it would be interesting to know what effect that has had on disposable incomes, benefit costs and investment using the Capital Economics model.

But the biggest challenge, whatever the logic of the analysis and the assessment of what is most optimal, is the question posed by SHOUT's Martin Wheatley at the launch of the report:

"How do you explain to a hardworking low-income tenant that their rent needs to rise above inflation every year, shouldn't government be investing in new social housing?"

As the Conservative chair of the LGA, Lord Gary Porter, made clear at the report launch: we have to let the state build and dispel the myth that state intervention is subsidy - it's not, it's investment in an asset, a security, and not just a debt.

Corbyn sets out Labour's housing stall

April 19, 2018

Today saw the launch of Labour's Green Paper focused on social housing - 'Housing for the many' - in Westminster. Together with Shadow Housing Secretary John Healey and the Leader of Leeds Council, Judith Blake, Jeremy Corbyn set out Labour's housing stall for the local elections at the start of May and the General Election whenever it comes.

Housing for the many' traces the history of social housing and its importance in meeting housing need, the failure to invest adequately in new social housing since 1980, and the Tories' efforts to remove it entirely since 2010. Without repeating the evidence of the scale of housing need, well documented in these pages, or summarising the whole document here - it is worth a read in its entirety - we would like to highlight some key issues that have been raised time and time again on Red Brick over the years. To mention just a few:

- Tenant empowerment will be a key feature of the new approach. A new national voice for tenants will be established, tenants' groups will be actively supported, and there will be consultation on a new requirement that tenants should sit on housing association boards. The regulatory regime will be strengthened to improve consumer standards and tenant involvement. Tenants' rights will be strengthened - with the ban on long-term tenancies ended.

- There will be a new definition of 'affordable' housing to tackle the increasing bizarre use of the word by the Conservatives. Labour will return to the key notion of 'social rent' with rents set by the existing national formula, and will scrap the Tories' bogus 'Affordable Rent' (with rents up to 80% of market rents) in favour of a new 'Living Rent' linked to one-third of local earnings aimed at key workers and people on moderate incomes.

- Recognising that building market homes alone will not tackle the housing affordability crisis, Labour will gear up to building 100,000 genuinely affordable homes a year, achieving one million over a decade. This is around six times the amount being achieved now and 'would reach levels last achieved in 1978'.

- There will be a proper focus on housing through a new stand alone Ministry and external checks on the progress Ministers are making towards meeting the housing targets.

- Building social housing makes good economic sense - the document references the SHOUT report by Capital Economics - and will improve the public finances in the long term by reducing the cost of housing benefit.

- One in eight social homes still fail the 'decent homes' standard despite the £20 billion investment improving 1.4 million homes made by the last Labour government. There is a new crisis - across all tenures, but here we are addressing social housing - in terms of fire safety and the urgent need to secure significant improvements following the appalling Grenfell fire. Grenfell survivors contributed to Labour's review, and the document commits Labour to installing sprinklers in high rise flats.

- Labour will act to stem the loss of social rented homes from the stock. This will include ending the scandalous practice of converting social rent homes to the much higher 'Affordable Rent' when they become empty, suspending the right to buy, and abandoning the Tories proposed policy of selling 'high value' council homes to fund a new housing association right to buy.

- The plans will herald the start of a major shift away from personal subsidies towards investment subsidies - from 'benefits to bricks'. Money will go towards ensuring affordable homes are built, not letting rents rip and letting housing benefit 'take the strain'. Critically, Labour will restore the £4 billion housing investment programme that was in place in 2010 and look to negotiate a new 10 year rent settlement to keep rents affordable for tenants as well as supporting a sustained investment programme and a new 'decent homes 2' programme.

- Labour's investment policies will also include lifting the council HRA cap to prudential levels, and reviewing the way borrowing is recorded in the national accounts. New development on public land will be required to meet affordable housing requirements. Housing associations will be regarded as a key part of finding the solution to the affordable housing crisis, but there will be a renewed expectation that they will have social purpose at their core.

- In private developments, Labour will remove the 'viability loophole' which allows developers to dodge affordable housing obligations and will change other planning rules which inhibit the provision of affordable homes.
- Although not a paper that focuses on Labour's social security policies, there are specific commitments to end the hated bedroom tax, protect housing benefit for the under 21s, and to pause and fix Universal Credit.
- In regeneration, there is a repeated commitment to a ballot when demolition is proposed. There will be a minimum requirement that there should be no loss of social rent homes and new guarantees for existing residents.
- There will be new commitments to improve design and reduce carbon emissions, together with new minimum space standards and a further extension of the Lifetime Homes standard.

It should be noted that, as a Green Paper, Labour is still open to comment and to revision of the policies before they are finally agreed. Everyone is encouraged to address the outstanding questions that the document highlights.

For Red Brick readers, the document addresses positively many of the most common themes seen in these pages over the past seven or eight years.

Let our Municipal Dreams flourish once more

June 20, 2018

John Boughton's 'Municipal Dreams' website was a breath of fresh air when it first appeared four or five years ago. The Government had ended direct investment in new social rented homes, the housing sector had all but given up the struggle, and the council housing finance reforms, developed by John Healey when Labour was in power but implemented by the Tories in 2011, which had offered hope for a new generation of council homes, had been undermined to the point where they had become almost worthless.

It felt like a last act of defiance when the SHOUT campaign for social housing was launched in 2014 - although things were to get worse (the 2015 Housing and Planning Act) before they started to get better. And then Grenfell changed everything.

'Municipal Dreams' took a different approach from the economic and political arguments that SHOUT deployed. The website started with the aim of championing the pioneering achievements of local government but came to focus more specifically on council housing, looking at the social and architectural history of estates around the country. Although never pulling punches about the errors made, Boughton bred confidence amongst we readers that many of our council housing estates were good places to live, were well designed and well constructed, and could provide good homes for many years to come. It directly contradicted the characterisation by the media, some politicians, and even some people in housing, that council estates were all high rise concrete jungles, failed communities, brutal places that housed inadequate and workshy people that were 'dependent' on benefits. It became a must read.

Boughton's book, also called 'Municipal Dreams' but subtitled 'The Rise and Fall of Council Housing', pulls together his remarkable knowledge of council estates all over the country - their planning, their development, their design, and their occupation – to illustrate the history of national council housing policy and finance and to comment on the successes and failures. The book starts where it ends, at Grenfell. Describing the devastating personal tragedy for those involved, Boughton also puts the disaster in its historical context: Grenfell, he says, is 'an awful culmination to deeply damaging policies pursued towards council housing, and the public sector more widely, since 1979.'

The early chapters of the book describe the development of council housing and the ideals that drove those who planned, financed and built it to replace the old slums. He leads us into 'the great programme of council house building which transformed our country, overwhelmingly for the better, up to the 1980s'. For those that like it, there is architectural detail which sometimes passes me by, but each example is always firmly linked to the policy and politics of the time. He dwells on the high point of Aneurin Bevan's policy of building to high standards despite post-war austerity and the 1960s system-build revolution which provided so many homes but created as many problems, not because of the quality of the homes themselves but because of the quality of the build and structural flaws.

Later chapters, post 1979, become more political in nature, but that can be put at Thatcher's door because she managed to politicise and polarise everything. He describes the long process of 'residualisation' of council housing - the narrowing of the social make-up of estates - and the emergence of so-called 'problem estates'. I tend to disagree with his assessment of the impact of the 1977 Housing (Homeless Persons) Act. I don't think the Act changed the social composition of council housing in the way that is often assumed – I think that is largely down to mass unemployment and the collapse in supply - although it did bring more people classified as 'vulnerable' (sometimes very young households or people with frail mental or physical health) into a sector which did not have the resources to ensure that these households were properly supported and integrated into communities.

Boughton's assessment of the New Labour period is more of a lament. Council housing was hardly a New Labour thing. Very few new council homes were built, that job went to housing associations, but the Labour government did invest enormously and to its credit in bringing the long-neglected council housing stock up to a 'decent' standard, with millions benefitting from new kitchens and bathrooms and windows. But it was all done with an ideological edge that council housing should be distanced from the council either by transfer to a housing association or PFI body or by separation into an arms-length management organisation. His judgement, with which I agree, is therefore that 'New Labour and its chosen agents improved both its fabric and management, but in a way which perpetuated the prejudices against it and undermined the values which sustained it.'

Ultimately, Boughton sees council estates as the victims of 'our social and economic woes' and not a cause. Those problems are disproportionately visited on the poorest people, and they are disproportionately – and quite rightly - housed on council estates. We should view council estates, he argues, 'not as a problem but as a solution – offering secure and affordable housing – to the low pay and insecure employment which affects so many'.

Special attention is paid to the period after 2010, the huge rise in rents and therefore in housing benefit, abominations such as the bedroom tax and the welfare caps, and the removal of security of tenure in newly-let homes, culminating in the 2015 Housing and Planning Act which confirmed the government's apparent intention to eliminate council housing. And he lambasts some of the many 'regeneration' (ie redevelopment) schemes being pursued on council estates, taking particular exception to the description of council estates as 'brownfield sites' and David Cameron's rehash of every cliché and stereotype to justify his plans to redevelop 100 'sink estates'. Boughton believes some of these 'regeneration' schemes are 'a desecration'.

The book identifies a little light at the end of a very dark tunnel: in the small new schemes of council housing around the country, and the significant shift in the politics of council housing brought about by the rise of Jeremy Corbyn and the horror of Grenfell. He ends with the hope that 'a fuller and more nuanced understanding of both past achievements and current follies may yet shift this politics and allow our municipal dreams to flourish once more'.

For anyone with an interest in (or even an obsession with) housing policy, the book is a great read. It has the detail which comes with real research but never loses sight of the long-term or the political framework. It is both about the extraordinary legacy of council housing and – if the politics can change – the enormous possibilities that exist in the future.

Shifting Housing's Overton Window

June 26, 2018

It's a sign of a remarkable comeback for social housing that the new CIH report *'Rethinking Social Housing'* contains few surprises. Only 3 years ago this report would have seemed a radical contradiction of the dominant narrative. It probably would have been attacked for lacking realism and harking back to the long lost 1970s.

Social housing reached its nadir around and after the 2015 General Election. It was unaffordable, past its sell-by date, consigned to the history books as the government and most of the housing industry focused their concerns on 'the only game in town', building homes that did not require grant, at significantly higher 'Affordable rents' or market prices, pushing forward with policies (right to buy, 'conversions', market sales) that would feed the development programme.

Housing's 'Overton window' - the range of ideas tolerated in public discourse – had become very narrow indeed and those of us who argued for social housing were made to feel oddballs well outside mainstream opinion. So it was that the very expensive National Housing Federation 'Homes for Britain' campaign prior to the 2015 Election choked on the words social housing. Joining the newly formed SHOUT campaign for social housing felt like heading upstream without a paddle.

So, what explains the turn-round between then and now, when the government is allocating funds specifically for new social housing, everyone is reviewing and rethinking the purpose of social housing - coming to the conclusion that it is an essential component of a fair and functioning housing market - and CIH feels confident enough to describe it as 'a pillar of the welfare state' without provoking guffaws of laughter?

Here are several possible factors. First, the refusal of tenants, campaigners, many people working at the grassroots in housing, and a few brave housing leaders, to stop banging the drum for genuinely affordable (as opposed to joke affordable) housing. Second, over-reaching by the Tories so their housing policies and the consequent rise in homelessness just confirmed their lack of empathy for poor and disadvantaged people. Third, the advent of unashamedly pro-social housing

Jeremy Corbyn to the leadership, which changed the nature of the debate in the Labour Party. Fourth, the general public, who did not obey the rules of the Overton window because they never lost sight of the simple idea that council housing was a good thing – even if they also thought it was subsidised and not for them. And fifth, Grenfell, which changed everything.

The new CIH report reflects a lot of background work with tenants and the sector and demonstrates that social housing is firmly back within the spectrum of acceptable thought. It identifies three key themes:

- Social housing, its affordability and the security it offers to people living there, are highly valued
- It has much wider value by allowing residents to prosper and thrive, through its contribution to tackling poverty, the success of local and national economies, and individual health and well-being
- However, there is stigma attached to social housing as a 'product' and to the organisations providing it and the people living in it

And so,

"Social housing has a unique and positive part to play in housing people, helping to create thriving, mixed communities, and meeting needs that the market will not. Done right it does great things. But it isn't always the case that homes and neighbourhoods are well managed and well maintained and it's important that we own and address this.

"It's time to reclaim the role of social housing as a pillar of the society we want to be, along with free health care and education – and it must be at the centre of government plans to solve the housing crisis. And, having 'reclaimed' the role of social housing, we need to push on – creating an ambitious vision of what a plentiful supply of social housing can do help people thrive in communities that prosper."

Some of the information in the report might surprise a general reader. For example, registered unemployment amongst social housing tenants is only 8%. The vast majority are either in work, retired or unable to work due to physical or mental disability or carers. Homeless people also take up around a quarter of lettings, far fewer than might be imagined.

The report contains a helpful discussion of the question 'who is social housing for?' based on a wide range of views from the public and the sector. The answer seems to be that ideally people want the sector to be 'for anyone' but that pragmatically it will remain highly rationed for many years to come. Given the vital role that security of tenure plays in enabling people to become established in their neighbourhood and having a platform on which to build their future, it is remarkable to note that there are still widely differing views on whether social housing should be a long term solution or, given scarcity, a short-term, reviewable, stepping stone.

CIH look forward by identifying six areas for further action, with some detailed proposals attached to each - including, for example, a call to suspend the right to buy which might become the headline proposal for the report.

1. there should be a new definition of social housing to get away from the current confusion.
2. tenants must have a greater voice.
3. there should be an increase in the supply of 'genuinely affordable' homes.
4. everyone should be able to afford a place to call home, with a move towards income-related rent-setting.
5. homes and neighbourhoods should be better managed.
6. there should be greater efforts to challenge the stigma and stereotyping attached to social housing.

It's a reasonable agenda. And given the general drift back to accepting the importance of social housing it will be fascinating to see how far the government is willing to go when it releases its Green Paper before the summer recess.

Social housing green paper: not fundamental, and not much of a rethink

August 14, 2018

When it was announced by housing secretary Sajid Javid back in September, the social housing green paper was described as the start of a "fundamental rethink of social housing in this country". Now that it is finally published after several postponements, the strong impression on a first read is that there has been little thinking and certainly nothing fundamental going on in government over the past 11 months.

Three things in particular strike me from this first reading.

First, the top news is that it signals the abandonment of much of the 'Cameron Housing Policy' imposed since 2010 and enshrined in the 2016 Housing and Planning Act. If it was an honest document it would say 'we got it wrong' when the Coalition dismantled the social housing regulatory system when taking office in 2010. Now indicated are a return to proper regulation of consumer standards, proper tenant involvement, a clearer framework for dealing with complaints, more of a level playing field between council and housing association landlords, and a return to a 'tenant voice' type organisation.

In his introduction the new housing secretary James Brokenshire almost confirms the point: *"There is a powerful case for strengthening the Regulator so it not only focuses on the governance and financial viability of housing providers, but also on how residents are treated and the level of services they should expect."* Well, that is pretty much what the Tenant Services Authority and the Audit Commission were doing in 2010 before they were abolished. The idea that is floated of linking funding to performance also takes us back into new Labour territory.

Second, the government has said a lot about the stigmatisation of tenants since the Grenfell fire. And it says it again here. But there is a contradiction at the heart of their thinking. They cannot really understand why anyone would want to be a tenant and so there are proposals for yet more routes into home ownership. One section is headed "Ensuring social housing is a springboard to homeownership", enshrining the notion that the most important thing is to aspire to home ownership.

The attitude that people who rent are inferior to people who buy is at the heart of stigma. So the Prime Minister, in her introduction, is wrong to try to pin the blame on landlords: *"Many people living in England's four million social homes feel ignored and stigmatised, too often treated with a lack of respect by landlords who appear remote, unaccountable and uninterested in meeting their needs."* I think she should look more closely at the long-term attitudes of politicians in her own party and the mainstream media.

Third, and most importantly, the GP totally fails to show any grasp of the ways in which social housing could help overcome the housing crisis, and especially the desperate need to provide many more genuinely affordable homes. Here there is a total contrast between this GP, prepared and delivered with all the resources of government, and the one produced by Jeremy Corbyn and John Healey for Labour earlier in the year. One fiddles at the edges and is going nowhere, the other is a genuine agenda for reform and the re-establishment of social rented housing at the heart of the housing system.

Some other points that strike me on this first reading of the green paper include:

It shows little understanding of how social housing estates have evolved since the Right to Buy. In some places RTB has brought about sustainable home ownership, but in too many others it has simply led to the enrichment of individuals who have either let at much higher rents or sold on for others to do so. It has been a huge policy error to allow social housing to become private rented housing in such large numbers. Mixed tenure estates involving high levels of private renting are harder and more costly to manage. The GP has no discussion of these issues let alone proposals to deal with some of them.

The GP says it is dealing with all of social housing including leaseholders, but the section on leaseholding is so scant it is almost insulting. It shows little appreciation of one of the key weaknesses of right to buy: service charges. Many leaseholders have faced financial ruin due to major works bills and, because many struggle to pay their service charges, they are often the group most likely to oppose local improvements.

There are several proposals that should be welcomed, even if they are really just ending a previous bad policy. For example, deciding not to implement the 2016 Act's provision that 'flexible tenancies' should become mandatory. The GP says these will remain open to local discretion. In addition the forced sale of 'high value' council homes to fund housing associations right to buy will not proceed. That is a relief. And finally, I would welcome the commitment to revise the Decent Homes Standard, which has not changed since 2006. It should incorporate wider standards for the estate environment and be much stronger on health and safety and especially fire safety.

I had hoped that there would be a clear announcement that the government will fund a replacement for the National Tenant Voice which it wound up in 2010. Instead it makes noises suggesting that support will be forthcoming for a new *'independent platform for tenants, based on widespread engagement, to enable them to have their voices heard more effectively at a national level.'*, which is what the NTV was.

There were two areas where a little chill ran down my spine. First the GP says that the government are considering *"a new stock transfer programme to promote the transfer of local authority housing particularly to community-based housing associations."* New proposals would be needed only if such a programme was not voluntary.

Second, there is a section on Universal Credit that is a work of fiction totally unrelated to the actual experience people are having with the benefit. It reads like a Duncan Smith speech from five years ago: *"Universal Credit is designed to mirror the world of work, to give people control over their lives and encourage* them to take responsibility for their financial affairs." Surely no-one believes that any more?

Finally, I note that the GP strikes a negative tone about tenant management organisations, which I think is not justified despite the debate about who was responsible for what prior to the Grenfell fire.

There will be no Parliamentary scrutiny of the Green Paper until the Autumn, and it may have passed into deserved obscurity by then. But there are a few areas where the government needs to be pushed to deliver, and a few others where it should be pushed to stop before it has started. Taken in the round, this Green Paper does not affect the debate about the housing crisis and the status of tenants in society one jot.

The Help to Buy gravy train

September 12, 2018

Some people suffer because of the housing crisis, others do quite nicely out of it thank you. Landowners are perhaps the best example of those who have traditionally coined it in. Nothing much has changed since Winston Churchill, way back in 1909, called land *'the mother of all monopolies'*, criticising *'the enrichment which comes to the landlord who happens to own a plot of land on the outskirts of a great city, who watches the busy population around him making the city larger, richer, more convenient, more famous every day, and all the while sits still and does nothing.'* And still they do.

But attention has been drawn more recently to another group of people who have been achieving great riches from the miseries of others – the housebuilders. You might say that at least housebuilders produce something of use, unlike the landowner, and the point is valid. But recently the vast profits being made by the volume housebuilders have been substantially donated by the government, free gratis and for nothing.

The housebuilders' own special magic money tree is called Help to Buy. In an excellent article in the Times on 8 September, Property Correspondent Tom Knowles showed how the average profit made by housebuilders on each home has doubled since the scheme was launched. Knowles' analysis showed that 'the top five builders in Britain are making an average profit of £57,000 on each house they sell, compared with a mean average of about £29,000 in 2007'.

On Red Brick we have criticised Help to Buy from the time it was launched in 2013 because it is a subsidy on the demand side of housing – it enables people to spend more on housing without necessarily increasing supply. A little bit of economics tells us that in the longer term it is likely to be self-defeating because more demand with no more supply will lead to price increases. Far better, we have consistently said, to apply whatever public finance is available to boosting housing supply, not demand.

At the launch of Help to Buy the argument was made that the scheme *would* boost supply by giving developers confidence that they would have buyers for their output – after all, no-one builds what they cannot sell. Yet Knowles confirms that the total number of new houses being delivered is much the same as it was ten years ago. He uses Barratt as evidence: profit per house has doubled since 2007 (he uses that date because it was the last full year before the global crash), but it is building only 411 additional homes.

Knowles quotes analysts who confirm that the largest driver of today's profits is Help to Buy. One assesses that housebuilders would be making £22,000 less profit on each house built for first time buyers if Help to Buy was not in place and concludes that 'someone is gaming the system'.

One of my favourite analysts, Neal Hudson, who puts good stuff on Twitter @resi_analyst, is quoted saying that shareholders had become *'the main priority'* for housebuilders since the financial crash. *'The over-arching factor has been big pressure from the City,'* he is quoted as saying. *'The priority for them is profit margin not the number of homes built.'*

One housebuilder chief executive was paid £75 million in a bonus last year, putting even bankers to shame. I suppose you could argue that no-one would turn down a nice earner, even if it is on the back of a government scheme designed to tackle the housing crisis. And, of course, it is government policy that is to blame. Since 2010 housing finance policy has been turned on its head. Instead of providing grant to enable genuinely affordable homes for those on low and medium incomes, Government help is now aimed at supporting the private housing market – and not very successfully it seems. The Chartered Institute of Housing's Housing Review estimated that support for the private market is taking nearly 80% of current investment compared to just over 20% going as support for affordable housing.

At local level, the riches flowing into the pockets of the housebuilders should stiffen the resolve of councils who are fed up with developers pleading that schemes are 'unviable' due to modest requirements that a proportion of new homes should be affordable.

In this debate, profits per home of around 20-25% of the cost are taken almost as a given, a fixed cost. I can remember a developer telling me that the rule of thumb in building costs was 'one-third for land, one-third for construction, and one-third profit'. In our Brexit-dominated world, construction costs are likely to inflate rapidly in the near future. So, if anything is to be done it must be to bear down on the other two elements: land and profit. We have posted a lot recently about land and taxation: another good step would be to tackle the Help to Buy gravy train.

'Happy clappy' is not the right response

September 21, 2018

It was a first for the National Housing Federation to get a serving Prime Minister to speak at one of their Conferences. It's obviously a feather in their cap, proving that government takes them seriously. But there was a degree of fawning in the audience – 'rapturous applause and a partial standing ovation' said Inside Housing, 'it's fair to say she is smashing it with this audience' tweeted Polly Neate of Shelter – that is not shared by those who need homes now.

So, are we to believe that one speech with some warm words means that housing associations are now 'a trusted partner' of government? And that an announcement of a tiny pot of money starting in four years' time means they will get long-term guaranteed funding sufficient to do the job? David Orr's inadvertently accurate comment that 'the penny has dropped' sadly told the real story. Yep, a penny, thanks Ma'am.

The truth is closer to this: 'the movement' has been played by the PM's political adviser Gavin Barwell, easily the best of the many housing ministers we have had over the last 8 years (for the simple reason that he actually knows something about the subject). He also knows how to get favourable headlines with a well-placed non-announcement, an unchecked promise of money, and a bit of flattery. May said what they wanted to hear and in glowing terms: she praised the movement's Victorian pioneers and the campaigning innovators of 50 years ago and commended the modern non-profit businesses. And no slagging off like there was from her predecessor.

Commentator Isabel Hardman saw this as one of a kind of speech that May makes. She is very keen to talk about her mission to tackle 'burning injustices' like mental health and housing. "What is missing from speeches on either topic is the sort of government action that might match up to a 'personal mission'" says Hardman in the Spectator. "This is the nub of the problem: there isn't enough money coming forward to solve these 'burning injustices', nor enough room for those who want to think radically about housing policy or indeed the provision of mental health care to do so."

Top housing blogger, Jules Birch, was feeling generous. "When was the last time a Conservative prime minister made a speech more favourable to social housing?", he asked in Inside Housing, whilst also noting that this week's promise of £2 billion was even flakier than last year's. Jules makes his judgement largely on the bit of the speech that was not about money. Here May spoke in carefully crafted Barwellisms, with housing associations taking more of a lead in developments, being more ambitious, being able to ride the business cycle, and praising the non-profit nature of their role.

It is also true, and a relief, that some of Cameron and Osborne's most extreme policies have been reversed or forgotten about. And I welcome the major contrast in her language with that of Cameron and Osborne, both of whom disliked housing associations and hated social housing. Speaking positively about social housing, especially if it is taken up in the media, is a start.

But what does it add up to? It feels like the boxer who has the opponent on the ropes, about to go down, and stops hitting quite so hard. The money means nothing and was not explained in the context of the next spending review, it is probably no more than existing puny budgets rolled through into future years. Jam tomorrow but spread very thin. It contrasts with a major report for London First this week showing the vast increase in both public and private capital spending that is needed to achieve the government's stated aim of 300,000 homes a year – a 40% increase is required with 65% in London, they estimate. Put another way, housing's share of UK GDP must grow from 2.3% to 3.3%. Unlike May's promise, these really are big numbers.

The love now showered on housing associations creates nothing more than a scumble, a thin veneer. Underneath, social housing is still seen as a holding pen for people who really should want to be home owners. And home ownership is where the real money is going. The view that people who rent are inferior to home owners is at the root of stigma, and it has not changed. Policy reversal is also very partial: the Osborne cuts in housing investment have not been restored, the welfare reforms are still destroying lives, homelessness is still rising, rents are far too high in all sectors, and the bedroom tax is still in place. And it was noticeable that she managed to irritate the Tory chair of the Local Government Association, Lord Porter, for implying that housing associations were the keepers of the legacy of council housing.

A few good headlines for the Prime Minister followed her speech, it must make a relief from Brexit. Most of the national press and broadcast media swallowed it whole, repeating the 'extra money' line with no analysis, as if the cheques would be arriving next week rather than 2022. But even with May's welcome new language the old tropes refuse to die. The BBC's commentary included the statement that in the 1980s 'those who couldn't afford to buy were left in sink estates', eliciting a complaint from vlogger John Popham who called it a slur on social housing tenants. As is their way, the BBC just denied that it was inappropriate, but also referred to another programme about sink estates to make their point. Of course, 'we value your feedback'.

Not being quite so battered is an improvement of sorts. The total hostility of the previous era towards social housing seems to be ending, and that creates an opportunity. But it requires an altogether more assertive stance which includes councils as well as associations. For the millions in desperate housing need, happy clappy is not the right response.

So, WHY can't you afford a home?

October 13, 2018

Occasionally you read something that challenges your firmly fixed views. Like most in housing, I fall easily into the simple analysis that there is a direct link between our inability to build new homes and the housing affordability crisis. If only we built more then everything in housing would gradually come right.

Josh Ryan-Collins'[1] new book 'Why can't you afford a home?' definitely makes you think in a different way. The traditional analysis fails to explain why the crisis has emerged in so many different countries at the same time despite widely varying policies and approaches. He says this outcome is based on two pillars: the priority given to private home ownership as the dominant housing tenure and what he calls the 'self-reinforcing feedback cycle'. On the first of these, most countries have promoted housing as an (unearned) source of wealth rather than just somewhere to live by reducing property and capital gains taxes on housing compared to other investments. On the second, Ryan-Collins asserts that it is no coincidence that the crisis has mushroomed since the deregulation of financial services. No amount of fiddling with the planning system or blaming migrants can moderate the huge global forces that have been at work.

The 'self-reinforcing feedback cycle' works like this:

'In order to afford a home, most people need a mortgage. But when mortgage credit is extended to buy an existing property, it inflates house prices as bank lending involves the creation of new money. If house prices rise faster than incomes, the demand for mortgages increase, banks lend more, prices go up and so on'.

Strengthened by the perceived global public debt crisis, which constrained direct building of homes by the state, governments increasingly looked to the banking sector to find new ways of satisfying both housing demand and the clamour for individual home ownership. Thrifty banking was replaced by almost unlimited lending relative to incomes. Bank lending, previously focused on business investment, became concentrated on lending for residential purchase. Banks liked it because loans had collateral, and, unlike business, there was no limited liability. Worst of all, after an initial consumption effect (people buying houses tend also to buy furniture and white goods etc) residential lending did not lead to much growth – mainly adding to price inflation. People were effectively borrowing against rising values, so everyone gets a stake in keeping values rising. But the system becomes more unstable and volatile, inequity between those who manage to buy and those who don't rises, and more people become priced out. Productive investment is frozen out in favour of speculative lending, and economies become more vulnerable to economic shocks.

Solutions therefore need to be much broader than those that governments and central banks have attempted to date. Crucially, Ryan-Collins argues, 'land and credit markets need to be shaped to create public value: in this case affordable, decent quality housing.' He notes that some successful modern economies have been rather less dependant on rising property prices, notably Germany, Japan, Korea and Singapore. Priority must be given to lending for productive investment by business, guiding credit away from property. Property taxes are needed to make it less attractive as a financial asset, including a land value tax, and we should learn from those countries where more land is publicly owned.

Curiously, after this long analytical journey, during which Ryan-Collins challenges my simple notion that the answer to unaffordability is that we must build more, he confirms my other long-held and deep-seated simple assertion when he says that one structural solution is "supporting alternative forms of tenure such as renting, social housing and cooperative home ownership where housing is viewed as a place to live, not a financial asset."

This is a stimulating read and the book (which also benefits from not being as long as most economic tracts) delves into areas of economic and financial policy that deserve far more scrutiny. I would have liked a little more analysis of market changes in the UK since 2003 which have led to a decline in home ownership and the resurgence of private renting. However the book's strength is that it goes beyond description and analysis to promote possible solutions. These are inevitably long-term and international but they could begin to influence government policies in the here and now.

[1] *Josh Ryan-Collins is a Senior Research Associate at the Institute for Innovation and Public Purpose, University College London.*

Home ownership is the most 'subsidised' tenure

November 21, 2018

It often seems that the term 'council tenant' automatically comes with the word 'subsidised' in front of it. It is part and parcel of the stigmatisation of the tenure by many politicians and much of the media – and even some within the social housing sector. Following Grenfell, the government in its Green Paper nodded in recognition of the unfair portrayal of council housing and noted that stigma has a deleterious effect both on the tenure and on the people who live in it. But even as they recognised it, they also repeated their underlying belief in the *superiority* of home ownership.

Despite overwhelming political and popular support, since 2003 or so home ownership has been in decline as the affordability of housing has deteriorated. For all its efforts, this government has not yet managed to reverse the trend. In his book launched last week, Josh Ryan-Collins showed that this was not just a UK effect, it has happened across what he calls the 'Anglo-Saxon economies' where banking systems have been deregulated in the same way and at the same time. Encouraged by the collateral of bricks and mortar, overly keen banks with liberal lending policies pushed prices up much faster than incomes, hugely stretching price to income ratios. Other countries with different types of bank – notably Germany where banks are regional and based more on co-operative principles – have experienced much less house price inflation and have much less emphasis on houses being investments rather than places to live.

In the UK since 2010 we have seen the amount of public money put into social housing slashed yet there have been many, often costly, initiatives to help slow the decline in home ownership. The net effect is that home ownership is now easily the most subsidised tenure, much more so than social housing, with private renting receiving the least help.

The conclusion that the state gives far more help to home ownership cuts against the grain of conventional thinking. But it has now been very well documented in a report entitled ***Dreams and Reality? Government finance, taxation and the private housing market*** published today by the Chartered Institute of Housing and written by housing finance experts Steve Wilcox and Peter Williams. The authors reached their conclusion after an exhaustive analysis, taking account of all types of government intervention in the market, not only spending on grants, loans and guarantees, but also tax reliefs, welfare benefits and regulatory mechanisms which aim to stimulate or control the three main routes by which people get access to housing.

They show that government is directing about £8 billion annually into private housing over the five years to 2020/21, with over half going specifically to support home ownership and the remainder being more broadly aimed at the private market. In contrast, direct funding for new social housing is less than £2 billion annually.

Wilcox and Williams accept that the analysis is bound to be crude because financial support for the sectors comes in different forms – for social housing it is mainly grant spending whereas much of the private market support is via loans or guarantees. Some specifics:

- In terms of tax reliefs, home owners benefit much more than private landlords: net tax relief for owners was some £29 billion in 2016/17 (£10 billion paid in tax; £39 billion received in tax reliefs) whereas private landlords paid net tax of at least £8 billion.
- Within the benefits system, tenants receive much more assistance than home-owners, with about £15 billion annually going to social housing tenants and £8.5 billion to private renters.
- Private renting has a big advantage in mortgage regulation because it can access interest-only mortgages whereas new home buyers have to navigate various restrictions on mortgage availability.
- Despite the huge increase in general support for the market, the government safety net for those homeowners facing financial difficulty has been much reduced. Support for mortgage interest will soon migrate from paying mortgage interest charges for unemployed home buyers to providing loans – a further erosion.

CIH chief executive **Terrie Alafat** CBE said:

"This report demonstrates just how much government support is going to the private market, and to home-owners in particular – probably contrary to many people's expectations. It takes a comprehensive look at the way the government supports our housing system – and we would urge ministers to do the same.

Currently just 21 per cent of government investment is going to affordable housing. Rebalancing this budget to support people on lower incomes who can't afford to buy could make a big difference. It is vital that the government supports councils and housing associations to build more homes for social rent."

Wilcox and Williams also sneak a look into the future. If home ownership is stabilised at around 60% and if the social housing sector does not grow proportionately, it follows that future net growth will come mainly in the private rented sector. This will lead to a substantial long term increase in the cost of housing benefit (especially as working private tenants retire and become eligible for rent support). Unlike social housing, where housing benefit is retained by landlords and surpluses recycled, HB to private landlords funds profits which are removed from the sector.

'It serves to make the point', the authors say, 'that the continuation of current trends is not a cost-neutral option for government'.

And in a massive understatement they comment that 'there are questions as to whether we are spending as efficiently as we can in the housing sector, a pertinent point given the general pressure on public finances.' In particular, they question the emphasis on intervention on the demand-side through Help to Buy and other schemes rather than supporting supply-side initiatives (ie directly building more houses rather than increasing buyers' purchasing power).

We may have to wait a long time to see 'subsidised home owners' replace 'subsidised council tenants' in the headlines. But this report demonstrates that government intervention has become critically important to the operation of the private housing market. It seems highly unlikely that the schemes chosen by the government will lead to less volatility and house price inflation. Whatever happens, in future a much sharper focus will be needed on private renting, both in terms of the cost to households in rent but also the cost to government in benefits.

2019

A vision based on evidence

January 9, 2019

Shelter's Housing Commission report published yesterday is undoubtedly a major contribution to the debate about how to solve the housing crisis, and I broadly agree with most of its conclusions.

Attending the launch, I found the most intriguing aspect was the frank admission by one of the commissioners, Baroness Sayeeda Warsi, a former chair of the Conservative Party, that her previously 'ideological view' and belief in the small state had been challenged and changed 'by the evidence' given to the Commission. For her, and the several other conservative-leaning members of the Commission, to support a huge social house building programme – more than 3 million over 20 years – represents an important shift in thinking on the right of centre.

Also noteworthy was the admission by former Labour Leader, Ed Miliband, that he had not been strong enough in his advocacy of social housing at the 2015 general election.

The report of the Commission is a well-written review of housing issues and how we got to the bad place we are now in. At its core the economic case for investment in social rented homes is made forcefully, based on a detailed analysis by Capital Economics which has been published separately.

In essence the case for investment is the same as that made by the SHOUT campaign in 2015 (with analysis also by Capital Economics)[1], which is that the cost of meeting the clear need for a large extra supply of homes for social rent is manageable if you take into account not only the long term costs but also the long term benefits - and especially the savings that will be made in benefits.

Shelter's Commission recommends and models building 3.1 million social homes over 20 years. You can argue over this number and how it is arrived at, but it is plain that we need to reverse the catastrophic switch that has been made over the last 40 years away from spending on investment in new homes towards helping people to afford or pay for homes at or near market prices.

The gross additional cost of the investment proposed by Shelter, estimated at an average of around £10.7 billion per year, is substantially offset by reductions in the costs of benefits, economic growth, spin off savings in health and other services, and increases in productivity, bringing the estimated net cost down to an average of around £3.8 billion per year. (One year's worth, as it happens, is less than the money being wasted on preparations for a no deal Brexit). The huge programme would only increase public sector net debt by 2%, a relatively trivial amount given the huge increase in human wellbeing that would flow.

The headline figure of 3.1. million extra social homes has dominated the coverage, but there are many more recommendations about other aspects of social housing. The report proposes a new system of consumer regulation to protect all renters (social and private), major changes to enable the enforcement of standards, and a transformation in the ability of tenants to make complaints and have them resolved. There are recommendations to improve tenants' ability to make their voice heard, with tenant panels, independent tenants' organisations and a revived national tenants' voice organisation.

In support of the programme of new building, the Commission makes some detailed proposals around planning, including reforms which would make land available at a fairer price and enable planning authorities to obtain a bigger planning gain contribution from private development.

These proposals are broadly very welcome although I couldn't always follow the logic between the discussion in the report and the final recommendations. There were important areas of debate from which no recommendations flowed at all. It does not undermine the report to set out some doubts and questions.

I am not convinced that the proposed consumer regulator should cover both social and private sectors. They are such different beasts and consumer regulation for social housing seems to me to be inextricably linked to economic and governance performance, which would remain with the existing regulator. The comparison that is made with banking, where financial and consumer regulation are separated, does not hold water, and I think it would be wrong to end up with 4 bodies (HCA/Mayor, economic regulator, consumer regulator, and Ombudsman) tripping over each other to hold housing providers to account. It would be too complicated and it wouldn't work.

The private sector absolutely needs consumer regulation, but I suspect it would be better done by a specialist organisation and be focused on finding ways of regulating small landlords.

Given that the report sets out a vision for social housing, I don't think it deals adequately with the question of rent. The economic analysis makes fair assumptions about the level of grant that would be available for new build, which would broadly maintain the current social rent regime, but a vision for the sector should include consideration of the best general level for rents – notably whether they should continue to increase faster than inflation - and whether there might be a better system, for example one that is more closely linked to incomes. There are associated questions about how the benefits system might change.

Similarly, the report discusses the problems but makes no recommendations about the terms and conditions of tenancy and the balance of power between landlord and tenant, which has shifted heavily to the former in recent years. I would like to see the return of security of tenure and the end of fixed term tenancies, and a detailed review of the various grounds for possession. It also fudges the issue of right to buy and does not address the increasing management problems being faced on estates by the rapid rise in high turnover private landlordism enabled by the right to buy.

As with the point about regulation, in some ways the discussion about private renting sits uncomfortably in the report. That is not to diminish its importance, but to observe that it feels too much like an add-on. Many good points are made, and important recommendations are made for example about no fault evictions. But it needs something more fundamental in a report which is concerned with a 20-year vision for housing. If the proposed social housing building plan came to pass, over time there would be a steep decline in demand for private renting. We need to think through what implications that would have in practice. How would private landlords react as their market changed? Would landlords generally seek an exit? Should we revisit the policy of encouraging institutional investors in private renting? If prices fell, what would be the knock on effect to home ownership? A major revival in social rent has broad implications for other tenures which need to be addressed.

The crucial thing about the Shelter Commission report, however, is probably not the specific recommendations. It is whether the work they have done, and the reach they have achieved into Conservative thinking, helps to create a change in the political climate which then leads to a far more balanced housing policy across the board.

Five years ago, the few left standing that defended social rented housing were mocked as living in the past and not facing up to the modern realities of market-driven housing policy. We were especially derided by some luminaries in the housing association movement who, thankfully, are more quiet these days. Social rent is back at the centre of the housing debate, in the mainstream where it belongs. The groundswell in favour of it is vitally important but the next stage is the vital one - because winning the political argument has not yet led to many homes being built.

[1] In March 2019 Red Brick reported on detailed evidence submitted to the Affordable Housing Commission by Dave Treanor and by SHOUT, the campaign for social housing. Both pieces are worth reading – Dave's on Red Brick and SHOUT's on Medium. SHOUT's submission makes the case that genuinely social rent is an exceptionally robust model of housing provision and remarkable in the degree of self-financing it involves. The submission can be read in full at https://tinyurl.com/SHOUThousing2019

Voluntary Right to Buy: should housing associations be 'proud to be involved'?

May 10, 2019

The headline is based on an Inside Housing article this week by a director of a national housing association, Stonewater, which is one of those taking part in the government's pilot scheme in the Midlands. Sue Shirt says they are 'unashamedly supportive of the VRTB' and 'proud' to be selling off their houses, estimating that around 170 will be sold in the pilot period (presumably in most cases houses currently let at social rents). She gives two main reasons for this. One is that they are giving tenants what they want. The second is that (unlike with council housing right to buy) they plan to replace every home sold. She says that it keeps tenants in their communities whereas otherwise they would move out to buy. In Stonewater's view, VRTB 'helps the social housing journey' by enabling financially secure tenants to buy instead of rent.

Superficially, of course, Ms Shirt has a point. No doubt the lucky buyers of Stonewater houses are over the moon, especially as they have qualified for discounts of up to 70% – or £82,800 outside London – the same levels as for council right to buy. They'll have to raise a mortgage but instead of paying rent they'll have a valuable asset to pass on to their children or to sell or let out at a later date. In many ways it's surprising that the pilot scheme isn't proving more popular. Stonewater has so far completed just 11 sales, and if it reaches its projected level of 170 it will have sold just two per cent of its stock in the region. That's a lot of effort to reach such a small proportion of tenants, and the government is said to be considering extending the pilot scheme to raise more interest.

What is missing from Sue Shirt's assessment is any examination of the wider picture if the pilot scheme does turn out to be successful. Of course, one reason why a housing association like Stonewater is willing to take part is that it gets full and instant recompense for the hefty discounts it has to give, so they can aim to have one for one replacement of their own stock. The money comes from a Treasury pot of £200 million created for the purpose. An extended scheme would need more money. Failing some magic by the chancellor, the only sources are the rest of the housing budget or reviving the Treasury's original plan, which was to force councils to sell their high-value council houses and hand most of the money over to subsidise housing association discounts.

Either way, a lump sum worth up to £82,800 to one 'financially secure' tenant who buys their home **comes at the expense of the same amount invested in new social housing for people who are struggling to rent**, let alone buy. It is not the narrow perspective of whether Stonewater replaces one for one, the essential point is that the money available in the housing system will produce fewer additional homes in total for people in need.

Sue Shirt says that the 'crucial point' about VRTB is that it helps more people into much-needed, modern, energy-efficient housing. But this is a very suspect argument. After all, tenants exercising VRTB are in a nice comfortable home already, and while the mortgage they will now pay releases a receipt that Stonewater can reuse, that's only because the rest of the sale price will be made up by the government.

A supposed advantage is that VRTB buyers stay in their home when they might have moved out to buy elsewhere. While this may be advantageous for the community in the short term, it ignores the issue of what happens when the buyer eventually moves. A house that could be relet at social rent may well end up in the private rented sector, as is frequently the experience with the council RTB. It will be let at higher rents – costing more in housing benefit if that is needed – and quite possibly with minimal management, causing problems for other tenants in the area.

While the pilot scheme might involve selling a relatively small number of homes, up to 3,000, the real danger lies in its potential success. This could have two effects. One is that it hastens the day when all housing associations are persuaded into a 'voluntary' scheme by attractive offers about how fast they can access the receipts, without answering the crucial question of where the money will come from once the Treasury's £200 million has been spent and what the impact of that will be on other programmes. Back in 2015, when it was planned to use 'council high value sales' to fund the VRTB, in *Selling off the Stock* CIH showed that a popular VRTB scheme might require all the receipts from selling high-value homes, leaving no money for replacements.

The second effect will be to prolong the right to buy in England when it should be on its last legs. It was scrapped in Scotland in 2016, it died in Wales earlier this year and soon it may be gone in Northern Ireland too. Only in Whitehall do politicians continue to find ways to breathe life into a policy that's not relevant to today's problems. Let's put some more nails in its coffin, not try to revive the corpse.

Labour's 'Land Grab'

June 4, 2019

In the middle of all the fawning over Trump, the newspapers got their teeth into a Labour story this morning. According to the Daily Mail it was about "the policies of Venezuela" and "Labour's garden tax: Party unveils new Corbyn cash-grab on your private green space and force the sale of vacant land on the cheap." The Daily Express said "Jeremy Corbyn proposes 'bombshell' tax RAID on hard-working homeowners who have a garden." The Telegraph's slightly more moderate headline but equally inaccurate story was: "Jeremy Corbyn unveils plans for 'progressive' tax raid on homes and gardens of the middle class."

Such disgraceful behaviour by Corbyn and the Labour Party attracted my interest, but when I tracked the actual report down I found it was a detailed and thoughtful analysis and set of recommendations around an issue which has huge implications for people who want affordable homes.

Called **'Land for the Many: Changing the way our fundamental asset is used, owned and governed'** it was produced for the Labour Party by seven contributors[1] including George Monbiot and Laurie Macfarlane - whose work we have covered on Red Brick before. Land is the hidden issue behind the housing crisis and the full report is well worth a read - because if you rely on media portrayals you might get the wrong impression of it.

Monbiot sets out his stall in a powerful preface, worth quoting at some length:

"Dig deep enough into many of the problems this country faces, and you will soon hit land. Soaring inequality and exclusion; the massive cost of renting or buying a decent home; repeated financial crises, sparked by housing asset bubbles; the collapse of wildlife and ecosystems; the lack of public amenities – the way land is owned and controlled underlies them all. Yet it scarcely features in political discussions.

"The sense that even in discussing land we are trespassing is so strong that this critical issue remains off the agenda. Yet we cannot solve our many dysfunctions without addressing it. This report aims to put land where it belongs: at the heart

of political debate and discussion. It proposes radical but practical changes in the way land in the UK is used and governed. By these means, it seeks to make this a nation that works for everyone, with a better distribution of wealth and power, greater financial stability, economic security and environmental quality, greater participation in the decisions that affect our lives, an enhanced ability to create our own homes and neighbourhoods and a stronger sense of community and belonging."

Despite the hysterical headlines, the report is not yet Labour policy: it contains proposals that will considered between now and the general election. But the reaction shows what a mountain of bias and misrepresentation Labour has to climb to get a serious debate going on this vitally important topic.

Is any of hysteria justified? Let's look at the key proposals

- free and open access to data on land ownership
- an explicit government goal to stabilise house prices to improve the long-term house-price-to-income ratio.
- redirect bank lending to productive sectors and reduce speculative demand for land.
- proposals for a Common Ground Trust to buy land underlying a house, to reduce house prices and bring in the idea of socialised land rents.
- major reforms to private renting with a cap on rent increases and an ambitious social housing programme.
- replace council tax with a progressive property tax payable by owners not tenants – with surcharges for empty and second homes and non-UK residents.
- phase out stamp duty land tax for owner occupiers.
- replace business rates with a commercial Land Value Tax.
- new Development Corporations buy sell and develop land to create new towns.
- enable public bodies to buy land at closer to current use value, estimated to be able to reduce the cost of affordable housing by 50%.
- remove permitted development rights that allow offices to be converted to homes without needing planning permission.
- stronger public involvement in planning.
- proposals to promote community ownership and control of land and buildings.

- greater provision of parks and stronger use of the public realm. And a stronger right to roam.

It's a detailed report, an instructive read, and in my view spot on in its analysis. It follows on from a lot of good work on the land question done by others in the recent past and covered on Red Brick, including Dave Treanor, London Assembly Housing Committee and Josh Ryan-Collins, Toby Lloyd and Laurie Macfarlane for the New Economics Foundation.

The Monbiot et al report is a serious contribution to a genuine debate, so it is enlightening to see how it is treated by the media. Most of it was hugely hostile, and I couldn't find a word about it on the BBC News or Sky News website. Let's see if Channel 4 can do a little better. But it shows the real difficulty Labour has in promoting progressive policies for wider debate, and the inherent bias in the mainstream media against leftish proposals, even when they are as strong and beneficial as these.

When the headlines say 'an end to council tax' or 'an end to stamp duty' then the public might have a chance of understanding what it's about.

[1] The seven authors are George Monbiot (editor), Robin Grey, Tom Kenny, Laurie Macfarlane, Anna Powell-Smith, Guy Shrubsole and Beth Stratford.

From social mobility to social justice: how a simple policy announcement started a small war

June 17, 2019

Most people reading or watching the media during the last few days would have been left with the impression that Jeremy Corbyn had launched a major attack on the last Labour Government. In fact, he made a forward-looking speech to teachers on moving away from an emphasis on social mobility to talking about wider social justice instead.

It got little coverage, no surprise there, until it was attacked by Tony Blair with a video and a fanfare, after which Corbyn was widely denounced for disparaging the last Labour government. Much of the vitriol was not in response to what he actually said, or even his own tweets on the issue, but to a strange and incoherent tweet from Momentum in reply to Blair's video, saying in effect that austerity was Blair's legacy. A little bit of displacement was all that was needed to make the charge that Corbyn had had a go at the last Labour government.

Blair's video is a hallmarked example of the spin at which he is so adept (a political talent Corbyn lacks). He takes **one line** from the social mobility speech – "for decades we have been told that inequality does not matter" – adds in a couple of quotes carefully selected from other speeches in the past, then claims Corbyn is constantly attacking the last Labour government and 'enough is enough', before laying out some of Labour's relatively good record on taking people out of poverty, spending on public services (focusing on health and education), throwing in Labour's excellent performance on overseas aid as well. So far as I know, none of these are disputed by Corbyn, indeed I frequently hear him attack the Tory record by quoting Labour's achievements in these areas.

But the facts of Labour's record was not what this was about. The media skirmish that ensued was remarkable for the lack of nuance. An exception was Sean Fitzsimons (@CroydonSean) who tweeted "My take on the Blair/Brown Government. Solid performer on most fronts. Excellent on NHS, education, and improving incomes of pensioners and middle/low pay with children. Poor on house building, class and wealth inequalities, and North/South divide. 7.5/10."

For virtually everyone else it was either 0/10 or 10/10. Hatred of Blair on the one hand and hatred of Corbyn on the other. The result of this madness will be no Labour government at the next election.

So, what about the substance of what Corbyn said? He was talking about inequality not just tackling poverty and he was talking about the weaknesses of the social mobility idea. Blair counters by saying inequality diminished under Labour. He compares the bottom decile with the top decile, but it is the top 1% that has become detached from the rest of society and that is what Corbyn concentrates on. Then again, this was not mentioned in his speech. Whether inequality rose or fell largely depends on which figures you pick, and it depends whether you include wealth as well as income. Blair also stresses that social mobility improved under Labour, rather missing Corbyn's central point.

Whether it is fair to include 1997-2010 in the '30 years in which we were told inequality doesn't matter' or 'dropping 40 years of political consensus' is of course a matter of judgement, but in my view it is fair because it has proved possible to reduce poverty (normally measured by comparing the poorest with the average) without reducing inequality. Andy Burnham on Marr yesterday used a similar rhetorical flourish, saying that governments have 'failed the north for many decades' including when he was in government. Is he to be denounced? Another expert in rhetorical flourishes, Peter Mandelson, probably did the most damage to Labour's reputation in this area with his notorious comment that he was "intensely relaxed about people getting filthy rich as long as they pay their taxes".

The idea of social mobility relies too much on counting how many people born into poor circumstances 'make it' into the richest group or into political power. Media often reduce it to whether someone born into poverty could become prime minister or find a 'route out' though football or boxing – the topic of many a film. It is often associated with the idea of 'meritocracy' and has been used to justify a wide range of both progressive and reactionary policies – including grammar schools and paid-for places in private schools, both of which are said to improve 'social mobility'.

Corbyn was building intelligently on a substantial debate about social mobility in recent months, including important reports by IPPR and by CLASS think tanks. There has also been debate in and around the current Social Mobility Commission, which has commented on issues to do with inequality, warning that without major reform social and economic divisions within Britain's society are set to widen. One of the current Commissioners, Sam Friedman @SamFriedmanSoc tweeted that "I would personally welcome a shift of political narrative away from upward mobility for some and toward a greater emphasis on inequality, individual flourishing, and tackling the reproduction of privilege."

I suppose I'm a good example of social mobility, brought up on a council estate in a one-illness-away-from-poverty family and ending up with degrees and well-paying jobs. But nearly all of the young people I grew up with left school at 16 and did not have the luck that came my way. In my view, the social mobility approach focuses on people like me and 'the ladder out', changing nothing structural, whereas the social justice approach cares about all the rest and how to create a rising tide that lifts all boats.

Corbyn plans to replace the social mobility commission with a social justice commission, sponsored by the Treasury, which would have a wider brief to undertake audits and impact assessments of policy and suggest changes to legislation.

The quote that caused the uproar was taken from this part of Corbyn's speech:

"For decades we've been told that inequality doesn't matter because the education system will allow talented and hard-working people to succeed whatever their background. But the greater inequality has become, the more entrenched it has become.

"The idea that only a few talented or lucky people deserve to escape the disadvantage they were born into, leaving in place a social hierarchy in which millions are consigned to the scrap heap, results in the talents of millions of children being squandered."

I think this is uncontroversial, not worthy of the fuss that's been made, yet grounded in reality, and the right way to go.

And the legacy of past Labour governments was fairly judged by shadow education secretary Angela Rayner, speaking with Corbyn, who said

"The Tories like to talk about people like me who had a difficult start but got on in life as evidence that anyone can succeed on their own. But actually my life shows the exact opposite. Any success I have had is thanks to Labour governments that provided the council house, minimum wage, tax credits and Sure Start children's centre that enabled me to achieve it. That is social justice."

Rayner also published an article making the case for the change in New Statesman.

So, despite the fury and the apparent division, this shift in emphasis away from social mobility towards social justice is actually something the whole Labour Party should be capable of uniting around.

There are many battlegrounds within the party, but this shouldn't be one of them.

Labour to modernise feudal leasehold system in response to Tory inaction

July 22, 2019

By Dermot Mckibbin[1]

On 11 July there was a debate in the Commons on the Government's response to the House of Commons Select Committee critical report on the leasehold tenure.

The Government claims to be bringing forward reforms to:

1. Ban the granting of new leases on houses other than in exceptional circumstances.
2. Restricting ground rents on newly established leases to zero.

3. Working with the Law Commission to look at ways to reinvigorate commonhold and improving the process for buying a freehold or extending a lease or exercising The Right to Manage.

4. By reviewing charges faced by both leaseholders and freeholders and professionalising and regulating property agents.

5. By clamping down on unjustified legal costs for leaseholders, ensuring all landlord freeholders belong to a redress scheme and giving freeholders on private estates equivalent rights to leaseholders to challenge communal costs.

6. By persuading developers to sign up a to public pledge to help existing leaseholders trapped in unfair and costly agreements.

The Government claim to be committed to introducing legislation as soon as parliamentary times allow. However due to the Brexit debate Parliament has been clocking off early and few bills are in fact currently going through Parliament. Ministers have repeatedly promised action to tackle the abuses that leaseholders face, yet with over 60 official announcements since 2010, no new legislation has been introduced. The Government lacks the political inclination to progress this issue as it is too close to the interests of property.

The Government claim in their response that leasehold is a legitimate form of home ownership. However, England is about the only country in the world that has not yet moved away from this feudal form of tenure. The leaseholder has to pay a ground rent to the freeholder and at the end of the lease the leaseholder becomes a mere tenant if no action is taken. The leaseholder can forfeit their lease if they break a term of the lease. There is no legal defence to the freeholder's right to remove the lease. The relationship is a landlord/tenant one which is feudal in nature and no longer appropriate for the 21st century

Alternatives to leasehold are available through co-operative flat ownership in Europe, strata title in Australia and condominium ownership in the USA. Closer to home, Scotland, Wales and Northern Ireland have all taken steps towards ending leasehold.

The Shadow housing front bench has recently produced an excellent consultation document called 'Ending the Scandal: Labour's new deal for Leaseholders'.

Labour plans five radical changes:

1. Ending the sale of new private leasehold houses with direct effect and the sale of private leasehold flats by the end of the first term in office.

2. Ending the ground rent for new leasehold homes, cap the ground rent for existing leaseholders at 0.1% of the property value, up a to a maximum of £250 per year.
3. Set a simple formula for leaseholders to buy the freehold to their home, or commonhold in the case of a flat, capped at 1% of the property value.
4. Crack down on unfair fees and contract terms by publishing a reference list of reasonable charges, requiring transparency of service charges and giving leaseholders a right to challenge rip-off fees and conditions or poor performance from service companies.
5. Give residents greater powers over the management of their homes, with new rights for flat-owners to form residents' associations and by simplifying the Right to Manage.

The document correctly refers to the growth in the number of leaseholders. The precise number is still surprisingly unknown, but is estimated at between 4.3 and 6.6 million: up to one in four of all homes. Over the past 20 years, the proportion of houses built as leasehold is thought to have doubled.

Over 90% of all leasehold house owners say they regret buying a leasehold property and almost two-thirds feel like they were mis-sold. Many leaseholders thought they had brought on the basis they could easily and cheaply convert to freehold ownership, only to later find that a complex and often expensive process makes enfranchisement impossible for them to afford.

According to the report it is increasingly clear that there is a systematic problem with the selling of properties on a leasehold basis. Leasehold mis-selling has the potential to be a new PFI scandal.

In 2018, the Conveyancing Association published research suggesting that 98% of sales of leasehold properties with onerous or doubling ground rents had been in breach of consumer protection regulations. The campaign group Leasehold Knowledge Partnership have estimated that up to 100,000 homes cannot be sold due to a high ground rents and other onerous lease conditions.

At the heart of Labour's plans to help leaseholders is the opportunity to obtain true ownership of their property through conversion to freehold or commonhold in the case of flat owners. Labour will legislate for a simple buy-out formula that will apply to longer leases, set at a proportion of freehold capital value. Labour will set the maximum ground rent chargeable at 0.1% of the ground rent, with a cap of £250 per year.

For a leaseholder currently living in a house or flat worth £200,000, Labour's simple new formula would mean they can buy their freehold for just £2,000. This is a significant saving compared to leasehold enfranchisement for a £200,000 property: with 90 years left on the lease and a £250 per year ground rent, the current cost for enfranchisement would be over £6,000 plus expensive legal fees. For properties with ground rents above £250, the cost would be significantly higher still.

Mis-selling of leases is a big issue in the North West. This region has 75 MP's of whom 20 are Conservative. Approximately two thirds of leaseholders live in London where there are elections in 2020.Hopefully this report will be read and acted upon by all Labour Party members. A House of Commons briefing paper is helpful and the accompanying table has useful regional and constituency statistics. (2)

[1]Dermot Mckibbin is a member of Beckenham CLP

A look back at Labour's Annual Conference 2019, from a housing perspective

October 22, 2019

By Sheila Spencer, Secretary, Labour Housing Group

Amid the gloom of Brexit, climate change, and reselection fever, Annual Conference this year was a rather more cheery experience for those who care about housing issues. For one thing, there were more fringe meetings about housing and homelessness (at least 20) than any other subject – even Brexit and the NHS. And the Priority Ballot for delegates to vote on which topics they want to see discussed at Conference saw housing get the highest vote in the Constituency ballot, and one of the highest in the Trade Union one. Finally, a large number of motions had been submitted about both housing and homelessness.

So, we were off to a good start, with the compositing meeting coming straightaway on the Saturday evening. Quite a few CLPs and some affiliated organisations had submitted the Labour Campaign for Council Housing model resolution, or variations of it. Labour Housing Group's own resolution, put together following a lively discussion of the outcomes of Shelter's Social Housing Commission at our AGM in March, contained many of the same issues.

There was fundamentally little disagreement between many of the delegates about what we should be doing to address the housing crisis. All agreed that we need a major programme of council house building, that housing should be at the heart of our campaigning efforts to win the next general election, and that the Right To Buy must end, though this could be accompanied by an option to buy a discounted home from private sector stock.

To my delight, no-one argued against compulsory purchase of unoccupied empty tower blocks, removing restrictions for councils to build new homes (by which LHG had meant counting investment against the PSBR), or abolishing Assured Shorthold Tenancies (ASTs). Nor was there any major falling out about the need for indefinite tenancies and the introduction of rent caps in the private rented sector whether Bedroom Tax should be abolished, or the need to build energy efficient homes.

There were, however, several contentious issues, and we took some time to explore them. Key amongst these were the question of whether it is necessary to state how much to spend on building the 155,000 public (social) rented homes to be built each year by the next Labour Government, and whether *all* new homes should be built to a lifetime homes standard.

Two other issues proved worthy of longer discussion, the first of which – retrofitting sprinklers and replacing combustible cladding in high rise tower blocks – will cause no surprise. Arguments were put forward for this to happen in all social housing tower blocks, to be paid for by the Government, and this view won the day.

The second issue was whether Housing Associations should be brought back under local authority control. From amongst the delegates present, there were several horror stories about the behaviour of these housing bodies which started their lives aiming to help to meet housing need and now seem, in the case of at least a number of the larger ones, to see themselves as private businesses beyond the reach of tenants, local councillors or indeed the government. The final wording in the composite, to "Give councils the powers and resources to take housing associations under direct council control" was intended as a last resort where the housing provider did not pay attention to the case made for them to mend their ways!

When it came to the housing session at Conference, the Housing and Homelessness composites [1] came on the very last day, somewhat overshadowed by the dramatic events at the Supreme Court the day before and the recall of MPs to Parliament that day. So in the event it was just as well that John Healey had not been down on the programme to speak – but I felt this was quite a disappointment, given the profile that housing *should* have in our General

Election campaign. I was also disappointed that Jeremy Corbyn mentioned only building council houses in his speech, ignoring the impact that could have come from telling young people that we will abolish ASTs and stop them having to move every 5 minutes. As John Healey often points out, for once, our current Leader needs no convincing about the importance of progressive Labour housing policies.

At LHG's two fringe meetings ("***Time for Public Housing Revolution***", and a second meeting with SERA and others, "***A home shouldn't cost the earth: How Labour can address the housing and climate crises***), people were in no doubt about the need for housing to be at the heart of our campaigning. As John Healey said, we must get across that only Labour can put in place what is needed, and give people hope once more.

And giving hope back to people about a decent approach to providing housing was very much called for this year at Conference. The visible need for this was obvious, since no-one can have failed to be dismayed by the large number of tents, people sleeping in doorways, and people begging that we passed every day on our way to and from the conference centre in Brighton. Despite going to several fringe meetings where homelessness was discussed, I uncovered no explanation for this big increase in the system failing to prevent people becoming homelessness other than the ones we all know about: sanctions, Universal Credit, Local Housing Allowance rates; sky-high PRS rents; and not building enough affordable public housing in the city.

I left Brighton feeling that we had done a good job on outlining what we must do when we are in office – but a little dismayed at what there is still to do to bring housing to the forefront of Labour's collective campaigning mind. Oh well, back to the doorstep for me, then!

[1] *The housing composite resolutions passed by Conference can be found on the LHG website at https://labourhousing.org/news/annual-conference-2019-housing-and-homelessness-composites/*

2020

Coronavirus and housing: Government doing nothing much

March 20, 2020

The government has been accused of being unclear in its communications around Coronavirus. But this headline appears on the Ministry of Housing website: *'Complete ban on evictions and additional protection for renters'*. Poor communication or a straightforward lie?

The policy is actually to **'suspend new evictions'** until after the crisis, initially three months. So, Minister Robert Jenrick's statement that 'no renter who has lost income due to coronavirus will be forced out of their home' is a short-lived commitment.

They call it a *'radical package'* which it plainly is not. They fail to address basic questions about possession proceedings that are already underway. Surely no-one should be evicted in the current crisis.

So far, no additional measures have been introduced to enable tenants to pay their rent, whether they are in work with reduced pay, laid off from work, or already not working. So, the best that can be said for the policy is that it will defer possession proceedings from starting and will therefore delay eviction. Protection from eviction during the crisis is of course important (although some people have noted that the Courts may well be closed anyway), but what is needed is a policy **to prevent tenants being forced into arrears** during the crisis, for which they may be evicted afterwards.

Landlords with buy to let mortgages have had the 'mortgage holiday' policy extended to them. This is something they can apply for and the devil might be in the detail. But if a landlord qualifies for a holiday, no arrangements have been announced to make sure the benefit of this is passed on or at least shared. Landlords who qualify will of course need to catch up with their mortgage afterwards, although many will add the three months to the end of their term, which might be 20 years away. It could be that tenants who pay rent will essentially be creating a short-term cash-flow boost for landlords. Meanwhile, those tenants who cannot pay will accrue arrears, which they may not have the income to repay, and might face possession proceedings when the crisis is over.

At that point the policy falls apart entirely. There will be a strengthened *'pre-action protocol'* before possession proceedings - engagement between landlords and tenants to establish a repayment plan and to *'resolve disputes'*, during which landlords should 'reach out' to tenants to 'understand the financial position they are in'. Almost unbelievably, "The government will also issue guidance which asks landlords to show compassion and to allow tenants who are affected by this to remain in their homes wherever possible." I have little belief that the protocol will work in practice as intended. And it is not a criticism of landlords – Twitter is full of both good and bad examples of landlord behaviour, that's how the sector works - to say that NO policy should be determined by hoped-for 'compassion' rather than rights and obligations in law.

In practice, many tenants may be saved by the fact that landlords will see value in hanging on to existing tenants even if they get into Coronavirus arrears. Given the broadly-based reduction in incomes and hence savings that is likely over the next few months, one predictable market correction might be a reduction in rents and the costs of starting up new tenancies. Under these circumstances, keeping a tenant on an existing contract might be an attractive option.

Given that the Chancellor was talking in terms of hundreds of billions of pounds in loans for businesses, the government should be pushed into actions like those taken in other countries to guarantee incomes, putting money directly into the hands of those who are affected by the crisis to enable them to maintain the basics of existence. I would argue that the same should apply to the biggest cost of all, housing. Affected renters must be enabled to pay their rent through direct support from government, not the goodwill of landlords (private and social) - although that is also to be encouraged.

I'm not expert enough to know the best detailed mechanism for achieving the aim of enabling people to pay rent, I assume it's a mix of entertaining new emergency housing benefit claims, changing Universal Credit rules (paying it immediately, guaranteeing that the housing element will cover all of the rent), and relaxing current policies like the bedroom tax (otherwise how are people to obey the government and 'sleep in the spare room' if they get Covid19?). But the purpose of policy must be to enable people to pay their rent during the crisis and to avoid the debt which will create a crisis later. Even the awful Iain Duncan Smith has called for benefit rates to be increased.

Jenrick's performance as Housing Minister during all this has been exceptionally poor and uncaring. Homeless people and tenants have been inconvenient afterthoughts with half-baked inadequate policy responses. Some loose change for rough sleepers, nothing that I have seen for people living in temporary accommodation (eg extra rooms), no workable special arrangements for people living in shared accommodation or overcrowded housing.

Of one thing I have no doubt: Jeremy Corbyn and John McDonnell would have risen to the challenge – indeed they are doing so in opposition – in a way that

Johnson is incapable of doing. Because today's Tories have not learned the lesson that was learned by the Victorians. Go back a century and more, and it was public health concerns about infectious disease spreading from insanitary slums that led to the rise of council housing and the birth of the welfare state in the first place.

If the Coronavirus is as bad as some are predicting, this lesson will have to be learned all over again.

NTV – the wheel waiting to be re-invented

April 2, 2020

Ten years ago this month, the new **National Tenant Voice (NTV)** appointed Richard Crossley as its new chief executive, appointed the National Tenant Council and its board, and started business.

Sadly, it was to be very short-lived, as the general election swept Labour and its dynamic housing minister John Healey MP out of office and installed the Tory/LibDem government with Grant Shapps in charge of housing.

One of Shapps' first acts was to axe the new-born NTV to save a miserable £1 million a year. Shapps, who could have invented double-speak, ludicrously claimed he wanted tenants to have a stronger say in things. But he saw the NTV as a waste of money as he laid waste to the social housing regulatory system, also abolishing the Tenant Services Authority and the Audit Commission.

The NTV had a long gestation and I had the privilege of independently chairing the Communities and Local Government department's project group, which brought together a majority of tenants with all the other key housing bodies and the civil servants to find a way of meeting the common goal of strengthening the voice of tenants within UK housing. It was a complex process because we wanted the new organisation to have the status of a non-departmental government body, and the rules for establishing one were suitably complicated and not easily adapted for an organisation which would be run by tenants and not appointed by government.

The idea for the NTV as an integral part of the new structure for social housing regulation arose from an earlier report by Martin Cave which was broadly welcomed and accepted by government. The project group conducted a major consultation exercise involving 16 regional meetings with over 1000 tenants, collecting over 160 written responses. There was a huge and occasional fractious debate about the precise role and function of the NTV but the consultation broadly supported the project group's proposals.

A lot is said about social tenants, and others who live on social housing estates, much of it based on ignorance. Tenants are stereotyped and stigmatised, especially in the media but also by some politicians and housing professionals. By grasping the opportunity presented by the NTV, there is a chance that the authentic voice of social tenants may at last be heard as citizens of equal worth. The NTV will be a voice for change and over time it could help transform the culture of social housing – and thereby improve the lives of nearly 10 million people.

From the introduction to **'Citizens of Equal Worth,** The NTV Project Group's Proposals for the National Tenant Voice', Report to Communities and Local Government, October 2008

The NTV's vision emphasised that it would be a resource for tenants (which included leaseholders and shared owners) of social landlords, an independent organisation that would be accountable to tenants, with clear values of inclusion, accountability, and transparency. It would not replace the existing national and regional tenant representative organisations but would be a business-like support organisation working for all tenants whether in existing organisations or not. It would not in the first instance cover private tenants, but the plan was to consult about if, when and how it would extend its remit.

The key roles of the NTV were

- advocacy – helping tenants collectively to speak *for themselves* to put their views to government and other bodies, placing particular emphasis on seeking and promoting the views of tenants whose voices are rarely heard.
- Research – identifying the impact that policies have on tenants and discovering the views of a wide range of tenants on policy issues.
- Communication – providing good information to tenants and developing a two-way dialogue with them.
- Support – for the existing representative tenants' movement to help it to develop and strengthen.

The working group and ministers believed that it was important to have a significant number of tenants involved in the governance structures of the NTV – to build its base, to encourage diversity, and to draw more people into policy discussions. It therefore had a National Tenant Council of 50 tenants to consider policy issues and a board of nine tenants and up to 6 independents to take legal responsibility for and to manage the organisation. An arm's-length accountability committee operated an open recruitment process for the organisation.

Over the last 10 years it has become clear to any observer that the decision made by the incoming Tory government to scrap Labour's regulatory structure, including the NTV, was a short-sighted knee-jerk mistake. Whatever Labour was in favour of, the new government was against. Despite the best efforts of some social landlords and many tenants, since then the voice of tenants has become weaker when it needed to be much stronger. The government (and much of UK housing) took its eye off the ball of maintaining and improving the quality of services to tenants.

It took Grenfell to open the eyes of much of the housing world, the government, and the public to the fact that tenants were not being listened to and their interests were not being served as they should be. Now, once again, there is some acceptance of the need to hear tenants' voices and to ensure that social landlords are monitored and regulated effectively (as all housing providers should be). But forward movement is even more glacial than the process ten years ago.

Ten years ago, the structure of regulation, with the NTV, was much closer to the right answer for social housing than anything we have now.

The NTV is a wheel that is waiting to be reinvented.

Domestic abuse: #MakeaStand

May 5, 2020

By Alison Inman [1]

I've spent the past few years talking to the social housing sector about domestic abuse, why it's an issue for them, and what they can do about it. The starting point for any discussion is usually that an average of two women a week are killed by a partner or ex-partner in England and Wales, a figure that hasn't really budged for years. Or, it hadn't until a few weeks ago. Since the lockdown started domestic homicides have soared, and the number of reports of abuse made to the charity Refuge has increased by 49%. This pattern is being repeated around the world; domestic abuse is itself reaching pandemic proportions and we must make sure that social landlords play their part in tackling it.

It has taken the lockdown to persuade the Government to agree with a coalition of homelessness charities, the women's sector, the Chartered Institute of Housing, the NHF and many more, that survivors of domestic abuse and sexual violence should automatically qualify for priority need when applying for housing. Good news, but too late for too many women who have had no choice but to return to their abuser rather than face life on the streets.

It is hard to completely disentangle domestic abuse from the wider housing crisis. Acute housing stress means that people often start living together far earlier than they would if there were other, affordable options. And when a relationship breaks down lack of alternative accommodation means people are forced to stay together. Labour's commitment to a massive programme of social house building will help but there is so much more we need to do. And many women and children do not have the luxury of time.

Work done by the domestic abuse charity Safe Lives for the Sunderland social landlord Gentoo (2018) estimates that approximately 13% of all repair jobs, and 21% of repairs spend, could be attributable to domestic abuse. This shows the business case for Councils and Housing Associations stepping up and making domestic abuse their business. It's shocking that most victims of abuse first come to the notice of their landlord when they are themselves reported as a perpetrator of noise nuisance. Just think about that for a minute. And almost two thirds of women with significant rent arrears are experiencing abuse in the home. Domestic Abuse really is a housing issue.

The work of the Domestic Abuse Housing Alliance has been key to the understanding of the relationships between physical, emotional and financial abuse and the housing system. They have free resources on their website and their eight stage accreditation guides landlords through a whole range of issues from case management to dealing with perpetrators. The CIH **#MakeaStand** campaign has hopefully shone a light on the issues for the sector, DAHA accreditation will make sure that local authorities and housing associations adopt the very best practice.

[1] *Alison was President of the Chartered Institute of Housing. She is a Board Member at Saffron Housing Trust and Colne Housing Society. Alison is also on the Board of TPAS, the engagement experts, and is a co-founder of SHOUT, the social housing campaign. Alison is a previous chair of Colchester Borough Homes and the NFA, the trade body for ALMOs. Alison is a former member of the Labour Housing Group's Executive Committee.*

Coronavirus: the poor must not be made to pay for the crisis

May 11, 2020

It seems likely that one of the groups that the Coronavirus pandemic is going to hit hardest is private tenants. The government's commitment to do 'whatever it takes' appears not to apply to them.

One of the biggest policy fanfares since the crisis began was their trumpeted 'ban on evictions'. It was a triumph of spin over substance because all they did was extend the normal period it takes to evict tenants for arrears, adding in a rather soggy new 'pre-action protocol'. People quickly grasped that this would just store up problems for a later avalanche of cases - unless the policy is extended, the avalanche will start at the end of June. It is an inadequate policy response to the huge additional housing problems being created for private tenants by rampant unemployment, reduced hours and furloughing at 80% wages.

While we wait for the 'eviction ban' to be extended or otherwise, an unknown number of private tenants are unable or significantly less able to pay their rent, including those on housing benefit or Universal Credit which only meets part of the rent. Given how high rents are, their debt will rise rapidly and quickly become unmanageable. For many there is little prospect of relief: the economic crisis arising from Coronavirus could last years not just the few months of lockdown. A survey for Shelter estimated that 1.7 million private renters fear losing their jobs this summer. This is a timebomb, not just for tenants but also for landlords and, if homelessness results, for the State.

In the absence of any new policy from government, Labour's new Shadow Housing Minister Thangam Debbonaire set out a 'five point plan' to tackle rent debt. This involves 1) extending the pause to evictions, probably to six months (when other measures should be in place); 2) offering more legal protection to people who got into arrears due to Covid; 3) allowing tenants 'at least 2 years' to pay back any arrears accrued during the crisis; 4) giving tenants greater protection from bankruptcy due to arrears; 5) making improvements to Universal Credit to help people pay their rents.

Of course, it is right that avoiding evictions should be the top immediate priority. The government seems likely to extend the ban beyond the end of June, but it has not said so yet. The weakness of Labour's position lies in 'two years to pay off debt'. This is not a holding position that can be addressed later: the debt is being incurred now and the issue must be tackled now before it is too late.

The policy has not gone down well in many Labour and tenant circles and there are calls for Labour to back a suspension of rent payments to mirror the mortgage holiday. If postponing rent simply creates debt for the tenant, cancelling rent passes the cost on to landlords. As a slogan, 'make the landlords pay' has an attraction on the left. I have never supported private renting as a tenure for people on low incomes, but making the sector even more volatile by denying landlords rental income will create conflict and more landlords will look to either remove tenants by any means or to escape from the sector. Good, some people will say to the latter, but this would not be the planned contraction I would like to see, and chaos will have bad outcomes for tenants. And there is an argument that government will end up paying anyway because it would be contrary to human rights legislation to deprive landlords of their legitimate income.

Two principles should guide Labour's response. First, private tenants should not be left in debt due to Coronavirus. Second, and related, it is the responsibility of the State to ensure that tenants have the means to pay their rent and not become homeless. Some are arguing that Labour should only propose pragmatic policies that the government might accede to. But Labour's analysis also shapes and informs public and media opinion, and at the moment Labour's message seems to be that private tenants should have to repay their Covid debts.

So, what policy would help tenants pay their rent NOW rather than slide into debt? Housing benefit used to do this and could do it again. It is a known system and would not have to be invented from scratch like the government's job protection schemes. HB should pay 100% of people's rent within reasonable limits by removing the freezes, caps and other restrictions. For those on Universal Credit the system would have to be amended to incorporate the principle of paying 100% of rent through the housing component. It could cater for people put out of work completely, people who face reduced hours, and people who are furloughed at 80% of previous income.

Reinventing housing benefit would mean: Landlords would get paid, there would be no crisis of evictions, no explosion of harassment, and no long term threat to supply; tenants would avoid large debt and its terrible consequences; and the State would help people in genuine distress due to the Covid crisis and avoid future homelessness. The cost would fall to government and they would be doing 'whatever it takes'. Labour is halfway to the policy already with its proposals to reform Universal Credit.

When housing benefit was introduced – by the Tories in the 1980s – they accepted the principle that the State should take responsibility for ensuring that tenants can pay their rent whatever their circumstances. This was not through generosity, but part of their ideological shift towards the marketisation of housing: reducing subsidy to 'bricks and mortar' (which kept rents low) necessitated increasing income support to enable tenants to pay much higher rents. It was the policy known by the shorthand of 'letting housing benefit take the strain'. Their deregulatory approach led to the resurgence of private renting that has carried on ever since. It is a free market system but with huge costs for the taxpayer. But it is suited to helping in the current crisis.

Cameron and Osborne, even more right wing than Thatcher, hated the idea of a benefit that covered all of the rent. Under austerity, an endless series of restrictions, caps and freezes forced millions to use a large slice of their money for other things, like food, to pay their rent. Many couldn't do it, so eviction from a private tenancy has become the most common cause of homelessness. But these policies can all be reversed, and it is not an extreme or fanciful position to call for HB to take the strain.

The idea is not dissimilar to that proposed by Congresswoman Ilhan Omar in the USA. She has proposed cancelling rent and mortgage payments with landlords and mortgage holders having their losses covered by Federal Government. That solution fits the USA – where 31% of Americans could not pay rent this month – but the housing benefit approach fits the UK circumstances better. The principle that it is the State's responsibility is the same.

Labour's policy must be driven by a simple rule. The poor paid for the global financial crash. They must not also be made to pay for the global pandemic.

Obituaries

Richard Crossley OBE

April 28, 2014

By Steve Hilditch

The first chief executive of the National Tenant Voice, set up by Labour but abolished by the Coalition Government shortly after the last election, has died of the rare peritoneal cancer aged 64. We were friends for 42 years.

Having worked at the front-line of community development for his entire career, Richard was seconded from the Priority Estates Project (PEP) to the Communities and Local Government Department to work on neighbourhoods policy before being asked to project manage the setting up the new National Tenant Voice (NTV), designed to make social tenants much more influential in the development of policy at local and national level.

Richard's networking and people skills - honed on estates around the country - were crucial in negotiating the minefield of civil service rules and procedures, and getting the Treasury and Cabinet Office behind the project - a quango run by tenants wasn't a concept they entirely understood. Richard made it happen but he also made sure that the tenants' movement stayed in firm control of the project. Following its establishment, which involved bringing together tenants from all over the country into a National Tenant Council, Richard was appointed as the first chief executive. Regrettably, he was hardly in post before the incoming Coalition Minister, Grant Shapps, abolished the NTV and pushed tenants out into the policy wilderness again.

Richard's career was unusual because he had no intention of climbing the greasy pole. He loved working with tenants on the ground and realising the untapped potential of community leaders in some of the country's most deprived communities. His first job, a rare step for a civil engineering graduate from Nottingham University, was with Cambridge Cyrenians, followed by a four-year stint doing community work in North Paddington. Then on to Stonebridge Estate in Brent, setting up the Charteris Neighbourhood Management Co-op in Islington and the tenant management scheme on Belle Isle Estate in Leeds (both still successful after 20-30 years). He then worked for PEP until his Government secondment, helping and advising tenants on estates all over the north of England.

Richard's decision to leave London and return to Yorkshire in 1984 was a watershed moment for him. He was a real, but not stereotypical, son of Yorkshire – West Yorkshire to be exact. Born and raised in Halifax, the son of a monumental mason, the area was in his blood. From there he could easily reach his beloved Yorkshire Dales and even the Lake District to indulge his other passion – walking the fells. He settled in Leeds with his partner Jane Williams, conveniently almost within touching distance of the cricket ground.

In Headingley Richard and Jane set about building a new community spirit, with a range of projects on the go at any one time. With others they formed the hugely successful Headingley Development Trust which now runs a series of projects including HEART, a large social enterprise centre packed with activities. Amongst other things, Richard loved organising the film club, with the selection of films decided by the members.

In 2012 Richard achieved one of his life ambitions, to go trekking in the Himalayas. His high point was Gokyo Ri, a peak 5200m above sea level commanding an astonishing view of the Everest range and much more. To get there he had to endure snow, severe temperatures of -20c and the effects of altitude. He took it all in his stride and, as a regular runner (having competed, for example, in the Great North Run) he seemed to be at the peak of his fitness.

Within a year of the trek Richard had fallen ill, had a bowel operation and then been diagnosed with a rare and incurable cancer of the peritoneum. Intensive treatments followed at 'Jimmy's' hospital in Leeds and the Christie in Manchester, but, as his health declined, Richard launched a new adventure. He started writing the most extraordinary blog[1], detailing his illness and treatment, but also his reflections on life and death: he was a humanist and did not believe in the afterlife. He praised the wonderful staff of the NHS and reflected on his career and housing policy, and on his love of the dales and mountains. He criticised the language of cancer: I'm not battling an external force called cancer, he would say, I'm living with it: when I die, it doesn't win, it dies too. He wrote movingly and inspiringly, completing his last entry days before his death.

Richard's blog stands as a testament to a uniquely strong and emotionally literate person, full of compassion and empathy but with the competitive streak of an activist. A long-term supporter of CND, his politics were a mix of red and green, but his distinctive contribution was as the unwavering advocate of much-maligned social tenants. He had an enduring belief in the ability of ordinary people to work collectively to take greater control over their lives and environments.

In January 2014 Richard received an OBE for services to neighbourhoods and tenants. It was a just award, even for a committed republican. But it took a superhuman effort (by him and his family) to come to London for the Investiture in March 2014. Despite his now extreme ill-health and weakness, Richard refused a wheelchair and walked the whole event, taking the family for a celebratory coffee and cake afterwards. He even managed to talk to Prince Charles about the advantages of tenant management.

Richard's wish was to spend his final days at home, which he achieved with the loving care of his partner Jane, daughter Emma and son Alex, and many other family and friends.

Richard Crossley OBE, born 11 January 1950, died 21 April 2014.

[1] Richard's blog can be found at https://richardcrossley1.wordpress.com/

Chris Holmes CBE

December 8, 2014

By Steve Hilditch

Chris Holmes, who died on 2 December after a long struggle with illness, was a towering figure in the housing world for more than 40 years.

Chris led many organisations in his extraordinary career: Shelter, where he was Deputy Director from 1974-1976 and Director from 1995-2002, tripling its income and increasing its influence commensurately; Camden, where he was a hugely influential and innovative Director of Housing from 1990-1995, putting into practice what he preached; the single homeless charity CHAR, where he was Director from 1982-87; East London Housing Association (Director, 1980-82); the Society for Co-operative Dwellings (Director, 1976-79), and North Islington Housing Rights Project (Director, 1972-74). He was also variously a Board Member of the National Consumer Council, the Housing Corporation, the Youth Justice Board and the Minister for Housing and Planning's Sounding Board (1997-2002). He was also active in the Labour Party and was a founder of the Labour Housing Group in the early 1980s.

Many tributes have already been paid to Chris, but there is one particularly noteworthy theme. So many people say he *inspired* them to work in housing and to campaign for the rights of homeless and badly-housed people. Whatever job he had, day and night he was a campaigner, a communicator, and a motivator.

Campaigns in which Chris played a major part included the extension of security of tenure in the 1974 Rent Act and the transformative Housing (Homeless Persons) Act of 1977, which changed government and public attitudes towards homeless people. In the early 1980s he led the campaign for comprehensive new rights for people living in houses in multiple occupation in a Bill which passed the House of Commons only to fall when the 1983 Election was called – what a difference that would have made. In the early 2000s he again campaigned for stronger homelessness duties, which led to Labour's 2002 Homelessness Act, then grasped the opportunity it created by launching Shelter into an enormous campaign to influence the practice of every local authority in the country as they wrote their new statutory homelessness strategies.

Chris inspired people though his leadership, his dedication, his encouragement of others, his sheer hard work, and his seemingly inexhaustible knowledge of his subject. But he was also a remarkable orator, capturing many audiences with his fluency and passion. He was a restless thinker, always ready with new ideas and new policies to debate, often controversially, although he never wavered from his core belief in the vital importance of social rented housing. He championed people's housing rights and spoke out against the use of discriminatory language referring to social tenants and homeless people. He wrote hundreds of articles and made thousands of speeches but he was always ready to sit quietly and talk through the detail of a point.

In 2000 he led Ken Livingstone's Housing Commission: as London had lacked a strategic authority for many years, he started with a blank canvass but steered a complex course through the new Mayor's untested planning powers to create (looking back from 2014) an extraordinarily progressive and ambitious set of policies.

In addition to his many articles, Chris wrote and contributed to a number of books. His tour de force, A New Vision for Housing, published in 2005, has become a standard text. It traced the avoidable policy mistakes over 50 years which led to the gross under-supply of homes and set out new ideas for creating housing justice and sustainable communities. He became a Visiting Fellow at the Institute for Public Policy Research and wrote an accessible but honest history of the Notting Hill Housing Trust, published in 2006, concluding privately that the organisation had lost sight of its founding moral purpose. He remained capable of stirring controversy, speaking out against excessive pay in the housing association sector when his term on the Board of the Housing Corporation ended in 2008 (when it was replaced by the Tenant Services Authority).